THE
NORTH WESTERN
AT WORK

Francis William Webb is often criticized for his 'obsession' with compounding, yet the reality is that his passenger compounds did their work competently and efficiently for 20 years, until, in fact, they were overtaken by rapidly increasing train weights, brought about by corridor stock, restaurant cars, electric lighting and suchlike. Contemporary engines on other lines suffered a parallel fate without their designers being ridiculed. The name bestowed upon 'Experiment' 2-2-2-0 No 301, depicted at Chester in the 1890s, was Economist. The choice of such a name was no accident, for it epitomized the compound era. An American engineer, Edward Dorsey, analysed British and US costs in the 1880s, and of six leading lines, the GNR, NER, Midland, LNWR, GWR and GER, only the GNR could show a fractionally lower running cost per engine mile. If loads were taken into account, the GNR too was easily defeated. LNWR engines, officers and men did a hard job capably and economically. They also did it with style. In the pages which follow, we will ask what they did, and listen to their opinions about it all. (R.H. Bleasdale)

THE
NORTH WESTERN
AT WORK
A PORTRAIT OF THE LNWR

Dr R. PRESTON HENDRY & R. POWELL HENDRY

Patrick Stephens Limited

© 1990 R. Preston Hendry and R. Powell Hendry

First published in 1990

British Library Cataloguing in Publication Data
Hendry, R. Preston (Robert Preston), *1912—*
    The North Western at Work: a portrait of the LNWR.
    1. England. Railway services: London and North Western Railway, history
    I. Title II. Hendry, R. Powell, Robert Powell, *1948—*
    385'.0942

ISBN 1-85260-129-9

385.0942
HEN

00113 6071

Patrick Stephens Limited, part of Thorsons, a division of the Collins Publishing Group, has published authoritative, quality books for enthusiasts for more than twenty years. During that time the company has established a reputation as one of the world's leading publishers of books on aviation, maritime, military, model-making, motor cycling, motoring, motor racing, railway and railway modelling subjects. Readers or authors with suggestions for books they would like to see published are invited to write to: The Editorial Director, Patrick Stephens Limited, Thorsons Publishing Group, Wellingborough, Northants, NN8 2RQ.

Patrick Stephens Limited is part of the Thorsons Publishing Group, Wellingborough, Northamptonshire NN8 2RQ, England.

Printed in Great Britain by Butler & Tanner Limited, Frome, Somerset.
Typesetting by MJL Limited, Hitchin, Hertfordshire.

10 9 8 7 6 5 4 3 2 1

Front endpaper *The London & North Western Railway offered immense contrasts. Its trains threaded their way through the industrial heartlands of England, and yet were equally at home in the quiet rolling countryside. They pierced the barren northern fells, and the Welsh mountains. It was a very down-to-earth, practical railway, eschewing the decorativeness adopted by many of its contemporaries, yet it possessed a style and elegance of its own, born from the conviction that it had nothing to prove to anyone. This previously unpublished study of a Class 'C' goods, No 1823, on a trip goods at Coventry in 1911, sums up that spirit. She was built in 1898 as a Webb Class 'A' compound, was converted to simple in 1905, and although engaged on quite mundane duties, manages to radiate style. The multiple track, overbridge, signal box and station buildings are in harmony with the engine. (H.J. Stretton Ward)*

Rear endpaper *Away from the bustling towns with their busy stations and yards, the pace of life was unhurried, and frequently unchanged for decades. This sylvan scene depicts the crossing gates at Clifton Mill station on the Rugby–Market Harborough branch. One of the authors built an O gauge model of these gates, coming to admire the sound design and economy of material in the process. (Dr R. Preston Hendry)*

Contents

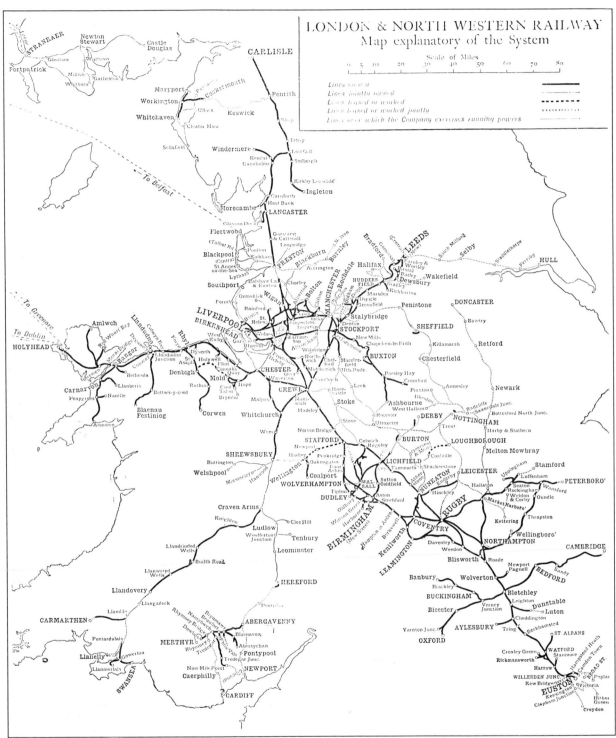

Right *The Company Secretary, James Bishop, held office from 1904 until 1921. His Euston office was double-glazed long before this was fashionable, and the early internal telephone system will be noted, along with the pile of* Manchester Guardian *newspapers on the desk — the latter entirely in keeping, as Bishop was a staunch Liberal! We see a stand containing writing paper, and by this is McCorquodale's calendar, secured open with an elastic band for June 1906, conveniently dating the illustration. The LNWR was noted for its frugality, and no doubt once expired, the reverse side of the diary leaves will do duty as a notepad. McCorquodale was printer to the LNWR, with a large works at Wolverton, employing the wives of the Carriage Works staff.*

Foreword by Peter Bishop, grandson of James Bishop

When Dr Arnold, the popular headmaster of Rugby School, beheld one of the first London & Birmingham trains that passed through Rugby, he is said to have exclaimed, 'I rejoice to see it, and think that feudality has gone for ever'. By 1914, this impression had been amply verified; the rapid development of the railway system, more than any other agency, tended to the breakdown of those natural or artificial barriers which for centuries had existed between nations and between men.

This book is quite unlike those we have grown used to over the last couple of decades, when so much has been published about the railways of Britain. The authors use unique sources to throw light on the attitudes, reasoning and methods of the people involved in running a pre-Great War railway; from a porter, through platelayers, footplatemen and Divisional Engineers to the Chairman of what became the largest company on earth, the men speak to us through the intervening decades — frequently using their own words — describing how they went about their work.

Like the best radio plays, one feels as though one is a fly on the wall, not only hearing what is said but also taking in the atmosphere of Edwardian and Victorian England. No finer example could have been chosen than the LNWR, since this was a truly universal concern, involved in all walks of life from basket-weaving to brickmaking, housing to shipping, catering to steelmaking. It pioneered mass-production in building nearly a thousand identical locomotives when few other lines possessed more than 50 engines of the same type. Before the welfare state, provision was made for those employees that were injured or fell ill, and not by merely giving them money and hoping the problem would go away; they were given lighter but useful tasks, thus remaining active members of their communities.

The fundamental reason why officers (the military vocabulary is not accidental) of other companies, and not only railway companies, studied the methods of the LNWR was the sheer efficiency of its ways; inherited from Robert Stephenson whose dictum was to 'obtain the maximum of result using the minimum of means', for three-quarters of a century this spirit led to outstanding results.

Others were keen to learn how it was possible to pull some of the heaviest trains using the cheapest locomotives, how third class passengers paying standard fares could dine in a carriage almost identical to that provided for the King — yet issue shares regarded as the safest in 'home rails' and produce profits unexcelled anywhere.

The secret seems to have been that the Company was a meritocracy, employing values finding favour once again in the United Kingdom in the closing years of the twentieth century. The ex-stonemason, George Findlay, was offered the Chair in 1891, not because of who he was but because of what he could do. Similarly, my grandfather (who was the son of a builder) joined the Company as a junior clerk in 1877, 27 years later becoming Secretary.

All this is very contrary to the popular myth, which many would have us believe today, that an 'old boy network' ran Victorian Britain; it is more along the lines of the American Dream.

These qualities go a long way to explain the regard held for each other by the management and staff, and indeed also explain the, to us, astonishing informality of method employed by the managers of the business, as brought out so vividly in this book.

LONDON AND NORTH WESTERN RAILWAY.

Third Instalment on £25 Shares, created in August, 1846,

Nº. *2406*

(CIRCULAR.)

7 Shares £*35*

OFFICE, EUSTON STATION,

5th June, 1849.

THE Directors of the London and North Western Railway Company, having in pursuance of the Provisions of the Act of Incorporation, and in conformity with the Regulations published on the Certificates of the said Shares, passed a Resolution, calling for a Third Instalment of £5 per Share on the £25 Shares, created in August, 1846, payable on or before the 2nd July, 1849, we are instructed to request that you will pay the Sum due on the Shares registered in your name as above, to one of the following Bankers, depositing this Circular with them at the time of payment.

We are also desired to apprise you, that should your Call remain unpaid after the appointed day, the Bankers have been severally required to demand Interest thereon, after the Rate of £5 per Cent. per Annum, from the 2nd July, 1849, to the day on which the payment shall be actually made.

London............Messrs. GLYN & CO., 67, Lombard Street.

Birmingham ...The BIRMINGHAM BANKING COMPANY.

Liverpool...... { Messrs. MOSS & CO. ; or
The BANK OF LIVERPOOL.

Manchester... { SIR B. HEYWOOD & CO. ; or
The MANCHESTER & LIVERPOOL DISTRICT BANK.

We are,

Your obedient Servants,

H. BOOTH,
C. E. STEWART, } Secretaries.

Elizabeth Holland

The LNWR formally came into being on 16 July 1846, the day the Act of Incorporation received the Royal Assent. Its initial capital, inherited from its constituents, stood at £17¼ m, but further extensions called for still more money, a process to continue throughout the company's life. This LNWR call notice, sent to Miss Elizabeth Holland, of Edge Hill, Liverpool, relates to these 1846 shares. (Authors' Collection)

Introduction

The London & North Western Railway was a dignified and respected institution in its day. Its admirers, and they were many, called it the 'Premier Line'. It was the largest joint stock corporation in the world — in other words, the biggest company there was. Through its associations with the Stephensons and the Liverpool & Manchester Railway, it called itself the oldest firm in the railway passenger business. Adjectives such as proud or majestic have been applied to it, and rightly so.

For many years after its demise, the North Western was ill-served in respect of literature about the Company. A definitive history is yet to be written, but recent years have seen many fine books upon a range of topics — locomotives, carriages, signalling, liveries, to mention but a few. Invaluable though these are, there are still many gaps, and perhaps the most notable of these relates to the character of this great institution, and of the people who made it all work.

In Victorian times, a number of accounts were published by railwaymen upon day-to-day life on the railways but, from the turn of the century, interest in what we would term anecdote or reminiscence died away, and it was not until the 1970s that railway reminiscence burgeoned forth once more. To anyone who has read even a part of the flood of reminiscences which have appeared in recent years, two things are apparent; with few exceptions, the reminiscences, however fascinating they are, relate largely to the Grouping and BR days, and most are confined to footplate or steam shed/workshops. The passage of the years is responsible for the first of these deficiencies, for it is over 60 years since the LNWR passed into history, and the number of its employees who survive today, all in their eighties and nineties, is dwindling by the year. Within a few years there will be none left. Already we can only quiz those who worked for the Company in its latter days, and what would we give for the chance of talking to a guard who had worked the notorious chain brake, or some of the strange grades of men who made up the North Western workforce, such as tunnel breaksmen?

The authors, a father and son team, have had a lifelong interest in the LNWR. The elder of the authors, Dr Robert Preston Hendry, spent his childhood on the Liverpool–Southport section of the Lancashire & Yorkshire Railway, which was absorbed into the LNWR in 1922. Apart from LYR electric sets, he also remembers the LNWR steam trains which instead of running into Liverpool Exchange diverged off at Bootle, and ran to Lime St. Shortly after the Grouping, his father moved to Rugby, and LYR electrics were replaced by the West Coast Main Line. It was early LMS days, but the Western Division of the LMS was still substantially LNWR, and within a few years a close acquaintance had been made with the LNWR signalling system, the most celebrated feature of which was the 44-arm signal gantry at the south end of Rugby station. That love of railways was inherited by the second of the authors, Robert Powell Hendry, whose first visits to the lineside were when he was but months old. He knew the standard block telegraph codes long before such mundane and boring things as the multiplication tables, and both authors have assiduously collected material relating to the LNWR over many years. They have spoken to former North Western men, and heard at first hand of the hostility towards the Midland.

However, those reminiscences alone could not provide a fraction of the material we needed for a truly balanced book, particularly as the work of most grades of railwaymen, other than footplate crews, has been so terribly neglected. What is really needed is a range of contemporary accounts by railwaymen of their working conditions, duties, wages, aspirations and frustrations. As reminiscence is so often subjective, a scrutineer would also be necessary to tell us if the story is true or perhaps coloured by prejudice or personal sentiment. As Victorian and Edwardian railway companies did not usually extend such invitations to their officers or staff, such a record was unlikely, *but*, in the case of the London & North Western Railway, it actually exists! It runs to 352 pages of small print. How it came to exist is one of those fascinating sidelights on railway history.

The full story behind this amazing document is told in Chapter 7, whilst the following seven

Above Cornwall *of 1847, despite its many rebuildings, takes us back to the dawn of the North Western, and the days when Elizabeth Holland was paying for those shares. She is seen in the paintshop at Crewe, surrounded, appropriately, by later North Western motive power.* (H.J. Stretton Ward)

Below *The final developments to LNWR motive power came after the company's demise, when Captain H.P.M. Beames rebuilt four 'Prince of Wales' 4-6-0s with outside Walschaerts motion, with a fifth engine added new to the same design. No 56, one of the rebuilds, is seen, still in LNWR colours, between 1924 and 1927.* (Attr J.N. Maskelyne)

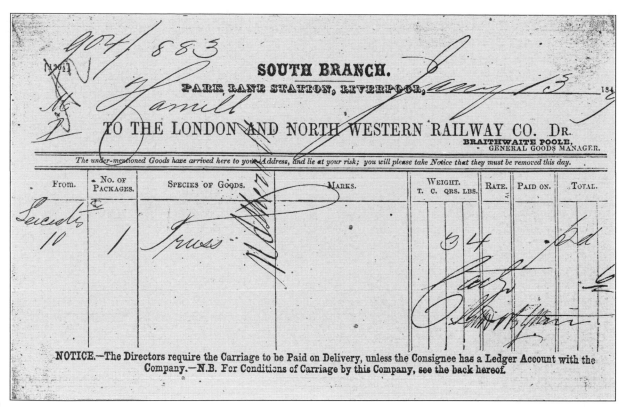

Above. *An LNWR 'Goods Received' note of 1849, printed in carmine on white*

chapters explore the evidence which it reveals. We discover not just what the pay and conditions were for North Western men, and what their working day was like, but what the attitudes of men and management were. We find senior North Western officers criticizing or turning a blind eye to their own rules, and see two of the most talented North Western men at work, C.J. Bowen Cooke and Herbert Walker, who was to carve out a brilliant career on the LSWR and Southern Railway. All this took place in 1908.

The next chapter reveals the crucial role played by the LNWR in averting a national rail strike in 1911. To most North Western devotees, *Sir Gilbert Claughton* is a locomotive which happened to be named after the Chairman of the LNWR. We see the *man* at work, talking to his fellow railway chairmen, to the Board of Trade, and the unions.

The next three chapters then look at different aspects of the Locomotive Department. Chapter 16, 'Steam Shed', tells us what it was like to be a locoman working for George W. Walton, whose '8 District' sheds provided power for such diverse workings as the 'Irish Mail' to Holy-

head, and coal trains from the Nottinghamshire coalfield. Much of this chapter is based upon interviews with the late Arthur Mason, who fired Webb Compounds, drove most later LNWR classes and finished his career on Stanier 'Pacifics', including Royal Train duties. In Chapter 17, we admire the 'view from the top'. We look at the kind of problems which landed on Charles John Bowen Cooke's desk! Enthusiasts are apt to see the Chief as devoting his entire time to designing new engines. Coaling plants, seniority and clogs were far more a part of the real world than high degree superheat or long lap travel! In Chapter 18 we visit an LNWR erecting shop, for once *not* Crewe, but the neglected Rugby workshop. The late Lew Walton provides a graphic account of a largely forgotten part of North Western history.

We wanted the portrait to be wider still, for a railway is not just locomotives, carriages, wagons, signals and the people who work them. It includes directors and shareholders, passengers and freight customers. Richard Moon is one of the most celebrated names in North Western history, and we wondered what it must have been like to have attended a shareholders' meeting, though the North Western had a far more dig-

The threat of competition on the Birmingham services, when the GWR Bicester 'cut-off' was completed, prompted the North Western to run an express into Broad Street, its North London ally's terminus in the very heart of 'The City'. The Civil Engineer ruled out use of the Whale 'Precursors', and in 1908 a Webb 'Jubilee', No 1918 Renown, was converted to a two-cylinder simple, and proved a splendid locomotive. The 'City to City' express from Wolverhampton to Broad Street, calling at Birmingham New St and Coventry, was introduced on 1 February 1910, Renown monopolizing the job for some weeks; but in March, another 'Jubilee', No 1913 Canopus, was converted, and she is seen on the approaches to Broad Street, passing some of the archaic NLR suburban stock. The train seldom loaded to more than four coaches. (Authors' Collection)

nified title than that — the Court of Proprietors! Chapter 1 takes us back to Victorian times, as we become a 'proprietor' in the 'Premier Line', paying calls on our shares, receiving dividends, and listening to Richard Moon. We felt that there could be no more appropriate way of concluding this portrait of the LNWR than by returning to the Court of Proprietors on the last occasion that it met; Chapter 19 tells us of the pride and sadness as we say 'goodbye' to the LNWR.

Generations of writers have emphasized the military precision and efficiency of the North Western, and we could be forgiven if we have a vision of an organization which was born perfect, and on which nothing ever went wrong. In reality, this efficiency was the product of hard experience. Chapter 2 gathers together a series of vignettes of life along the London & Birmingham line from the 1840s to the 1880s. There is efficiency, and humour and tragedy. Railway police show a professionalism fully up to modern police work, yet we discover incidents more in keeping with one of the Colonel Stephens lines! It would come as no surprise to hear of the floor of one of the Colonel's carriages falling apart between stations, but it actually happened on the North Western! A tiger chasing a railwayman up a tree would seem natural enough in India, but less likely near Kilsby Tunnel!

Chapter 3 looks at the passenger business, and an account of 1875 tells us about the latest word in railway travel, the sleeping car. Modern writers have spoken of the tantalizing lack of information concerning the first generation of West Coast sleepers. We have an eye-witness account of the panelling and even of the curtains. Chapter 4 takes us into the realm of the mail and newspaper

Equally important as Birmingham and the West Midlands to the LNWR was Liverpool, and out of the cramped and grimy streets surrounding Edge Hill came generations of superb enginemen. As steam and smoke drift across the yard at Edge Hill shed, LNWR No 1 Clive, *a 'Precursor' of 1907, pauses for her portrait in about 1922.* (Attr J.N. Maskelyne)

expresses, once again drawing heavily upon 1870s accounts.

In any work upon a subject as massive as the LNWR, there must be selection, and with it omission. Our publishers agreed a larger page size than initially envisaged, yet there is much more that could be said. If the reader should feel that his favourite topic is not covered, then it is possible that the authors regret the omission as much or more, but were forced into making choices. Also it is possible that sufficient detail has not yet come to light, and the authors would be delighted to hear from anyone who has material — whether illustrations, diaries or other items — which would further research into this aspect of North Western history.

With acknowledgments, it is hard to know where to begin. North Western employees who gave of their time for interview deserve our

thanks, including the late Arthur Mason and the late Lew Walton. Families of North Western men have helped, including Miss Greta Walton, Mr & Mrs Lea, and Mr R. Wilmshurst. Eddie Bray, himself a professional railwayman whose father started on the North Western, has been of immense help. Peter Bruce, whose career included a spell on the railways, has helped, as has Peter Bishop, grandson of the LNWR secretary, James Bishop. All are members of the London & North Western Railway Society. Other members of the LNWR society have contributed also. Useful signalling data has come from the late Mr Matthews and from Stanford Jacobs. A debt is due to the early photographers, whose work, often with cumbersome plate glass cameras, is so vital. Many of the illustrations in this book come from ancient sepia prints made when the LNWR was still in existence. In some cases we know the names of the photographers, and where possible we have given this information. They include Dr Roy Sellon, Henry Salmon, E. Pouteau, R.H. Bleasdale, J.N. Maskelyne and H.J. Stretton-Ward. Where illustrations from North Western days have been unavailable, we have utilized later illustrations if these show what

we need. For example, we know of no illustrations of the interiors of Rugby No 2 or No 3 signal boxes in LNWR days, yet these small but important cabins come into our story, and merit recording. Finally, we acknowledge, as always, a debt to the late Mrs Elaine Hendry, without whose patience the authors would never have been able to have gathered together so much material on the North Western.

Above *The LNWR reached many places via joint lines, as at Shrewsbury, where No 934 North Star, a six-foot 'Waterloo' of 1892, pauses with a northbound express in the early 'twenties. GWR No 4000, also North Star, was another regular visitor!* (Author's Collection).

Below *The North Western could be charmingly rustic, as at Liddington Crossing in Rutland. The old sleepers are worthy of Richard Moon, though the date is 1966!*

Wages and prices

In preparing this book, the authors faced a difficulty. With the adoption of decimal currency on 15 February 1971, the United Kingdom abandoned the pounds/shillings/pence (£sd) currency which had served it well for centuries. Whilst older readers will recall the traditional currency, a new generation exists for whom shillings and old pennies are as alien as the currency of ancient Rome. In any book depicting the lives of railwaymen, pay is an important topic, and we had to decide whether to use modern decimal currency, use the old pound/shilling/pence system, or both. Each method has its benefits and its drawbacks.

Today, the pound is divided into 100 new pence; until 1971, it was divided into 20 shillings, and each shilling into 12 pennies, so there were 240 old pennies in a pound. The system may sound cumbersome to those educated in the decimal system, but actually worked very well,

especially as many items were bought by the dozen. Without a calculator, the decimal system is indeed less convenient for many such transactions! Any currency change which replaces 240 old pennies with 100 new pence means that some amounts cannot be exactly converted, and conversion tables in 1971 only went to the nearest half new penny, a coin since abolished. A conversion error of a fraction of a penny may sound meaningless, but when weekly wages could be as little as 12 shillings and 8 pence, an increase of 4d — four old pennies — was a lot! In modern currency, which has lost the half-pence, the closest we can get is 1p (or 2.4 old pennies) or 2p (4.8 old pennies). The difference is trivial today but, to a labourer in the 1900s, an old penny, let alone a new penny, mattered. Indeed, the elder of the authors, when a medical student in the thirties, would sometimes walk 1½ miles to save a penny tram fare.

By using modern currency alone, we cannot recall an era in which a penny mattered, nor can we be sufficiently accurate. We also tend to obscure the link between wages and their own era if we confine ourselves to modern currency. It would be just as useful to express the wages of a Roman Centurion in pounds and pence. We would know what he was paid, relative to today, but not to his own time.

Such was the prestige of the LNWR that even the mighty Pennsylvania Railroad decided to try a Webb compound. As UK railways were prohibited from building engines for sale, Beyer Peacock built a solitary 'Dreadnought', No 1320 Pennsylvania, *in 1889. Despite excellent coal consumption, she was regarded as too light and complex for general service and was scrapped in 1898.* (Authors' Collection)

We could give old and modern currencies, for example 14s 7d (72.5p approx), but frequent insertion of dual amounts becomes tiresome.

The third alternative, which we have adopted, is to refer sparingly to modern currency, and usually quote only the traditional currency. This will be a little harder for the younger reader to grasp at first, but converting a single sum to modern terms is not helpful. The question one truly wishes to ask is not how does a driver's income of 1908 compare to modern wages, but how did it compare to wages and prices of the time. We offer the reader two guides; one is a pounds/shillings/pence conversion table, and the other is a range of sample wages and prices about the turn of the century. We suggest that the younger reader uses the conversion table to begin with, but as soon as possible abandons it, to say instead, 'How does that prices or salary compare with other figures of that time?' After a very short while, the pound/pence conversion will cease to be of any interest as one relives the prices and wages of Victorian and Edwardian England.

Conversion Table

New	Old	New	Old
1p	2.4d	25p	5s 0d
2p	4.8d	30p	6s 0d
3p	7.2d	33⅓p	6s 8d
4p	9.6d	35p	7s 0d
5p	1s 0d	40p	8s 0d
6p	1s 2.4d	45p	9s 0d
7p	1s 4.8d	50p	10s 0d
8p	1s 7.2d	55p	11s 0d
9p	1s 9.6d	60p	12s 0d
10p	2s 0d	65p	13s 0d
		70p	14s 0d
12½p	2s 6d	75p	15s 0d
15p	3s 0d	80p	16s 0d
17½	3s 6d	85p	17s 0d
20p	4s 0d	90p	18s 0d
22½p	4s 6d	95p	19s 0d

The accepted methods of showing traditional currency were as follows;

One shilling and sixpence = 1s 6d or 1/6d

One pound, four shillings and sixpence = £1/4/6d or 24/6 or 24s 6d.

Note Wage rates over the pound were often shown as shilling amounts, as above, ie 24/6d or 35/- (35 shillings or £1/15/0d).

In the chapters which follow, we will discover what North Western men were paid, and what they thought about it, but as a preview, a Loco Department apprentice aged 14-15 received 4 shillings (20p) *a week* in 1903. An express pass-enger driver earned 8 shillings (40p) per ten-hour day, or about 48 shillings (£2.40) a week. North Western shunters' wages ranged from 18 shillings (90p) a week to 35 shillings (£1.75).

Incredible though these wages may seem to the younger reader, railwaymen were relatively well paid. The average wage of railwaymen in England and Wales in 1906 was 25 shillings and 11½ pennies, or a fraction under £1.30 per week. An agricultural labourer was then earning 12 shillings (60p) to 18s 10d (94p approx) a week. An engineering labourer in Birkenhead took home one pound a week.

The daily pay of an infantry private was 1s (5p); of a sergeant, about 2s 6d (12½p); of a Second Lieutenant, 5s 3d (26p approx); and a Captain, 11s 7d. An engine driver on 8 shillings a day was considerably better paid than a junior army officer, and when allowance is made for trip work payments and other benefits, was comparable in income to an Army Captain. A Lieutenant-Colonel then received 18 shillings (90p) a day, and moving very high up the tree, a Major-General's daily remuneration was three pounds.

What was the cost of living? A four-room LNWR cottage in Camden cost 10 to 12 shillings (50 to 60p) a week. The freehold land for a labourer's three-room dwelling in Tooting in 1904 cost £28 15s (£28.75) and building the house cost £234 15s (£234.75). Hand-knitted socks, made by Irish peasantry, sold for 7d to 1 shilling (3-5p) a pair, and the charges for a tailor to make and trim a hand-tailored gent's suit, excluding cloth, varied from 21 shillings to 35 shillings (£1.05-£1.75). An off-the-peg jacket nowadays costs more pounds than a hand-tailored suit did in shillings then! The post for a 1oz letter was 1d (at the time of writing, the first class letter rate is 19p, or a 45-fold increase for a somewhat slower service today!) A newspaper or postcard could be sent for ½d. The cost of Stallard's seven-year matured Scotch Whisky was 21/6d (£1.07½) *per gallon*. If houses at £250, postal charges of ½d, or whisky by the gallon did not appeal, there was always the 'New World'. White Star Line were advertising passage from Liverpool to New York for as little as £15 to £30 winter rates. For those taking a holiday rather than emigrating, 5s (25p) a day provided a good standard of accommodation; for the affluent, a 45-day Mediterranean cruise was 45 guineas (£47.25)!

C.D.—No. 446 R

L. & N. W. R.
THE BUSINESS AND PLEASURE LINE

WHITSUNTIDE HOLIDAYS.

On Friday, May 13, and Saturday, May 14,

CHEAP EXCURSION TICKETS
WILL BE ISSUED AS UNDER TO

BLACKPOOL   KESWICK
MORECAMBE   GRANGE   CARK
WINDERMERE   BARROW
FURNESS ABBEY
And other Stations in the Lake District.

Fares there and back.

4, 5, & 6 Days Tickets issued on May 13, and 3, 4, & 5 Days Tickets issued on May 14.

FROM	To all places. May 13 & 14. a.m.	To Blackpool only on Saturday May 14. p.m.	Blackpool Lytham, St. Annes, Southport, Morecambe. 3rd Class.	Grange, Arnside, Kent's Bank, Silverdale. 3rd Class.	Windermere and Kendal. 3rd Class.	Keswick. 3rd Class.	Cark. 3rd Class.	Ulverston. 3rd Class.	Furness Abbey, Barrow-in-Furness. 3rd Class.	Coniston, Ravenglass, St. Bees, Seascale, Silecroft, Whitehaven. 3rd Class.
Sutton Coldfield	11 47	8 25	9 6	11 6	13/-	16/-	12/-	12 6	13 6	14 6
Bedworth	10 10	8 70								
Coundon Road	9 56	8 44								
Coventry	12 5	9 30	11/-	12 6	14/-	17/-	13/-	13 6	14 6	15 6
Leamington (Avenue)	10 20	9 0								
Warwick (Milverton)	10 23	9 5								
Kenilworth	10 30	9 13								

FIRST CLASS DOUBLE THE ABOVE FARES.

Fares there and back.

11 Days Tickets issued on May 13, and 10 Days Tickets issued on May 14.

FROM	To Blackpool, Fleetwood, Lytham, St. Annes, Southport, and Morecambe. 1st Class.	3rd Class.	To Arnside, Grange, and Silverdale. 1st Class.	3rd Class.	To Windermere and Kendal. 1st Class.	3rd Class.	To Keswick and Penrith. 1st Class.	3rd Class.
Sutton Coldfield	25/-	14/-	28/-	15 6	33/-	18/-	37/-	20/6
Bedworth								
Coundon Road								
Coventry	26/-	14/6	29/-	16/-	34/-	18 6	38/-	21/-
Leamington (Avenue)								
Warwick (Milverton)								
Kenilworth								

Children under Three free, over Three and under Twelve years of Age Half-fares.

Tickets not transferable.

Personal luggage under 100 lbs. free at Passenger's own risk.

Luggage should be fully addressed with name and destination of Passenger.

RETURN ARRANGEMENTS.

Passengers holding **3, 4, 5,** or **6** Days Tickets, return the following Sunday (where train service permits), Monday, Tuesday, or **Wednesday**. Those holding **10** or **11** Days Tickets, return on any succeeding day, up to and including the second Monday after the date of issue, by any Ordinary Train having a through connection, except the 1.37, 5.20, and 10.0 p.m. from Blackpool, the 1.27 and 4.50 p.m. from Penrith, and the 4.20 p.m. from Windermere, the 1.5 p.m. and 4.13 p.m. from Barrow, the 1.15 and 5.5 p.m. from Morecambe, and Trains in connection.

Tickets can be obtained in Birmingham at the following Excursion Offices:—

Stephenson Place,	45, Snow Hill,
Swan Office, 137, New Street,	1, George Street, Parade,
Bridge Booking Office, New Street Station,	41, Hall Street, and at the Stations.

Small Bills can also be obtained at any of the Stations, and Company's Parcels Receiving Offices.

Euston Station, London,
April, 1910

FRANK REE, General Manager.

McCorquodale & Co., Limited, Printers, London—Works, Newton.—

ROBERT TURNBULL.
Superintendent of the Line

DC

London & North Western Railway,

Office of Superintendent of the Line.

Euston Station

IN YOUR REPLY PLEASE REFER TO

CR. 63 W.C.A. *London,* N.W. August 11th, 1899.

16/8/99

Dear Sir,

On July 4th last a young man named John Faragher, a Sheeter in this Company's employ, lost his life in the Waterloo and Edge Hill Tunnel, Liverpool. On July 19th we sent to his father

Mr Jno.Faragher,
c/o Mr G.Moore,
Balladoole,
Castletown, I. of Man.

a cheque for £7.10.6. in payment of what was due to him from this Company, and also forwarded to him a receipt form, of which the enclosed is a copy, to be duly stamped,signed,and witnessed. That receipt has not been returned to me, and although I wrote for it on Aug. 2nd no reply has come to hand.

May I ~~xx xx xxxx~~ ask you to be so good as to instruct your Agent at Castletown to call upon Mr Faragher at the address given herein and obtain the receipt, or if it has been mislaid, get the enclosed stamped, and signed,and send same to me?

I hope I am not giving very much trouble, but it seems useless to write direct again; and moreover I feel satisfied that I may rely upon your kind assistance in the matter.

Yours faithfully,
R.Turnbull.
per G.H. Colley

G.H.Wood Esq:
Isle of Man Rly.,
Station Buildings,
Douglas,
Isle of Man.

Above *For the railwayman, a moment's forgetfulness can lead to tragedy. In 1899, a young sheeter, who had come from Balladoole to Liverpool for a job, lost his life on the Waterloo freight branch. This letter tells the story.*

Although tragedy was the railwayman's companion, farce was equally close to hand. In 1881, a village feud at Marton in Warwickshire dragged station master John Lawlor into fisticuffs! It was 29 July, and Lawlor was in his office working on some papers. An angry shout came from outside. 'You b. . ., you stole my whip!' Rather than allow a fight, Lawlor went outside and saw Tom King, a waggoner, snatch his whip from John Cooper, a labourer from the village. He called Cooper over to reprimand him, and got a mouthful of abuse, Cooper then walking off to tend his horses which were restive. A few minutes later, Lawlor glanced out of the office window to see Cooper striding towards the building, which also served as station master Lawlor's home. Despite protests, Cooper burst into the office, and when told to go, shook his fist in Lawlor's face. Eventually, he left, and Lawlor resumed booking parcels and passengers for the 4.19 pm to Rugby. The next day, Cooper returned shortly before 6.00 pm. Some days earlier, Lawlor had borrowed some hurdles from a Mr Hall of the village. Triumphantly, Cooper threw Lawlor

a note from Hall demanding immediate return of the hurdles. Hall, as it happened, was Cooper's employer, and his cousin. Lawlor, incensed by Cooper pestering him, tore the note up, and returned to the booking hatch to deal with passengers for the 6.19 pm. Cooper followed him. Lawlor told Cooper to clear off as he was busy, only to be told, 'No, you b. . ., we shall have this whip out now. I've come for the purpose.' The harassed station master invoked the aid of the driver of the Southam village bus, one Baskett, who told Cooper to clear off. Tempers were short on all sides, and as Lawlor and Baskett tried to push Cooper out of the door, he turned on Lawlor striking him in the face. The bawl spilled out on to the platform, where Cooper did his best to push Lawlor on to the line, but eventually fell on to the tracks himself. Fortunately the train was still some distance away, Cooper made off, and was later fined £2 12s for obstruction and assault. Had the fight broken out minutes later, there could have been tragedy; instead a village feud caused mirth for years.
(Dr R.P. Hendry)

1 The Court of Proprietors

Any great railway company was an amalgamation of interests, the promoters who conceived the idea, the shareholders who provided the funds, the engineers who laid out the line and who would maintain it after it was open, the officers who managed it, and the staff who worked it. The customers who used it, though not a 'part' of the company, were a vital ingredient too, as far too many companies found to their cost! Without sufficient passengers and freight customers, ruin ensued. Railway history abounds with references to the promoters, engineers and officers, and occasionally speaks of the staff, yet the shareholders and customers,

Right *The seal of the Secretary of the LNWR, reproduced to approximately twice actual size.*

Below *Income tax was deducted from dividends even in 1863, but it was not so high as nowadays; the rate was between 3 and 4 (new) pence in the pound!*

Right *This 1849 dividend statement, sent to John Holland of Edge Hill, shows a sizeable holding of stock, £1,944 in one class alone, and, of especial interest, calls on new stock being offset against dividends on older stock.*

---

35. ☞ **This portion of the Sheet to be retained by the Proprietor.**

Thirty-Fifth Half-yearly Dividend to 30th June, 1863.

	Dividend.			Total.		
	£	s.	d.	£	s.	d.

Consolidated Stock..............................Dividend at £4 5s. ℈ Cent. ℈ Annum on £ *120* —   2 | 11 | .

Coventry and Nuneaton Consolidated Stock... do. „ £5 ℈ Cent. ℈ Annum „ £ _____

£30.   Shares   Huddersfield & Manchester   do. „ 0 8 11 ℈ Share *(a)* „ _____

£10.   ditto   Ditto .... do. „ 0 2 11¾ „ „ „ _____

£50.   ditto   Leeds and Dewsbury .... do. „ 0 14 10½ „ „ „ _____

£25.   ditto   Ditto .... do. „ 0 7 5¼ „ „ „ _____

Income Tax at 8d. in the Pound (Being 3 months @ 9d and 3 months @ 7d.)   1 | 8

NOTE. SHARES.
(a) { £30 (H. & M.) / £10 do. / £50 (L. & D.) / £25 do. } 7-10ths of £4 5s. per cent. per annum.   £ 2 | 9 | 4

(CIRCULAR.)

OFFICE, EUSTON STATION, 25th August, 1863.

Referring to the Resolution of the Court of Proprietors of the London and North Western Railway Company of the 21st instant, declaring a Dividend on the Consolidated Stock and Shares of this Company, entitled to participate therein payable this day, out of the net Profits of the Company, for the Half-year ending 30th June last, I am instructed to send you the above Statement, and the Draft for Dividend due.

    I am also desired to request your *particular attention* to the Notes at the foot of the Draft, and to beg that you will not fail to give timely notice of any change in your residence, that the Warrants for your future Dividends may not be mis-sent.

    I am, your obedient Servant,   C. E. STEWART, *Secretary.*

London and North Western Railway.

Seventh Half-yearly Dividend, to 30th June, 1849.

						Dividends.			Total.		
							s.	d.	£	s.	d.
Consolidated Stock	Dividend at £3 10 0 per Cent......on £ *19414* SEE NOTE.					*18*	—	*9*			
£20. Shares of the late London and Birmingham ...	do.	„	5 0 ᵖ Share (*a*)	„	*1*		*5*	*1*			
£40. ditto Grand Junction	do.	„	1 3 0	„ (*b*)	„						
£10. C ditto Manchester and Birmingham	do.	„	2 6	„ (*c*)	„						
£25. ditto London and North Western	do.	„	2 9½	„ (*d*)	„ *13*	*1*	*16*	*6*			
£13. 10s. ditto Coventry and Nuneaton	do.	„	3 7	„ (*e*)	„						
						76	*2*	*0*			
Income Tax............			*2. 0-11*								
Deduct Arrears, with Interest *3 Call on £25 — 65. 9. 11*						*67*	*10*	*16*			
								£	*2*	*11*	*2*

NOTES.	SHARES.					£	s.	d.			
(*a*)	£20. at 7 per cent. per annum........................... *is £1. 8s. 0d. For the half-year*					0	14	0			
	Less—Interest at 5 per cent. per annum, for six months,........on £18 unpaid					0	9	0	£	s.	d.
									0	5	0 ᵖ S
(*b*)	£40. at 7 per cent. per annum............ .... *is £2. 16s. 0d. For the half-year*......................					1	8	0			
	Less—Interest at 5 per cent. per annum, for six months,........on £10 unpaid					0	5	0	1	3	0 „
(*c*)	£10. (C) *Interest at 7 per cent. per annum. on £10*............... *is £0. 14s. 0d. For the half-year*......................					0	7	0			
	Less—Interest at 5 per cent. per annum, for six months,........on £9 unpaid.............					0	4	6	0	2	6 „
(*d*)	£25. (L. & N. W.) *Interest at 4 per cent. per annum, on £7*.........*is £0. 5s. 7d. For the half-year*.............								0	2	9½ „
(*e*)	£13. 10s. (C. & N.) *Interest at 5 per cent. per annum, on £7. for six months*...............					0	3	6			
	Ditto ditto *on £3. from 16th to 30th June—14 days*					0	0	1	0	3	7 „

(CIRCULAR.)

OFFICE, EUSTON STATION,
17th August, 1849.

REFERRING to the Resolution of the Court of Proprietors, of this day, declaring a Dividend on the Consolidated Stock and Shares of this Company, entitled to participate therein; payable the 27th instant, out of the net Profits of the Company, for the Half Year ending 30th June last; we are instructed to send you the above Statement, and the Cheque annexed for Dividend due.

We are also desired to request your *particular attention* to the Note at the foot of the Cheque; and to beg that you will not fail to give timely notice of any change in your residence, that the Cheques for your future Dividends may not be mis-sent.

We are,

Your obedient Servants,

H. BOOTH,
C. E. STEWART, } *Secretaries.*

Name _____

☞ This **HALF SHEET** to be retained, the **OTHER** to be presented to the **Bankers entire.**

both vital ingredients in the mix, are often ignored.

From 1846 until 1923, the shareholders of the London & North Western Railway met regularly to elect their Directors, approve their accounts and dividends, and to sanction additional capital and extensions. Most companies referred to General Meetings, but the LNWR, with its regal overtones, adopted the resounding title of the 'Court of Proprietors', a name more in keeping with one of the Royal Chartered Companies of the seventeenth or eighteenth centuries than with up-to-date business methods! Until 1913, the Court of Proprietors met twice yearly, as the accounts were issued at six-monthly intervals, but for the last years of the Company's existence,

LONDON AND NORTH WESTERN RAILWAY.

£12 : 10/- SHARE, No. 103794

These are to Certify that *Thomas Holden*

of *Hull*

is the Proprietor of the Share Number 103794 of the

London and North Western Railway Company,

subject to the Rules, Regulations, & Orders of the said Company.

Dated the 30th day of April in the year of our Lord One Thousand Eight Hundred and Fifty-three.

REGISTERED No. 361

HENRY BOOTH,
CHAS. E. STEWART, } Secretaries.

Above *An LNWR share certificate of 1853; sadly the company cancelled its certificates, which were printed on paper watermarked 'LONDON & NORTH WESTERN RAILWAY COMPANY'; by tearing off the printed seal on the left.*

Below *Passengers and stockholders were familiar with the grand approach to Euston, with the Doric arch flanked by the two wings of the Euston Hotel, as depicted in this LNWR engraving used by the company in the 1890s.*

THE EUSTON HOTEL (IMMEDIATELY OPPOSITE) THE STATION.

This Hotel, which is lighted throughout by Electricity, contains 220 Bed Rooms and 20 Sitting Rooms; it is fitted with Telephone, and communication is thus established with all parts of the Metropolis

Above *This magnificent Bleasdale print of a 'Lady of the Lake'
single, No 818* Havelock, *shows the engine in early Webb condition, retaining the slotted Ramsbottom splasher and open safety
valves, but Webb livery, cab and chimney. A virtually identical
view exists of No 618* Princess Alexandra, *the engines having been brought to the camera, not vice versa.*

Below *This second Bleasdale print from the late 1870s recap-
tures a 'Newton' 2-4-0, No 1523* Marlborough, *in the transition period. She still has the open Ramsbottom cab. Predictably,
Bleasdale secured other views in the same location, one showing
another 'Newton', No 1525, with a cab.*

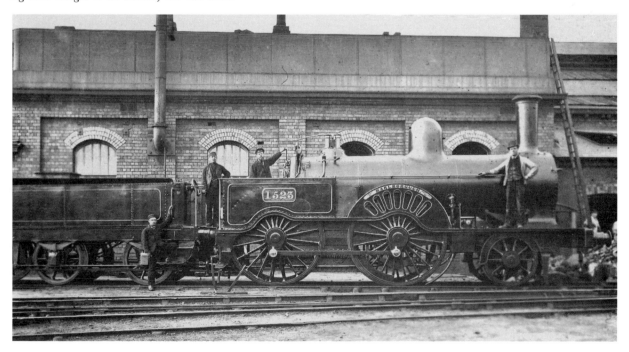

London and North Western Railway.

REPORT of the PROCEEDINGS of the HALF-YEARLY GENERAL MEETING held on the 19th FEBRUARY, 1870.

RICHARD MOON, Esq., in the Chair.

Mr. STEPHEN REAY, the Secretary, having read the notice convening the Meeting, and the minutes of the General Special Meetings on the 21st August, 1869, which were confirmed, the report of the Directors was taken as read.

The CHAIRMAN said his next duty was to move that the report, with the half-yearly statement of accounts, be received and adopted. Before doing so, he would say a few words. It was not necessary to say much, because the accounts in their new form were so full and complete, and the comparisons made gave the Proprietors so much information, that he was sure they would see the state of the Company at a glance from the details. In truth, it had always occurred to him that there were only three points Shareholders cared for: the first was the dividend, the next to see that it was honestly earned, and the third, that the capital expenditure was kept as low as possible. With regard to the first, looking to the state of the times, and remembering that the country was only slowly returning to a state of activity and trade, he thought they had reason to be satisfied. They had for some time been depressed as far as they were likely to be by the effect of the panic and the course of events in this country. They were now on the move upwards, and had returned to a point at which they were earning at the rate of 7 per cent. per annum for the past half-year, or 6¼ per cent. for the year, That they had reason to be satisfied with the course which the Company was taking he thought was abundantly clear. Some time ago there was a good deal of uncomfortable feeling amongst the Proprietors of the London and North Western Company generally, as to what would be the result of the competition which they would experience from their new neighbours, the Midland, coming into London. Amongst some of the Proprietors there was a notion that the North Western Company was going to receive great damage, and that the Midland would take away some £108,000 a year for the coal traffic. On this subject he might refer to what he had said at the Meeting on 21st February, 1868. The Proprietors were told then that it was not likely that anything of that kind would occur,—that the London and North Western had the markets on their line, and that, if the Midland neighbours did take some of it, other traffic would come on the line. Some returns had been now got out, which had been read to a Special Meeting of the Board this morning, and in them the most remarkable thing was that the increase in their traffic was in the very mineral and coal traffic, which it was supposed their Midland neighbours were going to take away. He thought, therefore, it might be said that the growth of the country and the development of the line by what had been done to increase its local and other traffic, might be taken as a guarantee that they had seen the worst. That the dividend on the present occasion was honestly earned he could assure the Proprietors most positively; and not only so, but practically the accounts were even better than appears upon the face of them, because it was thought advisable to go prudently and slowly forward rather than pay a larger dividend with the chance of coming back again. With regard to the position of the Company itself and its accounts, they now saw for the last time the remnant of the celebrated renewal of Road account, which for many years used to trouble the Proprietors. At one time it increased to something over £300,000, and he believed in the year 1862 the account stood against them for over £90,000. That was now entirely wiped out, and there would be no more relaying fund in suspense, or other account of the like kind. They had charged in the accounts the compensation, which had been paid up to the end of January, and had £10,000 in hand to meet any casualty. They had paid off all law debts, and had something in hand there also. The lawyers were paid up to the day. When he first became chairman they had a debt of about £120,000 in suspense to be recouped by revenue, and they had also a year's law bills in arrear. That £120,000 had been recouped, they had paid the bills off, and there were no lawyers' bills now in arrear He thought, therefore, that nothing could be more satisfactory than the position of the Company. He then came to a difficult point, and that was the question of the division of expenditure between capital and revenue. That was a subject which was open to discussion, and with regard to which nothing but rough justice could be done. But what they had taken care to do was, to tax the current Proprietors, so that at the end of the half-year the property, taken as a whole, was rather in a better position than it was at the beginning. In that way they had now for a long time been taking from revenue a considerable sum for the enlargement, improvement, and extension of the works, and it had been done to a very great extent during the last year. It would be readily seen that with an old line like theirs, when they came into competition with new lines, having all the first-rate appliances of modern science, it was necessary, to meet the competition at their stations, to keep the line in as good order as their neighbours. To accomplish that object they had spent very large sums, and he was sure no. gentleman could go from one end of the line to the other without seeing that the revenue of the Proprietors had been largely taxed in order to accomplish that which the new Companies were doing. They hoped very soon to complete their stations, and he believed they had undertaken the worst of them, so that there were scarcely any others of importance to be dealt with. One or two had cropped up recently, and the Wolverhampton and Walsall stations required some improvements, but he thought there were no others which needed any greater expenditure than had been already contemplated. They were improving the Euston station. They were going to have a new arrival platform, to raise the roof for a little ornamentation, that they might look as well as their neighbours, and making an approach through the square. They were going also to enlarge the station by taking in the carriage shops; and altogether, from one end of the line to the other, their stations were equal and probably superior to those of any other line in the kingdom. They had accomplished that whilst seeing that the income was rightly developed, so that the current Proprietors had, to a certain extent, the advantage of new works which following Proprietors would have to maintain. They had in every way done that which seemed advisable to make the property secure, in the hope that it would gradually mend in value. If the Proprietors looked to the maintenance of way account, they would see that it had increased very considerably. But out of that increase what had been done? The Company had spent for the protection of the public £48,000 in the single item of concentrating and locking points, so that there should be no accidents from facing points, and their system was simplified as much as possible. They had laid something like 72 miles of double line of rails in steel upon revenue account, and 15 miles upon capital account. The revenue account had contributed about £230,000 in the course of a few years, and this very half-year had taken £15,000 out of the revenue being the extra cost of steel over iron. That extra cost was now diminishing very much by the ceasing of Bessemer's patent on the 12th of the present month, and it was proposed to do a larger quantity in mileage, though possibly not more in money than had been actually spent last year. They would relay with steel rails something like 43 miles this year. Again, in the course of a few years they had done away, at the expense of the Proprietors, with 37 level crossings upon the line. Some of them were very costly, but still it increased the safety of the travelling public, to which their attention had been greatly directed. Further than that, they had spent £9,000 in the year, in fishing rails on certain of the branches not originally fished, and they had also spent something like £11,000 in additional weight of iron rails. Some of those charges had come to an end. They would very shortly have renewed all the bridges that were wood with iron and stone, and had nearly done all that was needful in the way of fishing. Whilst doing this they look forward to a future of considerable prosperity if the country answered to the improvements which had already begun in it. He believed the whole stock was practically rather more than maintained. But they had taken care to err on the safe side. The auditor was not able to put his hand upon a black spot. There was nothing in the accounts of the Company that could be challenged by any person whatever. He would just refer to the benefit which they had derived from the good credit which they had had for a great many years. Even in the worst times of difficulty the credit of the London and North Western Company had always been maintained with the greatest and most scrupulous exactness. They derived benefit from that in every way. They had been known as the best, most exact, and most punctual payers in the country. They were in consequence now able to get out their debenture stock in larger quantities,

---

The LNWR stockholder in the Moon era received reports such as this. Although the print is small, we have left it in its original 1870 format, to retain the full flavour of the original.

meetings took place once a year. Extraordinary meetings were also held, often on the same day as the ordinary meetings, to consider raising fresh capital and other special matters. Annual reports and the proceedings of meeting are often thought of as being dry-as-dust, yet in reality they show the interplay between Board members and the ordinary stockholder, then a far more significant figure than in today's companies with their mass of investment trusts. They can also provide an insight into the thoughts and hopes of the great and the ordinary, and give us an understanding we would otherwise be denied. To cover even a fraction of this world would take several volumes, so all we can do is to dip into this well which most readers will never have visited before.

Let us become, by proxy, a stockholder in the London & North Western Railway. Twice a year, an envelope would drop on our mat containing the half-yearly report and accounts of the Company. We might, of course, have told the Company to send the report to our bankers. If so, we

3

and at lower rates, he believed, than any other Company. During the half-year just ended they had issued £800,000 of that stock, in the previous half-year £700,000, making something like a million and a half in the year. Since the 1st of January they had issued £250,000 more, and it was now going on at about the same rate at which he hoped it would continue until the whole amount was converted. The Proprietors knew that they were redeeming debentures at 4 per cent. by an issue of perpetual debenture stock, and he might say, to show that there was no security like it in the world, that their income would now more than meet all the debentures of the Company, if they had to pay them off as they fell due. Therefore there was every security that it was possible to imagine for their debentures and debenture stock, and the Directors believed it was so well appreciated that within a very short period they would be able to convert the whole of the debentures into debenture stock, and that the stock would go off more quickly as the facts were better known. There was one point with which they had been rather annoyed during the half-year. It would be seen that the rates and taxes had increased. No doubt there was some hope even there; not from any legislative enactment, but because the great towns were getting frightened at their own extravagance. As a notable instance he might mention that the town of Liverpool had withdrawn its bill this year. So that he did hope the great town rates, at all events, would not increase, if they did not diminish. It had been shocking to see the towns wasting their money, and spending it, without taking any account of how it was to be got. With regard to the telegraphs, they had secured the services of one of the most efficient officers of the late Electric Telegraph Company; and their arrangement for carrying out the telegraph system on the line was complete, and would be very materially improved. He thought the public ought to see the difference between Government and Railway management. If the Railway Companies had been guilty of what the Government had done, they would never have heard the end of it. They would have taken the thing as it was, spent a large sum in making it suit the wants of the public, and gradually work it into shape. The Government had taken it, and without trying to work it gradually they had worked it out of shape and into a difficulty. He had stated already what the Company were doing for the public. The Company were keeping their road up, and spending great sums of money upon its improvement. They were now trying the experiment whether the line could be worked upon the actual block system. It must be observed that no system whatever would infallibly prevent accidents. That was an impossibility. The Company did the best they could to have as few as possible, and he believed, as he had often told them, there was no mode of travelling in the world so safe as railway travelling. They were trying the experiment of the absolute block upon 14½ miles of a most difficult portion, the Stour Valley, and had worked 9½ miles of single line upon it. They had, also, 310 miles of line worked upon their own telegraph caution system, and they believed that to be the best and most effectual. At the same time, Parliament seemed inclined to be most tyrannical, and make the Companies do all manner of things; if they were all to be carried out it would be a very serious item against the railway. In fact they were now spending many thousands a year to carry out their own improved system. He then came to a point which was mentioned every year, though they had never been able to make anything out of it, namely, compensation for accidents. They knew that in this country we were all governed by parliamentary talkers and doctrinaires. Good management would have enabled the Board of Trade to guide and direct the Railway Companies, instead of being, as at present, in antagonism with them. But he believed he had now got a man of common sense at the head of the Board of Trade in Mr. John Bright; and he (the chairman) had a great hope that a reasonable view would be taken; and at all events the matter would be fairly discussed. The railway Companies had agreed that they would promote a bill in Parliament to raise the question, and it would be seen what would come of it. He could give instances without end of the apparent iniquity of the present law. A blind man went into one of their stations near Birmingham, he had nobody with him, he caught his foot in a nail which happened to have started, he fell down stairs, and the Company had to pay him compensation. At one of the stations, a boy got on to the mantelpiece, it fell, and the Company had to pay compensation. The North London Company had been mulcted in £4,000, and the sum total which they received for the fare, was five-eighths of a penny. They all knew the case of the Brighton Company, and their liability for £50,000 for a train which earned only £17. In point of fact, the pecuniary liability attending the carrying passengers was so great that he believed it had a great deal to do with diminishing the excursion traffic of the country. But, as

showing the great inequality of the present law, he would refer to an accident which occurred on the Great Northern Railway. Because a man had not made a will, his eldest son took all the property, and the whole of the younger children came upon the railway Company. If the will had divided the property, his children would have had a beneficial interest in his death. As it was, they lost by his death, and the Great Northern had to pay compensation. So again, with regard to the Abergele accident: some people really benefited by it. But the point which had always struck him most forcibly was that the common law did not provide for the case; and Parliament was obliged to legislate specially for the purpose; and then the railway Companies were obliged to pay everybody, and the prejudices of juries were against them. In one case, a sum had been offered to a man who pretended to have been injured, he declined to accept it, and it was afterwards discovered that he had not been in the accident at all; and the same thing had occurred with the Midland Company. But, in fact, at present the responsibility for accident rested largely with the Board of Trade, who approved the Bye-Laws, and some of the Regulations, and the Works and Signals before allowing a line to be opened for passenger traffic. The railway Companies were like outcasts, and judges and juries were sometimes prejudiced against them. He also complained of the remarks made by Vice-Chancellor James on the previous day, in granting an injunction against the company at the instance of the Duke of Bedford, which he said were extra-judicial, and as they were founded upon a misapprehension, he expressed his confidence that that learned judge would, on reflection, regret what he had said, there being no justification for the imputation of improper conduct on the part of the London and North Western Company. He would not trespass further upon the time of the Proprietors, but should be happy to answer any questions, and would conclude by moving the adoption of the report and statement of accounts.

Sir HARDMAN EARLE seconded the motion.

Mr. MICHELL called attention to the large amount paid for passenger duty, and said they might fairly urge on Parliament in mitigation of that duty the great expenses to which Companies were put by providing smoking carriages, warmers in cold weather, and other matters for the accommodation of the public.

Mr. HELPS suggested that it would add very considerably to the convenience of the Shareholders and to the value of the stock to have fixed days for the payment of dividends—say the 1st of March and 1st of September in each year.

THE CHAIRMAN said they always paid the dividends as early as possible; they would be payable for the past half-year on the 23rd inst. As to the passenger duty, he believed their tolls were lower than those of any other Company and so they were authorised to add the duty to the fares. He thought it was more a question for the public than for this Company. If the duty were removed the public would reap the advantage in lower fares. With regard to the compensation bill, he hoped it would be supported by the Shareholders as a most desirable measure for railway Companies and the public.

The report was then unanimously adopted. A dividend of £3 10s. per cent. for the half-year ending the 31st of December last, out of the net profits, was declared upon the ordinary stock and shares of the Company. The proposal to provide additional steamboats and to execute the works stated in the report was approved, and the addition to the capital of £317,795 for those purposes was sanctioned. A formal resolution to exercise the borrowing powers of the Company was adopted. The retiring auditor, Mr. R. W. Hand, was unanimously re-elected. The four retiring Directors, Mr. R. Birley, Mr. W. N. Hodgson, M.P., Lord A. Paget, and Mr. W. Tipping, M.P., were re-elected. The two vacancies at the board were filled up by the election of the Earl of Caithness, and Mr. W. Lowther, M.P.

The meeting was then made special, and two bills promoted by the Company were approved, one for conferring additional powers on the Company in relation to their own undertaking and the undertakings of other Companies; the other was to make further provision for steam communication between Holyhead and Ireland. Two bills promoted jointly with other Companies in respect of steamboats and the Preston station were approved; and four bills, promoted by the Birmingham canal Navigations, the Dublin, Wicklow, and Wexford railway, the Ellesmere and Glyn Valley Railway, and the Great Western Railway Company, were also approved.

The proceedings concluded with a vote of thanks to the chairman and Directors.

---

would probably have arranged to have the dividends sent to the bank as well, so would miss the excitement of the dividend warrant, with its orange and white Britannia seal, landing on the mat. If we had been an early shareholder in the LNWR, we would have seen C.E. Stewart's name as Secretary, though it is doubtful if we would have been aware of his extraordinary career, running away to sea as a youngster and becoming a China Seas smuggler, before returning home as the valued adviser to a diplomatic mission, and finally to the Secretaryship of the London & North Western Railway!

Stewart's name might also appear on our share certificate, along with that of Henry Booth, whose long association with the Liverpool & Manchester Railway spoke of the antiquity of the LNWR as a railway even in the 1850s.

The Court of Proprietors met in the stately offices above the Great Hall at Euston, and whether we have come there by train from the far reaches of the line, or by cab, the dignity of our surroundings will have reminded us of the prestige of this great railway. Waiting for the meeting to begin, we are surrounded by the tall hats, flowing beards and sideburns of Victorian

Swaylands.
Penshurst
Kent
Sep. 29th 1870.

Sir,

May I hope for your voted support at the Annual Election in February 1871 in favor of my Step-son, who is duly qualified, & is a Candidate for a seat at the Board of Directors on the London & North Western Railway.

From long & intimate knowledge I can strongly recommend him, as likely to make a very good Director, with leisure (having recently left the Navy on the score of health) to devote to the Duties involved, & energy and ability to perform them successfully. I believe him to be one worthy of your confidence should you honor him with your support.

I am Sir
Yours truly,
Edward Cropper

Shareholder

Late Director on the London and North Western Railway Board. J.O.

The Cropper family's involvement with the LNWR at Board level spanned several decades. In this letter, Edward Cropper is canvassing support for his stepson, H.D. Macaulay, late of the Royal Navy.

high society. The conversation ebbs and flows; world events, the price of consols, greetings to old friends, all assail our ears. As the time draws near for the meeting to begin, the hubbub subsides. If we are present each year, the ritual will be familiar to us, but in our proxy journey, we cannot make the trip a score of times.

We could hark back to the days of George Glyn, Lord Wolverton, as Chairman, or of the Marquis of Chandos, but greatest of all North Western Chairmen was the formidable and austere Richard Moon. Much has been written

LONDON AND NORTH WESTERN RAILWAY.

(No. 1255.)

(2080)

Secretary's Office, Euston Station,
London, N.W. 9th Nov 1893

Sir,

Enclosed herewith I beg to hand you the undermentioned Certificate No. 5535 for £ 450 3 per cent. Debenture Stock. This Stock has been duly registered in the Company's Books, together with a notification that the Holder is in respect thereof entitled to the benefits of the Forged Transfers Acts, 1891 and 1892, in accordance with the Resolution of the Directors of the 5th October, 1893, copy of which is printed on the back hereof. I have to request that you will be pleased to sign and return to me the subjoined form of acknowledgment.

I am,

Your obedient Servant,

THOMAS HOUGHTON,

Secretary.

Edward W. Catin Esq

about Moon, but the modern reader seldom has the chance of listening to Richard Moon himself, speaking across more than a century. But the document on pages 24-25 takes us back to 19 February 1870, when Richard Moon, his knighthood still many years in the future, tells us about his railway, his objectives, likes and dislikes.

Above *New capital was still being issued regularly in the 1890s, and Thomas Houghton sent out this slip with Debenture Stock certificates in 1893.*

Below *This 1906 dividend warrant was issued by the then secretary, James Bishop, whose entire career was spent with the LNWR, save for a spell as secretary to the LNWR Chairman, Lord Stalbridge. Bishop became secretary in 1904, and retired on the fusion of the LNWR and LYR.*

London and North Western Railway.

(No. 53.)

DIVIDEND STATEMENT.

No. 5732

Name *Francis H J Darbyshire + Thomas M Clutterbuck*

Secretary's Office,
Euston Station, London, N.W.,
22nd February, 1907.

In accordance with your instructions, I have paid to **The North & South Wales Bank, Limited,** *Castle Street, Liverpool* the amount due to you for Dividend, as per statement at foot. *credit of Income a/c*

I hereby certify that the amount of Income Tax deducted will be paid by the Company to the proper Officer for the Receipt of Taxes.

Proprietors requiring exemption from Income Tax are informed that the Inland Revenue will receive this Statement as a Voucher in claiming the same.

NOTWITHSTANDING THAT YOUR DIVIDEND IS TRANSMITTED TO YOUR BANKERS DIRECT, IT IS VERY DESIRABLE THAT YOU SHOULD INFORM ME WITHOUT DELAY OF ANY CHANGE IN YOUR FULL POSTAL ADDRESS, IN ORDER THAT COMMUNICATIONS AFFECTING YOUR HOLDING MAY NOT FAIL TO REACH YOU.

JAMES BISHOP, *Secretary*.

One Hundred & Twenty-Second Dividend—Half-Year ending 31st December, 1906

This Statement to be forwarded to the Proprietor by the Banker.

	£	s.	d.
CONSOLIDATED GUARANTEED STOCK.........at 4 per Cent. per Annum £			
CONSOLIDATED PREFERENCE STOCK.........at 4 per Cent. per Annum £			
PREFERENCE STOCK (1902).........at 4 per Cent. per Annum £			
CONSOLIDATED STOCK ....at 7¼ per Cent. per Annum £ 2890	104	15	3
Income Tax at 1/- in the £	5	4	9
E.&O.E. £	99	10	6

2 Growing Pains

'The Directors are happy to report that the Act to consolidate the London & Birmingham, Grand Junction and Manchester & Birmingham Railway companies received the Royal Assent on 16 July last.' Thus began the first Directors' report of the London & North Western Railway. At its birth in 1846, the new company possessed 420 route miles and 120 stations. It carried six million passengers, excluding 'seasons', 1½ million tons of goods, and gave employment to 10,000. Its passenger trains regularly loaded to 12-14 carriages, and as many as 50 wagons could be seen on its freight trains.

Inspector Faulkner, stationed at Rugby, had scarcely had time to get used to the new title that autumn when, on 10 October, he held a telegraph form in his hand. It was shortly after 8.00 am that the message had come in. It began 'Thomas Trotter from Derby states that he has been robbed'. The miscreant was expected upon the next train from Derby, due about 11.00 am. As Faulkner paced up and down waiting for the train to arrive, he must have thought of the sensational Tawell case on the Great Western Railway the previous year. Tawell had led a double life, a married and respected philanthropist in London, and keeping a mistress in Slough. Tiring of the liaison, he paid his mistress a farewell visit armed with cyanide, but her dying screams alerted a neighbour, and he was seen boarding the Paddington train. His description was telegraphed to London and he was in due course arrested and sentenced to death. As the hands of the clock drew near to 11.00 am, the Derby train rolled over the impressive viaduct on the outskirts of Rugby. William Eltinon was in a jubilant mood; he had put many miles between himself and the scene of his crime, by the fastest conveyance known to man. No pursuit was possible. The wires stretched along the lineside meant nothing to him. The train stopped in Rugby station, William Eltinon climbed out of the carriage, perhaps a little stiffly, for it was a long journey, and the springs were none too good. A man in a frock-tailed coat with polished buttons was waiting for him. The wheels of justice moved fast, and a few days later, William Eltinon was commencing six months' hard labour; he had ample time to reflect just how much those innocuous-looking wires had mattered.

The fledgling LNWR police had another feather in their caps that same month. A country butcher, travelling perhaps for the first time, bought a ticket and boarded the train. The booking clerk saw his dog jump into the coach, and went over to request the fare. An altercation broke out, during which the butcher jumped out of the train. As he and the booking clerk stood arguing, the train moved off, and the butcher scrambled back in, gleefully chortling to the other occupants of the compartment about how he had 'done the beggars'. Like Tawell and Eltinon, he was in for a shock, for when he arrived in Birmingham, a railway policeman greeted him: 'Sir, you have a dog with you, for which the fare has not been paid. You must either fob out the needful, or I take you into custody'.

Today, the duties of the policeman and railway signalman are quite different, but in those early days the policeman's lot covered a multitude of duties, not just security work. The railway policeman could himself fall foul of the law, as Bernard Fossey discovered the following year. Fossey was stationed at Wolverton, and on 5 June

The original L&B station in Rugby adjoined Newbold Road, across which the line was carried by a handsome mock-Tudor arch, a wise gesture in view of the influence of Rugby School in town affairs.

Right *From 1839, the L&B made con-*
nection with the Birmingham & Derby
Junction Railway at Hampton, 103 miles
from Euston. The B&DJ lines curve
towards Derby in the right distance.

Below *Tile Hill station, on the outskirts*
of Coventry, started life as an L&B cross-
ing keeper's cottage, became a stopping place
in 1847, and remains of the L&B cottage
survived until March 1966.

1847 was in charge of a set of facing points on the main line. Somehow his mind wandered, with the result that an express ran into some coal wagons in the siding, with seven fatalities. On 2 August, Fossey stood before the Buckingham Assizes, charged with so negligently and carelessly conducting himself, 'as to turn a train of passenger carriages from the main rails on to a siding of goods wagons, whereby a collision occurred between the said train and certain coal wagons on the said siding'. Fossey received two years with hard labour.

The early years of the nineteenth century were marked by periods of acute labour unrest, and various attempts to found trade unions. These culminated in the Chartist outbreaks, the last and greatest of which was in 1848. The Chartists sought redress for various grievances, and made use of processions, marches, petitions, meetings and strikes. There was also a small but unpredictable extreme fringe, from whom trouble was feared. Violence or even sabotage was a possibility, and the LNWR ordered a large supply of police truncheons just in case. The enginemen, being a skilled body of workers who could easily meet at the sheds, were relatively easy to bring out on strike, and as the unrest mounted the LNWR took the precaution of providing for replacement men. Naturally the emergency men did not have the same route knowledge as the regular staff, and Mark Huish issued orders that the Guards and Breaksmen were to join the new crews on the footplate. The Board later indicated its appreciation by means of a gratuity and a certificate, which is a fascinating reflection upon labour conditions of the time:

LONDON AND NORTH WESTERN RAILWAY

Extract from the Minutes of the Board, under date 9th September, 1848.

The Manager having brought before the Board the names of the Guards and Breaks-men, who, under his Circular Notice of the 7th August, took their stand on the footplate of the Engines with new Drivers; and having reported the good conduct of these men in the novel and somewhat trying position in which they were unexpectedly placed.

It was Resolved:-

That this Board has much pleasure in recording its sense of the excellent conduct of the Guards and Breaksmen, during the period of the Line being worked by the new Drivers;

That the ready and cheerful manner in which the whole of them undertook the duty suddenly imposed upon them merits the approbation of this Board;

That the freedom from accident, in the conduct of the service during the period alluded to is in no slight degree to be atttributed to the active assistance of this class of their Servants — and that their attention to orders under very peculiar circumstances, deserves this testimony from the Board in corroboration of that general good conduct which has so long characterised them as a body.

Ordered:-

That a Gratuity be given to each man employed on this extra duty. That this Minute be printed, and that a copy of it be given to the Guards and Breaksmen, endorsed with the name of the party to whom it specially applies.

By order of the Board of Directors,

MARK HUISH
General Manager.

Euston Station, 11th Sept. 1848.

One of the problems facing Mark Huish in the early days was the multiplicity of local banks, often one or two-man affairs, and the frequency with which they collapsed, leaving their notes valueless. A favourite way of getting rid of worthless notes was to unload them on the railway in payment of the train fare! Instructions were issued from time to time cautioning station masters and booking clerks against accepting notes unless the bank was known to be sound, and reminding them that they were held responsible. Another 'dodge' perpetrated on the railways was to shave tiny clippings off the gold sovereigns which were then legal tender. After a few such escapades, the amount of gold built up, and so long as the sovereign was accepted, it was a useful way of picking up some money. Light coins became such a problem that most merchants kept scales on the counter to weigh them, and would deduct a few pence for a light coin.

The LNWR adopted similar precautions, but one precaution can sometimes be used to create a new trick, and an instance of this led to some unwanted publicity in June 1850. A young man was booking a ticket at Coventry, and when he tendered a gold sovereign, the booking clerk told him it was under weight, and that he was deducting 8d. The passenger protested and handed the clerk another coin, which was said to be 4d under weight. At this stage, Isaac Benoliel, a jeweller and frequent passenger, joined in. The clerk angrily demanded what it was to do with him. Benoliel retorted, 'A great deal; I am often travelling up and down the line, and were I to submit to such an imposition, I should be robbed to a great extent by fellows such as you.' Hearing raised voices, the station master hurriedly intervened, found out what was the matter, weighed the coin himself and, finding it in order, returned the 4d. Such episodes were not uncommon, and whilst there were light coins in circulation, and the clerks had to protect themselves, it was widely believed that a number of clerks kept underweight coins to hand to switch for correct sovereigns in order to make a little on the side. It was rumoured that the trick had even spread to Euston itself. As the century drew on, the practice declined, due to better currency standards and judicious use of the railway police turning up as would-be passengers!

The animal kingdom could give the North Western almost as many problems as mankind! On 7 September 1850, a cow decided to put George Stephenson's famous dictum about the effect of a collision between cow and train — 'It would be too bad for the coo' — to the test. It strayed into the path of the 7.00 pm Rugby to Euston. The cow did not live to tell the tale, but whilst it was unable to derail the locomotive, tender or the three first class carriages at the head of the train, it thoroughly derailed the remaining six coaches. Although they were derailed into the 'six foot', no train was coming in the opposite direction at the time; however, a down train was expected within a few minutes. Whilst the driver ran on light to Wolverton to summon help, the rest of the crew provided front and rear protection for the stricken train. Had there been a train in the opposite direction, or had the coaches derailed to the side of the line, which was on a 25-foot embankment, there could have been heavy loss of life, instead of just bruising and shaking. Despite its demise, it was undoubtedly a moral victory for the cow. The carcass was deposited by the lineside for the farmer to collect, but the countryfolk, who had gathered to watch the excitement, had other ideas, and it had vanished piecemeal into many a stewpot ere morning!

On a much lighter note, but in similar vein, a pair of water wagtails provided the District Engineer with some headaches, as they concluded that the ideal place to build their nest was at the foot of one of the large ventilating shafts of Kilsby tunnel. A less suitable location is hard to envisage, for apart from the steam, smoke and noise, which would hardly contribute to bringing up a well-balanced fledgling, the parents had to fly in a corkscrew fashion up the shaft! The District Engineer's men, with the traditional English sentimentality over animals, resolutely refused to do any work which would disturb the nest, and spent a good deal of time seeing that the eggs came to no harm.

As with a number of tunnels, the risk of collision was such that a form of block working was

Above *Until the BR rebuilding of Coventry station, an Edward Bury water column of L&B vintage stood at the end of the down platform. The joint between the horizontal pipe and the 'bag' was poorly designed, and many enginemen recalled a shower from a split bag!*

Below *An early engraving of one of the ventilating shafts in Kilsby Tunnel. Either single line working was in force, or the engraver did not know the rules of the road, and put the engine on the wrong line!*

instituted at an early date, but on Monday 14 June 1852, the precautions were to prove inadequate. A ballast special left Birmingham early that day, and passed Rugby at about 11.00 am. At 11.50 am, the Bletchley coal left Rugby as usual. Not being signalled to stop at the north portal of Kilsby tunnel, the latter's driver proceeded normally, but near the centre of the tunnel saw a train ahead of him. He barely had time to shut off steam, throw the engine into reverse and jump before the heavy coal ploughed into the rear of the ballast train. It was then common for permanent way men to travel on top of the ballast wagons, and as the coal engine smashed into the train, several pw men were thrown off and injured. One of their number, Thomas Williams, was trapped between two vehicles and seriously injured. He was rushed by train to hospital in Coventry, but died at six o'clock that evening. At the inquest, Mr Coulter of the Superintendent's office described the rudimentary block system in force, which involved telegraph posts at each end of the tunnel. The north end man, William Chappell, who had worked on the line since 1838 without previous misconduct, should not have admitted the coal until he had received 'train out' for the ballast. The inquest jury found Chappel 'guilty of negligence in suffering the goods train to enter the tunnel while the ballast train was there, before receiving the usual and necessary train out'. He was committed to the Assizes for trial.

The haphazard signalling system, even at a busy junction, was demonstrated at Rugby a few years later. On 7 January 1856, Michael Steel, driver of the down 'Brum Goods', was rather annoyed. He had arrived in Rugby to time at 5.20 pm, but here he was, sitting in a siding at the north end of the station near the Trent Valley Junction, at 6.30 pm, when by rights he should have been in Coventry. Just then, John Baker, the goods foreman, gave the 'all right' to the guard, who showed Steel a green light. Michael Steel gave two blasts on the whistle to attract the pointsman's attention.

The tall fixed signal further down the line remained at red, but this was according to the rules, for one of its varied functions was to hold trains on the down line when a train was signalled from the siding. When, in response to his whistles, he saw the pointsman's white handlamp flash, he eased open the regulator. Jonathan Abbott, his fireman, saw the white light as well, and called out, 'All Right, Mickey, go on'. Slowly the heavy goods moved forwards, but with 50 wagons and a greasy rail, it took some effort to get under way, and Abbott scrambled forward to place sand on the rails from the buffer plank. As they were nearing the junction with the Leamington line, 270 yards away, they had picked up to 5 or 6 mph. To his horror, Michael Steel suddenly saw a Leamington passenger train cut across right in his path. Before he had time to do anything, the engine ploughed into the ducket of the guard's van and the first/second composite behind it. Abbott, out on the buffer plank, concentrating on his sanding, was seriously injured, and died a few hours later.

At the inquest, the Superintendent of Police, Mr Bedford, explained the signalling system. On the approach of a Leamington train, the pointsman was to turn the Trent Valley and Birmingham signals to red, and give a green to the Leamington branch. For a train to pull out of the down siding, he was to turn a red on to the main line and the Leamington, and hand signal the goods out with his white handlamp.

Henry Eldridge, the pointsman at the junction, had commenced duty at Rugby on 2 January, having previously worked on the Buckinghamshire line for two days, at Roade Cutting for two nights, and a few days at Northampton. He explained that his duty, when it was clear for a train to leave the siding, was to 'put on the red signal and wave a white light to indicate the line was clear'. He denied giving a white handsignal to Steel, but admitted having his lamp lit 'as it was dark'. He was adamant that he had held it in front of his body, and shielded it from Steel. Robert Ray, the driver of an up ore train, confirmed the statement by the Leamington driver, John Cryer, that his signal had gone from red to green when he was about 300 yards away, but he was unable to say what the fixed signal for the main line gave. He did recall that Eldridge has walked halfway over the bridge towards Steel about the time the latter whistled.

Shortly after the accident, it seemed that Eldridge thought he was to blame, and had remarked to John Whittle, the locomotive foreman, 'If I get over this, I'll not turn another train'. His subsequent denial of the statement, and the fact that he had turned an engine into the 'cut' at Oxford some time previously, told against him. The inquest finally concluded that the 'collision between the Birmingham Goods and the Leamington Passenger train was occasioned by the incompetency of the pointsman Eldridge to discharge his complicated and difficult duty'. The LNWR did not escape censure, and a rider was added suggesting 'a special signal post erected to apply to the Goods Siding exclusively'. Clearly, the system was as much to blame as Eldridge, for the chance of a pointsman accidentally showing a white hand-signal to the siding was too high, particularly as the red on the main signal was as likely when a train was coming from Leamington, as when one was signalled from the down siding. It was

J.E. McConnell was the first Locomotive Superintendent of the Southern Division. His engines had vanished before the end of the Webb era, but several tenders survived on the Cromford & High Peak section as water carriers into BR days. Less well known was this tender, which was running as LMS 05396 in the 'thirties, as part of a 'vacuum cleaning train'. This peculiar formation is seen at Bletchley. (H.J. Stretton Ward)

also quite possible that an engine crew, irritated by a long delay, and keen to get away, might take the most momentary flash of a white lamp as the 'All right' signal, and immediately direct their attention to getting under way, instead of pondering whether the white had been for them.

An accident on the Birmingham line between Long Lawford and Church Lawford on 4 May 1856 resulted in no fatalities, but demonstrated the flimsy nature of the freight stock of the day, and could easily have had dire consequences. A down 'luggage' train was in the section when the 'axletree' (or W-iron) on a gunpowder van collapsed. Ten wagons were derailed, six being smashed into fragments. Thankfully, the gunpowder van did not catch fire. A gang of labourers was hurriedly dispatched to the scene. The loads in the wrecked wagons had included two pianofortes, which lay at grotesque angles, thousands of tin whistles, bonnets, shawls, rolling-pins, and scores of dolls. The latter had fared badly, and the accident site was likened to a battlefield, with limbs and bodies bestrewing

the ground. The villagers of Lawford had turned out to watch the proceedings, and as the labourers set to work, dense clouds of black dust rose up, for the wrecked wagons had also contained several cases of lampblack which had burst open, and within minutes everyone on the site had assumed the complexion of chimney sweeps. By this time, the labourers had discovered a far more interesting cargo — several cases of rum, which had not been improved by their sudden decanting on to the ground. Labourers and villagers alike, all were seized with a firm resolve that this precious liquid, albeit mixed with lampblack, should not go to waste, and the foremen and gangers faced an infuriating task, throwing

drunken villagers off railway land, and goading their somewhat merry men back to work. It was later estimated that damage came to well over one thousand pounds.

The 1866 Watford tunnel accident has been recounted from time to time, but what is seldom highlighted is the size of the train. On Monday 21 May 1866, an excursion left Northampton (Bridge St) station at 8.00 am. It was well filled, but at Bletchley coaches from two other trains, from Banbury and Oxford, were added. Two engines were needed, the train engine being a big McConnell goods, and the pilot an Allan 2-4-0, No 89. By this time, the train consisted of 40 carriages, into which had been crammed *two thousand* passengers. At Tring, the train was turned on to the slow line which extended as far as Watford tunnel, where it was gauntleted with the fast line. The fast was protected by a trap,

Below *A Parcels Way Bill from Coventry, dating from the 1870s.*
Bottom *An 1873 LNWR Parcels Way Bill from Euston.*

An 1883 engraving looking from the Doric arch across Drummond Street to Euston Place and the Euston Hotel.

but the train was unable to pull up; it ran through the trap and into a bridge abutment a few yards north of the tunnel portal.

A bizarre accident a few years later suggested that it was not merely in brakes that the North Western could err. On 23 January 1871, just after the 3.40 pm Euston to Birmingham had left Leighton Buzzard, the flooring in one compartment of a second class coach started to disintegrate. The solitary passenger hastily scrambled on to the seat, where he was bombarded with splinters as the floor was progressively smashed to pieces against the wheels. He leaned out of the window to pull the communication cord, but was unable to attract the attention of the enginemen, despite clearly hearing the gong ringing himself. As the floor looked even more threatening, he finally decided to jump for it, as the lesser of two evils, and, apart from a few bruises, survived his ordeal. That the floor of a passenger carriage should fall apart in motion does not speak too highly of the carriage examiners, or Wolverton, at the time.

A still more bizarre incident which took place a few years later become a legend on the 'London & Birmingham' section, and was still talked

of 30 years and more later. On 10 July 1877, the breaksman of a down goods burst into Station Master Allen's office at Rugby to say there was a tiger loose on the line somewhere between there and Wolverton! One can imagine the station master's thoughts, confronted with an excited and incoherent breaksman babbling about a tiger, but the man went on to explain that the tiger had been in a cage on his train at Wolverton, but had vanished by Rugby. A light engine was hurriedly sent on safari, and at Buckby bank the beast was spotted. Sadly, the only two written accounts differ. In one, a porter got off the engine to consult with the signalman, in the other it was the signalman who came down from his box; but both versions agree that when the tiger showed interest, the railwayman scaled the nearest pole at record speed.

The engine crew, feeling that discretion was the better part of valour, departed in haste in the direction of Wolverton 'to get assistance'. Fortunately for the unlucky soul up the pole, the engine did not have to go all the way to Wolverton, but merely as far as Weedon, where a large barracks existed. A contemporary account noted that apart from a 240,000 stand of small arms, Weedon depot possessed extensive powder magazines, etc. The railwaymen explained to a somewhat incredulous barracks duty officer that they

L. & N. W. Rly.   Standard Double-end Tank Local Engine, used
on all Suburban Trains and Metropolitan Rly.

Regular travellers in the London area became used to the busy little 4ft 6in 2-4-2Ts on the various suburban services. Often called the 'Mansion House Tanks', because a batch was built to work via Kensington and the District Railway to Mansion House, they were widely used on suburban and branch duties. No 136 ran from 1882 until 1915.

required assistance on a Tiger Shoot, and a party of three army officers were duly dispatched to deal with the problem.

In the meanwhile, the tiger had been circling the pole, making encouraging noises, much to the joy of the man who had taken refuge there. The accounts differ once more. In one, the army officers arrived, and the tiger was duly shot. In the second version, the officers found, to their chagrin, that they had left their ammunition at the depot, and a local farmer had to be roped in to do the job. It was sad that a fine animal had to be shot, but it was felt that the tiger, which was probably somewhat bruised and angry after the shaking of a train ride and its escape, was too dangerous to attempt to recapture.

A constant theme throughout the nineteenth century on the L&B section was the growth in through and local traffic. Triple, then quadruple track was laid in over much of the line, and new sidings were added to meet public demands or to cater for factories, works and quarries. It will

suffice to tell the story of one of these. A band of iron-producing strata sweeps in a curved path across the South Midlands. At one time, the ironstone workings around Corby, on the Midland Railway, were well known, as were the workings in the direction of Banbury. The North Western main line, however, is not usually associated with iron ore workings in the way that these other routes are, but south of Weedon the L&B runs close to the village of Heyford. In the 1850s, George Pell opened the Heyford Iron Works, although these were not at first rail-served. A second plant, the Stowe Iron Works, opened in 1866. As output rose, Plevins & Co, who owned the works on the up side of the line, negotiated with the LNWR for a private siding. Agreement was reached in July 1870, and a siding laid in. By November 1870, a siding had also been provided on the down side for the Castle Dykes Iron Ore Co. A branch off this siding, which was worked from a 'point box' on the up side of the line at the south end of the sidings, ran to the Stowe Iron Works. With the pressure of freight on the main line, numerous refuge sidings were necessary, and Heyford soon boasted a 75-wagon refuge on the down side. In 1874, this was extended to hold 95 wagons — or in other words to comfortably hold at least two full freights. The primitive point box was replaced by a proper signal box, 'Heyford Sidings', which provided greater safety and an additional block post.

These improvements were soon overtaken by events, and by the summer of 1877 plans were in hand to extend the refuge sidings, convert them into goods loops, and add new signal boxes. The plans were finalized by the Signal Department at Crewe on 13 September. After doing the rounds of the other departments for scrutiny, they came before George Findlay, the LNWR Manager, on 13 October, then, two days later, Richard Moon initialled his sanction. He may have winced at the cost, £572 for signalling work at the south end alone! An oversight in the Signal Department caused great concern, for no names had officially been bestowed upon the boxes. In later years, the LNWR was to develop a firm tradition of numbering multiple boxes at a single location — well into double numbers in the case of Edge Hill, Liverpool. Numbering was already in fashion in the 1870s, but it was not yet paramount, and the District Signal Inspector was to write plaintively, 'What is cabin to be called? — Heyford Loop or Heyford No 1, and present Heyford Siding box to be Heyford No 2?' In the event, neither name was selected. The sidings box became Heyford Middle, and the two new boxes, when they opened on 15 April 1878, did so as Heyford South and North boxes! What did the LNWR get for £572 at Heyford South? A new cabin, four distants, four home signals, four points and a facing point lock, all connected up and complete.

Further changes came in 1884, with proposals to remove the 1878 North Box and rename Heyford 'Middle' box as Heyford North. This would be 1,260 yards away from the south box. Whether this Middle box was the original 1874 structure, or a new 1882-83 box, is not clear. The alteration necessitated shortening the up loop, and making alterations on the down side. Previously, access to the down sidings, one of which served the 'Corporation of the Sons of the Clergy', had been controlled by the North box, but as this was to come away, a connection was laid in from the down loop to the down sidings, the down loop terminating near the old Middle box. Other than for the telegraph instruments, electricity was virtually unknown in signalling work at the time, but with the removal of the 1878 North box, a crossover by that box was to be worked by ground frame, electrically released from the new North

(ex-Middle) Box!

Aside from its complex history, which does, however, mirror the piecemeal way in which extensions were found necessary to cope with traffic, and its strangely named siding, Heyford possessed a further claim to fame, for until its closure in 1940, the Heyford Brick Works traffic was shunted by an Aveling Porter 'traction engine'-type locomotive. This lay by the lineside for many years, until rescued for the Clapham Museum.

The LNWR was not noted for its enthusiasm for special excursion traffic in the early days, but a vivid impression of what sort of pressures existed is given when we recount the events of August Bank Holiday 1881. It would have been an important day in any case, for with ever-increasing traffic, the LNWR had decided to put in a loop line from Rugby to Northampton, where it would join the existing Blisworth-Northampton-Peterborough branch. This would finally put Northampton on a through route, and avoid quadrupling the Kilsby Tunnel section. The 'New Line' opened to goods on the Bank Holiday Monday, 1 August. Excursions had been arranged to a variety of destinations, and by 4.00 am Rugby station was thronged with passengers. Over the next few hours, 1,000 passengers went to Blackpool, 1,100 attended a Temperance Meeting at Stanford Park on the LNWR Rugby-Market Harborough line, 500 went to a Godiva Procession in Coventry, and 200 went via the Midland to Leicester. Others went to Euston and Stoneleigh. For several years, the Rugby Co-operative Society had run an excursion to North Wales for the Bank Holiday, but fashions were changing, and Blackpool was the new venue. The special was to commence from Market Harborough at 3.30 am, call at wayside stations to Rugby, which was reached at 4.20, pick up at Brinklow on the Trent Valley line, and then run to Blackpool for 8.45 am. The fare from Harborough was six shillings for a one day excursion, or five shillings from Rugby. The return trip was to leave Blackpool at 7.00 pm, reach Rugby at 11.15 pm, and Market Harborough at midnight.

Bookings were so heavy that it had become apparent to the Co-op officers and Rugby Station Master Allen that two trains would be needed. The first of these left Rugby at 4.30 am with 20 carriages. The second train, which had originated

G—185.

LONDON AND NORTH WESTERN RAILWAY.

SUMMER EXCURSIONS, 1874.

On SATURDAY, August 15th,

FROM THE UNDERMENTIONED STATIONS TO

LIVERPOOL, MANCHESTER,

STOCKPORT, BIRKENHEAD, WARRINGTON, CHESTER, DENBIGH,

Crewe, Nantwich, Oswestry, Shrewsbury, Wellington,

WELSHPOOL, MINSTERLEY, NEWTOWN, MONTGOMERY,

LLANIDLOES, HEREFORD,

LUDLOW, LEOMINSTER, CRAVEN ARMS,

Returning MONDAY, August 17th, or on THURSDAY, August 20th.

Fares for the Double Journey :—

FROM	Hour of departure. a.m.	Liverpool, Manchester, Stockport, Birkenhead, Denbigh, Warrington.		Chester, Crewe, Nantwich.		Oswestry Welshpool, Minsterley, Hereford, Ludlow, Leominster, Craven Arms.		Wellington.		Shrewsbury.		Newtown, Montgomery.		Llanidloes.	
		3rd Cl.	1st Cl.	3rd Cl.	1st Cl.	3rd Cl.	1st Cl.	3rd Cl.	1st Cl.	3rd Cl.	1st Cl.	3rd Cl.	1st Cl.	3rd Cl.	1st Cl.
OXFORD... ... ... 8.45 BICESTER 9. 8		13/	26/	12/	24/	11/	22/	10/	20/	10/	20/	12/	24/	13/	26/
BANBURY(*ViaN.&B.J.R.*)10.5 BUCKINGHAM ... 9.18		12/	24/	11/	22/	10/	20/	8/6	17/	9/	18/	11/	22/	12/	24/
LEAMINGTON(Ave.)11. 5 ,, Milverton 11.10		11/	22/	10/	20/	9/	18/	7/6	15/	8/	16/	10/	20/	11/	22/
COVENTRY 12. 0		10/	20/	9/	18/	8/	16/	6/6	13/	7/	14/	9/	18/	10/	20/

CHILDREN UNDER TWELVE YEARS OF AGE, HALF-PRICE.

Tickets NOT TRANSFERABLE. Personal Luggage under 60 lbs. Free, at PASSENGERS' OWN RISK.
The Company cannot in any way be responsible for detention on the Line; at the same time, EVERY EXERTION will be made to ensure punctuality.

NOTICE OF RETURN.

The Return Train on Monday, Aug. 17th, and Thursday, Aug. 20th, will leave Liverpool (Lime Street) at 9.20 a.m.; Warrington, 10.10 a.m.; Denbigh, 7.15 a.m.; Chester, 10.5 a.m.; Birkenhead, 9.20 a.m.; Manchester, 9.50 a.m.; Stockport, 10.5 a.m.; Oswestry, 8.5 a.m.; Shrewsbury, 10.20 a.m.; Wellington, 10.40 a.m.; Crewe, 11.10 a.m.; Nantwich, 8.52 a.m.; Hereford, 7.30 a.m.; Leominster, 8.7 a.m.; Ludlow, 8.31 a.m.; Craven Arms, 8.54 a.m.; Llanidloes, 5.10 a.m.; Newtown, 5.52 a.m.; Montgomery, 6.13 a.m.; Welshpool, 6.35 a.m.; Minsterley, 9.15 a.m.

Tickets and Small Bills may be obtained of the Booking Clerks at the Stations on the Line.

NOTICE.—Passengers will be booked from Liverpool, Manchester, and other places, on August 17th to Oxford, Banbury, Leamington, Coventry, returning on August 21st.

By Order,   G. FINDLAY,

EUSTON STATION, August 1st, 1874.   *Chief Traffic Manager.*

M'Corquodale & Co., Printers, 6, Cardington Street, London, N.W.

at Market Harborough, and picked up *en route*, collected the left-overs from Rugby and the Brinklow party, and ran 10 minutes after the first portion. Both arrived at Preston to time, but thereafter things went awry, for with 100,000 passengers funnelled into Preston for the Blackpool line, delays were endemic, and the Rugby trains did not reach the seaside until 11.00 am. In the evening the first special was very fortunate. It left almost to time, and only took 90 minutes for the 18 miles to Preston. Once on the West Coast Main Line, there were no further delays and the train pulled into Rugby at 1.00 am, less than two hours late. The second train did not fare so well, for Blackpool station was so inextricably jammed up that the relief service did not reach Rugby until 3.00 am, almost four hours down on its schedule.

The 1,100 passengers on the Temperance outing to Stanford Park had a less hectic time, although a last-minute rush caught the LNWR on the hop, and Station Master Allen had to scrape up the stock for a relief train with next to no notice. The Godiva procession at Coventry had been condemned by the local papers and attacked by the Mayor of Coventry, but it too was well attended, with 500 from Rugby, and thousands more from Birmingham, Nuneaton and Leamington, etc. After the procession, the crowds streamed back to the station, and as the 9.45 pm local to Birmingham backed into the platform, John Aitchinson, a trooper in the 5th Dragoon Guards (Princess Charlotte of Wales'), missed his footing in the jostle, slipped and fell beneath the train, and was killed. At the inquest it transpired that the crowd had become boisterous and excited and, despite the efforts of the platform staff, had made a rush for the carriage doors as the train backed down.

August 1881 was not a good month for the North Western on the L&B section. It had got off badly with the dreadful delays to the Blackpool excursions and the death of trooper Aitchinson. On 13 August, a freight train derailed on the Northampton loop. On the 18th, an engine turner was crushed to death at Rugby shed. On Sunday 21 August, the 9.00 pm down 'Scotch' express lost time as far as Wolverton, despite double heading, and at Roade came to a stand with the train engine a failure. The pilot was unable to take the train on, and an engine from the Northampton local at Blisworth had to be com-

mandeered to handle the express, whilst the pilot took over the Northampton local! Another accident at Rugby on 29 August resulted in a severe grilling for local officers. Edwin Goode, a greaser, went on duty at 6.00 am for a 12-hour shift. During the day he was asked by William Lane, the Wagon Department foreman, if he minded doing a double turn, as his relief, due on at 6.00 pm, was tending his father, who was ill. Goode agreed to the double turn — of 24 hours — as it would give him a clear day later on. That evening, at about 11.50 pm, as he was working on an up Ashby goods at the north end of the station, the down Birmingham came in, and he started across the lines to join Andrew Barnacle, the wagon examiner. The two freights were separated by one road, and with darkness, engines blowing off, and his own tiredness, as he had been on duty almost 18 hours already, Goode failed to notice an engine propelling a wagon down the line as he stepped into the 'four foot'. He was run down, and died in the early hours of Tuesday morning in the local hospital.

At the inquest, the coroner, W.S. Poole, was scathing. In response to Lane's statement that the men made it the rule to do the double turn, he snapped back ' . . . and it is a very bad rule. It is almost impossible for any man to work 24 hours; he might have fallen asleep at his post.' Allen and Lane were in further difficulties when a juror asked if the practice was known to the Superintendent of the Line; their reply that they could not manage without it was rightly condemned. 'It is a system that won't stand: I don't see why, at a large station like Rugby, you can't have extra men.' Allen, who for most of his 20 years in charge at Rugby, was highly thought of by townspeople and staff alike, could only finish by saying that he hoped the system would not be regarded as prevalent on the LNWR. The jury had the final word, finding that Goode had been killed whilst working on a double shift of 24 hours, and they considered the practice highly dangerous.

The episodes in this chapter cover a period of almost 40 years, from the inception of the LNWR in 1846 to the early 1880s. They relate to one line. A similar story could be told for any other section of the LNWR. Unlike great events or great accidents, they are not the kind of story which normally reaches the history book, yet because they provide a glimpse of the LNWR

Above *This 1875 engraving from the LNWR official guide predates effective 'action' photography. The artist's proportions for the locomotive are slightly out, but technical details in other illustrations from the same source are usually sound. The engraving is probably a reasonable source of data on train formation. The first brake vehicle is the fifth coach, at first a peculiar placing, but the chain brake was not reliable beyond four or five vehicles, so that a brake placed here with double brake fittings could brake rakes in front and rear. It could therefore brake two-thirds of this 15-coach train, the rear brake handling the rest. Two different types of luggage coach are also shown, with a centre or end luggage locker.*

Right *The entrance to Rugby station circa 1881. This was the second station at Rugby, opening when the Leicester line was built, and surviving until 1885-86. Three imposing residences, the first of which is seen on the left, provided accommodation for senior officials stationed in the town. (Warwickshire Library)*

growing up, and of how things could go wrong, they tell us much. We see the railway police on crime prevention and signalling duties, the rudimentary block and signalling system, labour unrest, the pressure at Bank Holidays, and the kind of hours which were worked. The theme is straightforward; this is how it was for passengers and staff alike, and it was out of the errors made then that the smooth-running railway of the twentieth century emerged.

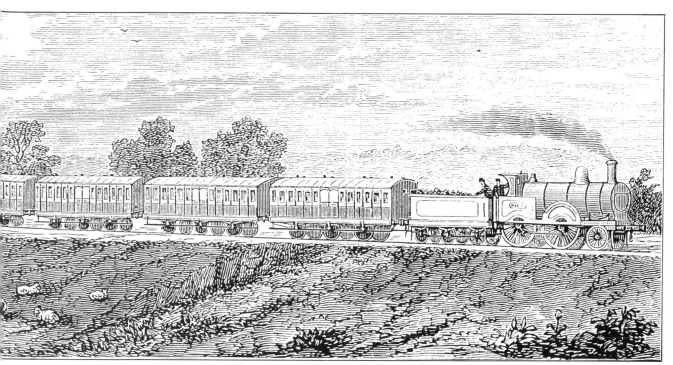

3 The Passenger Business

Incised into the dressed corner-stones of the two lodges which have guarded the entrance from Euston Road to Euston station itself since 1870 are the names of just some of the myriad of destinations to which it was possible to book a ticket: Aberdeen, Aylesbury, Banbury, Blackburn, Bury, Peterborough, Preston, Rochdale... To the passenger, approaching Euston, it was a graphic reminder of the ramifications of the line he was about to travel on.

Today, we mourn the appalling official vandalism which led to the destruction of the Doric portico and Great Hall, and their replacement by architecture memorable only by its supreme forgetability, but let us go back to 1875, when the Doric arch and Great Hall were still young. This is what the LNWR official guide said in that year: 'Euston station, at once the great starting-point and terminus of this system, is approached from Euston Square between two lodges, one of which [the western] is a branch office of Messrs Norton & Shaw, the celebrated tourist agents and guide book publishers. Midway between these lodges stands a statue of Robert Stephenson. Crossing the northern division of the square and passing between the two great railway hotels, the *Euston* and the *Victoria*, the severe but imposing entrance portico of the station, with its ornamental iron gates, rises before the spectator with a dignity becoming its position, in front of the chief station of the London & North Western Railway Company. On each side of this portico, which is built in the Doric style, from designs by Hardwick, are two offices — one is used for the post and postal telegraph office, and the others respectively for the Royal Mails, parcels office, lavatory, etc. Passing from this entrance to the station, a carriage area, about 135 feet long by an average of 66 in width, is crossed, this having at its northern extremity, verandah work of iron and glass to protect passengers from the weather as they alight from their vehicles.

'On entering the station the tourist finds himself in the large entrance hall, a spacious room, 126 feet long by 61 feet in width and 62 in height, at the extremity of which is a staircase leading to the board room and various offices, and near the foot of this staircase is a statue of the elder Stephenson. On each side of the hall are doors leading to the booking offices, and thence to the waiting and refreshment rooms, and also to the platforms, which, together with the lines of rails within the station, are covered over with a glazed roof of great extent, supported by iron pillars. The cost of this station was upwards of £100,000, and its extent is above six acres.

'The shareholders' meeting room at Euston station is large, and contains a painting, by Joy, of the late Lord Wolverton, formerly a chairman of the company, and a bust by Wyon, of Admiral Moorsom, who also held that office. The room is used for the meetings of the board of directors, a number of gentlemen chosen from the most important of the proprietors... At the present time [September 1875] there are 1,587 miles of line opened in connection with the London & North Western Railway, and 90¼ miles of new branches are in course of construction and approaching completion.'

The Doric arch and Great Hall were victims of the modernization of the West Coast Main Line in the 1960s. Once upon a time it would have been fair to assume that virtually every devotee of the 'Premier Line' would have stood in the Great Hall at some stage, and taken in the magnificence of this wonderful room, dominated by its heavily ornamented flat ceiling, said to be the largest of its kind in the world, and the imposing staircase rising a few feet, then bifurcating into two flights at right angles which opened on to small landings. Reversing direction, the twin flights of stairs merged before another landing, from which a final broad flight of steps led to the upper landing and galleries which stretched back down the hall. Polished double doors, beautifully panelled and topped by an ornate frieze, guarded the inner sanctum, the Board Room. More than six decades have elapsed since North Western shareholders ascended those stairs and entered the meeting room, more than four decades since LMS shareholders did so, and more than two decades since the official vandals struck at our national heritage. How many of the readers of this book will have mounted those stairs, have passed through those wooden doors, and seen what was once the meeting room of the London & North Western Railway? The authors, to their great joy, once made that trip. One did not 'walk up the stairs', one *ascended*, and it was only as one did so that the subtle genius of the approach stairs became apparent. The broad shallow flights of stairs and change of direction with the intermediate landings, allowed the eye — indeed forced it — to take in the grandeur of the surroundings. A comparable approach is made to some of the most lavish of England's stately homes.

Passengers came under the grand heading of 'Coaching Traffic', which also included parcels, fish, meat, poultry, milk, carriages, dogs and any other items handled by passenger train, and left luggage, lost property, cab rents, and fees from badge porters, lavatories, time tables, guide books and 'salvage', which was the name given to proceeds from the disposal of perishable lost property. Many readers will be familiar with the Rule Book, if not of the LNWR then of some railway company or perhaps of British Railways, that pocket-sized bible of operating and other rules. Less familiar will be the far bulkier instructions

issued to cover Coaching and Merchandise traffic, as the LNWR termed it. The 1881 issue of 'Rules and Regulations for the guidance of Station Masters and Others', issued by the North Western Secretary, Stephen Reay, ran to 177 pages, each more than twice the size of a rule book page. Lawyers, when they wish to be pedantic, which is always, will often use the word 'hereinafter', conceding the 'hereafter' to those of clerical garb. The North Western had no such qualms.

The section upon passenger traffic opened thus: 'Although only three classes of carriage are provided, four classes of tickets are in use, viz, 1st Class, 2nd Class, 3rd Class, Parliamentary. Parliamentary receipts and fares differ from 3rd Class by reason of their exemption from Government Duty, and tickets for such traffic are only to be issued, unless otherwise directed, to those Stations where the Passengers can travel throughout by trains against which a thick black unbroken line is shewn in the Company's Time Tables and Local Bills. On Sundays, the service being different, care must be taken to see how the trains are marked.'

The Doric arch from an LNWR engraving of 1875.

Looking along the Great Hall to the stairs leading to the Board Room. The flat panelled ceiling was copied from the roof of St Paul's-outside-the-Walls in Rome.

LONDON & NORTH WESTERN RAILWAY.

_____

EUSTON STATION,

22nd June, 1881.

The following is a Copy of the Code of Rules and Regulations
referred to in the Resolution of the Board of the 21st day of May,
shewn on the next page, subject to any alterations which may at any
time hereafter be made therein by the authority of the Directors.

S. REAY,
Secretary.

Eighteen basic types of ticket were then listed, ranging from printed or blank cards, through tourist coupons and soldiers' paper tickets to sleeping car tickets and tri-lingual tickets issued on the continent! One of the most interesting sections related to platform tickets.

The use of automated ticket printers, which produce an individual ticket with the correct destination, fare and category, is now so widespread that the traditional pre-printed Edmondson card ticket has recently disappeared altogether from modern railway operation. The use of separate children's tickets where the Edmondson ticket did survive means that the North Western method of dealing with half-fare tickets will be unfamiliar to many readers. The 1881 instructions, shown

opposite, complete with contemporary illustrations, make fascinating reading.

The instructions about sleeping carriage tickets were, in contrast, quite brief (see top of page 46). Many North Western devotees will be familiar with the magnificent 12-wheel sleeping saloons built at Wolverton, some of which survived in Royal Train use well into the diesel era. Information about the earliest sleeping facilities is scant, but the 1875 issue of the LNWR official guide includes a series of engravings and descriptions. The most basic approach was the convertible carriage: 'Fig 15 shows the manner in which a first-class carriage attached to the Scotch and Irish mail trains is converted into sleeping compartments, each compartment being made by this arrangement to provide sleeping accommodation for three travellers. The elbow rests, it will be seen, are thrown up so as to enable two persons to lie at length upon the ordinary seats of the carriage, whilst a third couch is provided by a seat which slides out and forms a communication between the two opposite seats on the right-hand side of the carriage. This arrangement leaves the door on the left-hand, or platform side of the compartment, free for the ingress or egress of the passengers.'

The idea of removable arm-rests was in use prior to 1871, but the sliding seat, to provide a third longitudinal berth, seems to have been introduced following discussions by the West Coast companies in 1871. The idea of a proper sleeping carriage, which could be modified to ordinary service if not successful, was mooted at the same time but not taken up. An experimental LNWR saloon appeared on the Anglo-Scottish services in 1873, and this led to four pioneer six-

Above *This LNWR ticket of 1898, printed on green card, reminds us of the fourth class of tickets, the 'Parliamentary' or 'Parly', mentioned in the LNWR instructions of 1881.*

L. Platform Tickets—These are used at Crewe, Dudley Port, Edge Hill, Lancaster, Llandudno Junction, Northampton, Rugby, Stafford, Stockport, and Warrington. They are issued to all persons on entering the Station other than by train, whether they intend travelling by train or not, in order to ensure that a ticket of some description may be given up by every one on leaving the Station, otherwise excess is to be charged. All persons on booking from these Stations must be asked for their Platform Tickets, unless the latter are issued at an inner door after the booking office has been passed. Passengers arriving at any Station without Tickets, and asserting they have come from the afore-mentioned places, are to be required to produce their Platform Tickets in corroboration.

CHILDREN.

When carried free, and when at half-fare. 129. Children under three years of age if accompanied by a Passenger are carried free. Children over three and not exceeding twelve years of age are carried at half-fares.

Certain exceptions. 130. Exceptions to the issue of tickets to children at half-fares exist in the case of certain bookings to Paris and some descriptions of Excursion traffic, which are intimated in the special announcements relative to such bookings.

Detection of fraud. 131. Booking Clerks and Ticket Collectors are expected to exercise reasonable promptitude in detecting children palpably over age travelling without tickets or with Children's tickets. In such cases, the full or half fare is to be demanded, and if not paid, the names and addresses of the parties are to be obtained and reported to the District Superintendent.

Ordinary tickets to be cut. 132. When tickets for children are applied for, the practice is to issue one of the ordinary description, cutting out of it a small portion as hereafter

Whole tickets to be issued to even numbers. described, to indicate that it is issued to a child. When two or a larger number are asked for by the same party, one whole ticket for every two children may be issued; but in the case of Return Tickets, the applicant should be asked whether the children will come back together.

53

Manner in which to be cut. 133. The manner in which Single and Return Tickets are to be cut is indicated on the following specimens :—

On no account is the small piece to be issued to the passenger, but only the larger and numbered part of the ticket.

Ticket Cutter. 134. The Company provides for each office a Ticket Cutter, with which whole tickets are to be cut for children. If it becomes blunt or out of order, the fact must be reported to the Audit Office.

Cut piece receptacle. 135. At every Station two receptacles should be provided in which to place cut pieces—one for the current day's pieces, and one to which they can be transferred day by day until the end of the month, the latter being under the sole custody of the responsible clerk.

Station issued to, printed on cut piece. 136. All Card Tickets now supplied, with the exception of Blank Cards, have the name of the Station to which they are available printed in small type on that portion of the Ticket to be taken out by the cutter, but on many old Tickets this is not the case, and in such instances, as with Blank Cards, the Station issued to is to be written on the face of the cut piece.

Cutting of Paper Tickets. 137. At the right hand top corner of the Single and in the centre at the top of the Return *Foreign Paper* Tickets, appears a triangular slip, which must be cut off when the ticket is issued to a child. In addition to this notification that the ticket is issued for a child, the word "Child" must be legibly written across the portion or portions given to the passenger (except in cases where the following remark is printed across the corner : "When this corner is cut off this Ticket is only available for a *Child.*")

No. to be written on piece, and placed in receptacle. 138. Immediately after a Ticket is cut for a child, the *Number* of such Ticket must be written in ink on the back of the small cut piece (except with Foreign Paper Tickets, on which the number is printed) and it must be placed in the receptacle for the current day's cut pieces, credit is not allowed unless these rules be complied with. On closing the books for the day the cut pieces so placed should be balanced with the Traffic Book, and afterwards transferred to the monthly depository.

SLEEPING CARRIAGE TICKETS.

97. These are supplied to stations from which certain night trains, having Sleeping Carriages attached, depart, or at which they stop. A sleeping ticket entitles a person holding a First class ticket to a berth in the Sleeping Carriage on payment of an additional charge. The following are the series of tickets in use :—

From or to   ...   .   Holyhead.
     „   ...   .   Liverpool.
     „   ...   .   London.
     „   ...   .   Manchester.
     „   ...   .   Scotland.

The extra fares for such tickets are to be accounted for in the ordinary manner in the Train and Traffic books, and on the classification in the First Class Single column, care being taken not to cast in the numbers of tickets issued.

This sleeping-saloon (fig. 12), which far excels for its admirable arrangements and luxurious accommodation all others in use upon English railways, is divided into a single and double compartment. The former will accommodate four travellers, while the latter is capable of holding eight, each having its separate lavatory and w.c., while the entrance-passage, common to both, divides the double compartment from the single one (see plan, fig. 13). By this arrangement the more numerous party of travellers, whether ladies or gentlemen, could have the double compartment, leaving the single one for the smaller party. In the same manner the couches and berths could be allotted to a larger and smaller party of gentlemen.

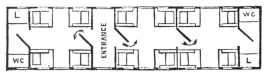

Plan of Sleeping Saloon Carriage. (Fig. 13.)

The sleeping-saloon is superbly fitted up with maple and walnut panelling, relieved with gilt mouldings. The seats, which resemble those of a first-class carriage, are covered with the blue cloth usually adopted by the London and North-Western Railway Company, but the seats are made to slide out and meet, thus forming one sleeping couch, running lengthways of the train, not transversely ; thus the four seats in the single compartment form two couches. Overhead are two chintz-covered mattresses with pillows, which by a clever arrangement of levers can be lowered from the roof, where they are packed during the day, and made to form two sleeping-berths. These, when in position, are reached by a low pair of steps, upon which a little table-top slides so as to be available during the day for writing, reading, chess, or other purposes. The windows of the carriage have crimson blinds, while a green shade covers the lamp, thus giving, in connection with the various fittings of the carriage, a pleasing variety of colour.

The fittings of the lavatory, with its large mirror, etc., are also most complete, and the water arrangements admirable ; the last remark also applies to the w.c.

Altogether this is one of the most magnificent specimens of railway carriage building yet produced, and carriages of this class are in great demand for long journeys. They certainly reflect great

wheel sleeping saloons being introduced for the West Coast Joint Stock during 1874. They became WCJS Nos 101-104, and were employed on the Euston to Glasgow and Perth night trains. As is so often the case with any pioneering venture, they were soon outclassed by later vehicles; were taken out of front line service in 1883, and partitioned between the LNWR and Caledonian companies, the North Western pair becoming family saloons. Official plans have long vanished, but Norton & Shaw's official North Western guide provides not merely a written description, down to such esoteric items as the colour of the lamp shades, but interior and exterior engravings as well! Thus we may, in imagination, and with the help of the accompanying illustrations board a WCJS sleeper of 1875.

Earlier in this chapter, the authors recalled personal memories of the Great Hall and the stairs leading up to the Board Room. We will close it with another personal reminiscence. The North Western was adept at altering and modifying carriages for use as picnic and family saloons, and as departmental vehicles. After the WCJS pioneer sleeping cars were taken out of service, one of the lavatory compartments was replaced by a twin door luggage compartment. Two saloons, identical in door and window layout to the original sleeping cars, survived in departmental use at Rugby into the late 'fifties or early 'sixties. The authors saw these vehicles, little realizing that they were almost certainly looking at the dawn of the sleeping car era on Britain's railways.

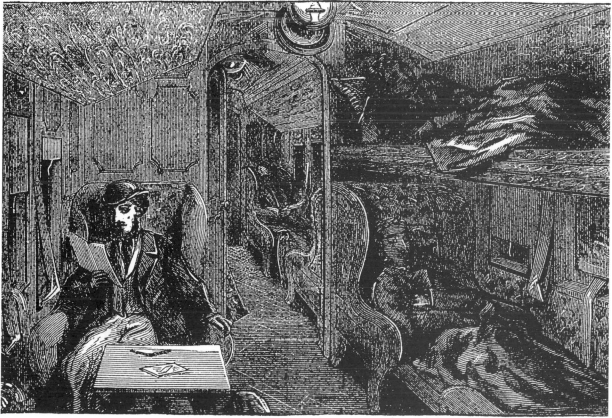

Above *An 1875 engraving of the West Coast six-wheel sleepers.*

Below *Departmental saloons M284669 and M284672 possessed a window and door layout identical to the first generation sleeping cars as rebuilt. Both are seen with the Rugby Breakdown Crane.* (T.W.J. Hayward Collection)

Above *A friend of the authors, Mr Tom Hayward, measured up the two Rugby coaches for an O gauge model built in the 1950s. Tom loaned the two vehicles to the authors for this portrait of the pioneer sleepers against a suitable 'North Western' backdrop, at the authors' Hillside MPD.*

Below *An 1875 engraving of a first/second/third luggage tri-composite six-wheeler.*

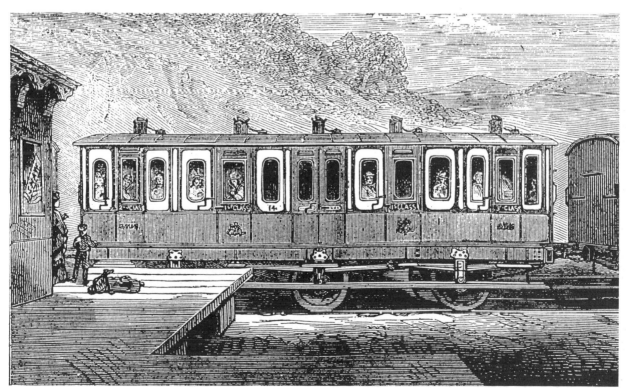

Reference to your

Letter of ....   (2079)

In your reply please refer to

E/A

FROM **ROBERT TURNBULL,**

SUPERINTENDENT OF THE LINE,

EUSTON STATION,

.... 189   **LONDON, N.W.**

TO

NORTH WALES GUIDE—SEASON

I enclose herewith a Copy of the last edition of the North Wales Tourist Guide, and shall be glad if you will have the descriptive matter carefully looked through, so far as you are concerned, and return to me early, with any alterations or additions you may consider necessary.

R. TURNBULL.

Below *The LNWR 'Lost Property' circulars, distributed to other lines, are virtually unknown. We now know what the fashionable Victorian Miss deemed essential travelling clothes!*

Above *A circular from Robert Turnbull regarding the 1898 North Wales Guide.*

Opposite *An LNWR season ticket application form of 1884.*

SPECIAL.

London and North Western Railway.

Reference
O S 707
31.7.1900

OFFICE OF SUPERINTENDENT OF THE LINE,
EUSTON STATION, LONDON,
31st *July*, 1900.

DEAR SIR,

MESSRS. SUTTON & CO.'S AND OTHERS MISSING PROPERTY.

Will you be good enough to have your Depôts searched and special enquiry made on your Line for the Luggage described on the other side, and let me know the result as early as possible.

Yours truly,

R. TURNBULL.

Station Masters are requested to make careful search in their Parcels Offices, Lost Property Offices, and Cloak Rooms for the Packages described below, also make enquiry at the Hotels and other places in the neighbourhood where the property is likely to have been taken in mistake.

DATE OF LOSS AND POINTS OF JOURNEY.	DESCRIPTION OF PACKAGE.	LIST OF CONTENTS.	NAME OF OWNER.
12th Nov., 1899. Dublin to Euston.	Wooden Case, addressed to Mrs. Bartley, 48, Tremadoc Road, Clapham, London	Picture, "An Army Surgeon in Regimentals." Size of frame, 2 ft. by 1½ ft.	Messrs. Sutton & Co.
8th May, 1900. Chester to Rhyl.	Brown Leather Hand Bag	Racing cards, gloves, &c. ...	Mr. Darling.
17th May, 1900. Longsight to Grimsargh.	Gentleman's Bicycle ...	Leader Cycle make, drop bar, pneumatic tyres	Leader Cycle Co.
20th May, 1900. Lime Street to Holyhead.	Canvas Bag, 4 ft. high, round, white, strapped	3 doz. white dress shirts, 2 suits pyjamas, 3 doz. collars, 12 pairs socks, 2 handkerchiefs	Mr. Walshe.
31st May, 1900. Lime Street to Euston.	Square Leather Hat Box, locked	Ivory hair brushes and clothes brush, opera hat and silk hat, straw hat, 6 collars, flannel shirt, 3 waistcoats, &c.	Mr. Wilson.
2nd June, 1900. Manchester to Whitchurch.	Brown Canvas Holdall, black and white check lining, 2 straps, with handle attached	Lady's costume, gentleman's morning coat, infant's coat and cape, 4 infant's frocks, cotton petticoat, flannel petticoat, flannel singlet, flannel bibs, lady's blouse	Mr. Cheshyre.
2nd June, 1900. North Wall to Mexboro'.	Black Leather Box, bound round with brown leather, locked, strapped, white letters on top "S. P. D. H."	Grey dress with white silk, 3 blouses, black satin skirt and bodice, crimson silk blouse, flannelette blouse, black skirt, 2 cotton blouses, shoes, 2 night dresses and gown, 3 combinations, collars, cuffs, &c.	Miss Jones.

(1933—Ordinary Season)
(Ticket Conditions Form.) # London and North Western Railway.

Conditions upon which ordinary Season Tickets are granted.

1. Any Season Ticket issued by this Company entitles the holder to travel by any of the ordinary passenger trains (other than the Irish and Limited Scotch Mails and those specially restricted by public notice), between the points and in the class of carriage named on the ticket, during the period for which it is available.

2. Season Tickets must be given up to the Company immediately on their expiration, otherwise the sum which the Company require to be deposited will be forfeited.

3. Season Tickets are not transferable; and should any ticket, from the default of the holder be used by any other person, it will be forfeited, and all advantages arising therefrom will cease.

4. In the event of the loss of any Season Ticket, immediate notice must be given at the Chief Office of the Company; and in consideration of a new ticket being issued the holder will be required to pay a fresh deposit, and ten per cent. on the unexpired value of the lost ticket to the end of the current year, half-year, or quarter, according to the duration of such lost ticket.

5. Season Tickets are not available for any journey unless produced to the Officers of the Company on demand for examination; and in the event of any journey being made without so producing the ticket, such journey is not considered part of the contract, but must be paid for as an ordinary passenger.

6. The holders of all Season Tickets must abide by all the Rules, Regulations, and Bye-laws of the Directors of the London and North Western Railway now in force or which shall hereafter be in force, especially those relating to alterations in the number of trains, or the periods of starting, or the arrival of the trains. The Company do not undertake to give any previous notice of such alterations, or future additional regulations; nor will the Directors hold themselves in any way responsible in consequence of any circumstances arising therefrom; nor answerable for want of accommodation in any train; nor for any stoppage, delay, hindrance, or change, whether arising from accidents or otherwise, which may impede the proper starting, running, or arrival of any of the Company's trains.

Date _____ 10 July _____ 1884

I hereby request to be supplied with a Season Ticket between the following points on the conditions named above.

Class of Ticket _____ Second _____

Name _____ William Henry Peacock _____ { To be written in full and distinctly.

From _____ Chester Road _____ Station to _____ Euston _____ Station.

Period _____ one _____ months, from first day of _____ August _____ to last day of _____ August _____ 1884

Residence _____ Fir Tree Cottage, Boldmere, S.E. Erdington _____

(Signature) _____ W. H. Peacock. _____

To the District Superintendent,
London and North Western Railway,

_____ Euston _____ Station.

The Government Passenger Duty of 5 per cent. is charged in addition to the amount payable on all Season Tickets.

4 Posts and Papers

Three times a day, North Western locomotives backed into Euston, their drivers knowing that their running would not only be studied by their own senior officers, but by Post Office staff at St Martin's le Grand, for the trains they would shortly take out, although running under ordinary express passenger headlamps and block codes, were no ordinary trains. They were the three down 'postals'. The first away was the 7.15 am 'Day Mail', conveying Irish and Scottish traffic. Often known as the 'Wild Irishman', the 'Day Mail' only conveyed first and second class passengers for many years, and then only on certain journeys, for with passenger accommodation limited by GPO instructions, local journeys were not permitted.

In the evening two mail trains made ready, most of the Euston porters being assigned to the work briefly. First away was the down night 'Irish Mail' at 8.25 pm. As with the day mail, the passenger restrictions were strict. In 1883, they provided that 'The night mail leaving London at 8.25 pm, conveys First and Second Class passengers to Holyhead and Ireland only; First and Second Class from London to Chester, and (if there be room in the train) First and Second Class passengers from Birmingham to Chester. Express fares are charged by these trains.' A few minutes later, at 8.40 pm, later 8.50 pm, the 'Limited Scotch Mail' was due away. Limited to four (later five) carriages, the rules were extremely complex: 'The Down Limited Scotch Mail, leaving Euston at 8.50 pm daily, conveys 1st, 2nd and 3rd Class Passengers (Tourist or Ordinary) from London to Carlisle and Scotland; and (if there be room) 1st and 2nd Class Passengers from any of the Intermediate Stations at which the Train calls between London and Carlisle. On Saturday nights, Third Class Passengers for Carlisle and Scotland can (if there be room) join this Train at Rugby, Tamworth, Stafford, Crewe, & Preston.'

Operating under penalty clauses for late running, the up and down mails possessed an aura unlike any other service on the line. They were the cream of North Western express working. Now we have set the scene, we will turn over the venerable pages of the North Western official guide for September 1875 to find out what it was like.

CHAPTER VI.

MAIL DEPARTMENT.

BY referring to the Post Office estimates for the year ending March 31st, 1874, printed by order of the House of Commons, we find that a sum of £446,532 per annum is set down as the cost of the conveyance of mails by railway in England and Wales. Of this sum no less than £136,740 is paid to the London and North-Western Railway Company, and it will be seen by a glance down the table marked " Sub Head (G) " in the official estimates that this is more than double that paid to any other of the forty railways (or thereabout) which carry her Majesty's mails. The next largest sum, £52,500, is paid to the Great Western, while the Midland claims £45,000, and the North-Eastern £44,030, six other companies getting various sums from £26,060 down to £10,450, and the remainder smaller amounts, some as low as £167. The total sum of the amount paid to the Great Western, the Midland, and the North-Eastern comes, therefore, to very little more than the single item paid to the London and North-Western Railway, leaving somewhat more than a third of the gross sum to be divided among about thirty-six smaller lines, a conclusive proof of the great postal and, consequently, commercial extent of the London and North-Western Railway system.

The immense district traversed by this railway causes such an enormous quantity of postal work to devolve upon its lines that were the trains marked in the time tables as mail-trains the only ones that carried letter-bags, the public correspondence would in these crowd out the public. For few persons besides those whose interest and duty it is to know, have any idea of the aggregate weight and bulk of the little ½oz. packets that flow in an almost continuous stream from all parts into the sorting rooms of the General Post Office at St. Martin's le Grand.

But some time back the post-office authorities acquired the power to send letter-bags by any train, and from Euston alone no less than twenty passenger trains per day carry the mails to various places on the London and North-Western Railway Company's line. This has, to a considerable extent, reduced the bulk and weight of those which are daily carried by the special Irish, the Irish and Scotch, and the limited Scotch mail-trains, by dispersing among many what would otherwise have to be carried by three. Still, by these special trains the bulk and weight carried are formidable enough, and the van loads of letters, etc., which arrived night and morning from St. Martin's le Grand, to be quickly stowed away in the post-office carriages, may be spoken of as tons ! Books and newspapers make up much of the weight, but not so much as many would suppose, for the starting of Messrs. Smith and Son's newspaper vans (see Chap. VII., page 75) every morning from Euston by the 5.15 train enables the country booksellers to supply daily papers at an early hour, and consequently newspapers are not posted and re-posted to friends from place to place, as in the days when there were no facilities for obtaining the *journal du jour*. This of course has lightened the labours of the post-office, proportionably, with regard to newspapers, and it will be found that one half of the daily tons of correspondence, etc., is made up of ½ oz. letters, circulars, and of post cards weighing 1/5 oz. each, while it may surprise the reader to learn that before now the springs of the railway post-office carriage have snapped under the united weight of the various missives sent by post.

The mail-trains from Euston with sorting carriages are the 7.15 a.m.—Irish and Scotch—the 8.25 p.m., which is special Irish, and the 8.40 p.m., the limited mail. The letters for Ireland are sent to the travelling carriage comparatively unsorted, and the correspondence for particular towns is made up *en route*. Some of this is done in the train from Euston to Holyhead, and some of it in the post-office cabin of the Holyhead and Kingstown mail steamers, as shown in illustration, fig. 24, page 73. Thus it is all ready for distribution by the various Irish railway companies directly the mail arrives at Dublin.

The limited mail, for Scotland, which leaves Euston at 8.40 p.m., is limited to four passenger carriages, one for Edinburgh, one for Glasgow, one for Aberdeen, and one for Inverness, with post-office sorting carriages, and two bag tenders, connected with each other by gangways, thus enabling the officials to pass from one to another. The sorting carriages are about 26 feet in length; the tenders are not quite so large, nor are they fitted for their whole length with sorting boxes, their chief use being for the stowage of direct mail-bags from London to Liverpool, Manchester, Edinburgh, Glasgow, and other large towns, until such time as the train reaches Scotland, when they are used for taking up and sorting the Glasgow and Edinburgh mails. The furniture of the sorting carriage is *nil*, if we except a small rack for books of reference and a swing seat in the shape of a saddle, on which the sorter may sit when he is tired of standing.

The most interesting feature in the post-office carriages is, however, the mail-bag exchanging apparatus, and of this we therefore purpose giving a short description. The machinery consists of a rope net, in a strong iron frame, fixed upright against the outside of the carriage window-shutter, as shown in fig. 20. This net at the proper time is let down, and then extends about 2 feet 6 inches over the side of the line. A strong rope in the shape of the letter V is permanently fixed from the side of the carriage to the outer side of the net, horizontally, thus <, the opening facing the direction in which the train is going, and this, passing under the post at the station on which bags to be received are hung (see fig. 21), sweeps them out of the springs which previously held them in position into the net, when they are lifted in through the window. The bags to be left at the station are made up in bales weighing about 70lbs. each (this being the weight proportioned to the tension of the springs), and the wrappers in which they are enclosed are of strong leather, secured by cross-straps. A short strong strap with an iron tongue is attached to each bale, and this is inserted between the springs of a lever at the side of the doorway. The bale is gently pushed out at the proper time, and its weight brings the lever down into an extended position. Passing over the ground net at the side of the line, the bales, one or more, according to the requirements of the town, are swept out of the lever springs and left on the ground net. By again referring to fig. 20, the manner in which the bag is inserted in the lever springs will be apparent to the reader.

Having described the mail-bag exchanging apparatus, we proceed to speak of the journey and the internal arrangements of the sorting-carriage and tenders. Some of our readers may have travelled by, and others may have seen, the " Wild Irishman " and the " Flying Scotchman," as these special mail-trains are familiarly called, and may be aware of the speed at which they travel. The time of their departure is fixed by the post-office authorities, as is also that of the trains which wait their arrival at the various junctions with North-Western branches and other companies' lines. These trains are allowed to wait a short but rigidly fixed time, in case the limited mail should be late. This may be the case in winter ; though in summer it passes or arrives at the various places on its route with almost the regularity of clock-work. Between London and Aberdeen the limited mail stops at thirteen stations, which are important junctions with other lines, and the mail-bags are exchanged at fifty-three stations by the apparatus we have described above. The sorting-carriage and tenders are exclusively for post-office purposes, and none but post-office officials are allowed to enter them. Relays of employés are here engaged in dealing with the correspondence. One clerk and four sorters start from London and travel as far as Preston ; they are joined by another five at Rugby, who go on to Carlisle. One clerk and one sorter join at Preston in place of those arriving from London, and in the same way those who joined at Rugby are replaced at Carlisle. Each officer is on duty about six hours, and is continuously engaged, the work being evenly extended over the whole of their respective distances. They return to their various head-quarters on the following night by the up mail, and usually perform four journeys, two in each direction, and then rest at home one night.

Postmasters sending bags to the travelling post-office divide their letters into two divisions, according to a list supplied to them, and label the bundles respectively 1 and 2. The object of this will presently be seen. The bags are opened at the newspaper desk, which stands in the middle of the sorting-space, and while bundles marked No. 1 are handed to the sorter on the bag-opener's left, those marked No. 2 are passed to the one on his right. The effect of this arrangement is that letters in bundles No. 2, when sorted, are found to be only for those towns the

labelled pigeon-holes for which are on the right, and those in No. 1 for towns whose pigeon-holes are on the left of the bag-opener ; and it also enables the authorities to tell approximately by whom a particular letter was sorted. While this is going on, the sorters of these respective divisions, Nos. 1 and 2, are preparing the mails for those towns whose names are before them, and the empty bags to contain the letters hang behind each man. Thus all passing and repassing is avoided. A view of the interior of the sorting-carriage on the London and North-Western Railway is shown in illustration on the opposite page (fig. 22).

Should the bag-opener find any registered letters, these, with the bills upon which they are entered, are handed to the clerk on duty. He also deals with the surcharged and the unpaid correspondence.

Such is the internal economy of the sorting-carriage and tenders as the limited mail flies on its way northward. We ought, however, to mention that, in addition to the clerk and sorters mentioned above, one man is continuously engaged with the exchanging apparatus.

On arriving at Carlisle, the train is re-marshalled, and the post-office carriages separated. One of the tenders being used as a sorting-carriage for Edinburgh and another for Glasgow ; and thus the letters collected between London and Carlisle for those cities are prepared for prompt delivery on the arrival of the train.

At Carlisle two sorters belonging to the Edinburgh and Glasgow offices, who have worked their way by the up mail, join the train from London, and proceed to do the work which formerly had to be done after the arrival of the limited mail at these two cities. On their way up from Edinburgh and Glasgow to Carlisle, they had sorted the Scotch correspondence for London into bags for its eight metropolitan districts ; then, waiting eight hours, they return to their homes, on the way sorting the English correspondence for Edinburgh and Glasgow. The down limited mail service ends at Strome Ferry, in the extreme north of Scotland, and here begins the up mail service to London, which is indeed the exact counterpart of the other.

The apparatus for taking up and delivering the mails *en route* is now so perfect that failures to receive into the train are very rare ; but it may upon occasion happen that the bag is not delivered, owing to the official in the darkness of the night failing to observe some well-known object by the way, a house, a bridge, or a church, which has usually warned him of his near approach to some station. It has been the case that a white horse, or a herd of cattle, having, perhaps, for months past fed in a particular meadow, has served as a cue ; and that the sudden withdrawal of either of them to another field has misled the post-office official and caused him to be too late in fixing the bag for delivery. When, however, a failure of this kind does take place, the bag is sent back by first train from the next station, and thus serious inconvenience is avoided. The run between some of the stations is very short, and hence considerable expedition is necessary to get the bags ready in time—we mean, to take those from one station out of the net, and to tie up, seal, and adjust others for delivery before reaching the next station. Sometimes a letter gets missent, but this happens so very rarely that such an occurrence must be looked upon as the exception which proves the rule ; and when we bear in mind the rude or obscure hieroglyphs, rather than handwriting, on some letters, and the imperfect knowledge of geography shown by the writers, we can only wonder that letters thus addressed in an unfamiliar scrawl should be as a rule so unerringly sorted by lamplight, in carriages flying at the rate of sixty miles an hour.

Lest some of our readers should be prompted by curiosity to attempt to witness the work of the mail-bag exchanging apparatus, we deem it right to inform them that, owing to the speed of the trains, any attempt of this kind will be useless, as the exchange of the bags is instantaneous, and even the practised eye of the post-office official fails to catch it. Moreover, some little personal risk is incurred if the head, or even the hat, of the curious traveller is thrust too far out of the window of the carriage. Under these circumstances he will do wisely to content himself with our description of it, supplemented by an inspection of the working model kept at the Euston station of the London and North-Western Railway Company.

As letters between America and Great Britain pass through Ireland, it may interest the transatlantic tourist to know something of the postal arrangements to and through the sister island. We have before spoken incidentally of the two special Irish mails from Euston, morning and evening. The appliances and internal arrangements belonging to the post-office vans of these are similar to those of the limited Scotch mail, and they convey letters over the London and North-Western line as far as Holyhead. Upon the arrival of the train at this port one of the four splendid steamers, *Ulster*, *Leinster*, *Connaught*, or

Munster, is in waiting to receive the mails. These vessels are expressly fitted up for this service, and are unrivalled as to speed and safety. Of one of the finest of these steamers, the *Connaught* we give an illustration, (fig. 23). The steamer is bound to start a few minutes after the mails are shipped, and in the post-office cabin, the process of sorting *en route* goes on as shown in fig. 24, in spite of wind and weather. Upon arriving at Kingstown the mails are carried by rail to Dublin, and thence are sent out into all parts of the island. The number of mail-bags conveyed weekly by the above steamers averages—

By day boats	- - -	339 bags
By night boats	- - -	788 ,,
Total	- - -	1,127 ,,

The advantages of sending and receiving the Anglo-American correspondence by the special Irish mail trains are obvious. If an ocean mail steamer start from Liverpool on the evening of the 16th instant, letters may be posted in London to go by it up till the evening of the 17th, the steamer calling at Queenstown and taking in the bags which have meanwhile been conveyed by the London and North-Western Railway Company's special Irish mail, and Holyhead and Kingstown steamers, and Great Southern and Western Railway to Queenstown. In like manner letters from America are landed at Queenstown, and, proceeding thence by fast mail train, reach London long before the steamer which brought them from New York gets to Liverpool.

Although overall dimensions, and even floor plans, have survived for many early LNWR and WCJS Travelling Post Offices, details of body styles are elusive. It is difficult, therefore, to be sure how these vehicles appeared, for the older examples predated the evolution of the Wolverton 'traditional' style of body building. Wolverton works opened in 1865, and within two or three years had developed a style which was so standardized that with a floor/window plan it is possible to prepare accurate side elevations. Wolverton had replaced the old Saltley works in Birmingham, which had created various styles of its own, some going back to the early days of railway carriage building, which had in turn evolved from the stage carriage. Reliable plans and illustrations of these pre-Wolverton vehicles, or of stock constructed in the transition from one style to another at Wolverton, are virtually non-existent.

In the absence of drawings or photographs, the researcher must therefore turn to such other sources as he can find, such as paintings or engravings. These can be a mine of information, or of dis-information, for artists are not always the most careful technical illustrators. If the accompanying 1875 engraving of a North Western TPO is accurate, its importance and interest can scarcely be overstated, but how can we evaluate it? Usually, in any engraver's work, there is a uniformity of fidelity or inventiveness, and if features we know about are accurate, then there is a likelihood that those we do not know about are equally reliable. The underframe of this vehicle is of especial interest, for both Saltley and Wolverton used a special form of hornplate, secured to the solebars by five bolts, and which is reproduced with commendable accuracy

LNWR Post Office van with mail-bag exchanging apparatus, showing the bags ready for delivery.

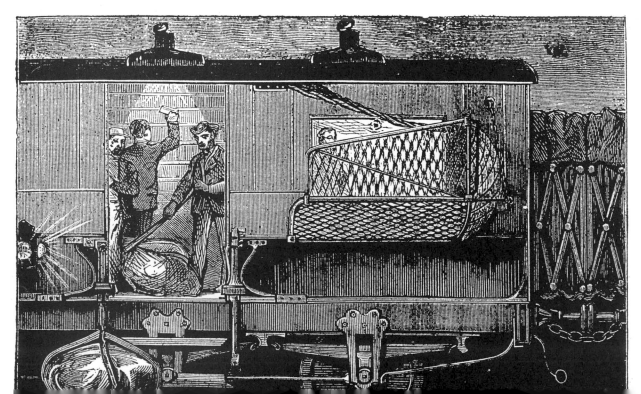

Isle of Man Railway four-wheel passenger brake E4, built at Saltley by Metropolitan in 1873 bears a remarkable similarity to the engraving of the LNWR TPO, even the end beading being identical with known Saltley stock. The part of the TPO not in the engraving was probably to this pattern. Other styles of Saltley stock also existed, but we at least have a reasonable basis to carry TPO styling back another 20 years!

in this engraving. A tie-piece joined the lower ends of the hornplate and, in latter days at Wolverton, this was straight, but there is evidence to suggest that Saltley had used a tie-bar which curved downwards (Bishop's Castle Railway). The spring anchors and tie-rods also reflect known Wolverton and Saltley practices, and in particular the manner in which the end tie-rod curves up to the inner face of the headstock. This is perhaps a slight exaggeration of known work, but certainly captures the technique, and with the dearth of definite information could even be correct. The proximity of the first and second axles demonstrates a minimum wheelbase six-wheeler, of which we see just two axles. This again conforms to known information. The TPO fittings are a reasonable representation of known practice, and the inference must be that the artist

had worked not from memory, but carefully from drawings or photographs.

Turning to the body, we are moving from the known to the unknown in some respects, but it is a reasonable assumption that if the underframe is correct, that the body is also. The square-edged panelling, upper and lower waist beads and unequal-width panels by the door and at the end are quite unlike Wolverton work, but it is known that Saltley used approximately one-inch half-round beading, with the lower bead curved up, stage-coach-style, at the ends of the body. Perhaps the most unusual feature of the bodywork is the distance between the upper and lower waist beads, for this was customarily much narrower, and the most noted exponent of such a deep waist panel was the Great Northern Railway.

Possible confirmation exists, however. After the LNWR ceased to use Saltley, the works were sold to the Metropolitan Railway Carriage & Wagon Co, which built coaches to traditional Saltley style for various companies. The largest surviving group of early 'Metro' stock is on the 3-foot gauge Isle of Man Railway, which opened in 1873, and whose Directors included two members of the LNWR Board, and whose first General Superintendent was a Crewe man.

Above Post Office sorters at work.

Below The inclusion of an engraving of the PS Connaught in the North Western's Official Guide is intriguing, for although she was one of the finest vessels afloat at the time, she was not owned by the LNWR, which was strenuously developing its own Irish sea services, but by the rival City of Dublin Steam Packet Co, which held the mail contract from 1850 until 1920.

The Connaught *was one of four single expansion paddle steamers, all built by Cammell Laird & Co of Birkenhead in 1860 for an accelerated Irish Mail service. 338 feet in length, with a breadth of 35 feet, she was intended for a 3 ¾ hour passage, but was the fastest of the quartet with a 3 hours 14 minutes crossing to her credit, between Holyhead and Kingstown (later renamed Dun Laoghaire), just south of Dublin. She had a turtle-backed forecastle, visible in the engraving, and remained in service until 1898.*

Above *Victorian artists and engravers had a propensity for showing steamships in rough weather conditions. The engraving of the* Connaught *at sea, shows her in surprisingly calm waters, but the artist has more than compensated for it in the portrait of the Post Office Sorting Cabin.*

Below *Sadly, none of the 26-foot Saltley TPs have survived, but an example of a later generation of Travelling Post Office was preserved in 1938. This was a West Coast Joint Stock 42-foot eight-wheel radial coach, one of the first three radials introduced to the WCJC TPO fleet in September 1883. No 186 remained in WCJS service up to the Grouping, and then in LMS operation up to its withdrawal in 1934. It was restored for the Centenary of the London & Birmingham Railway and of mail services by train in 1938, and is depicted at Birmingham New St station on display immediately after restoration. The full-length waist panel was a normal feature of the TPOs, but quite alien to the majority of Wolverton stock of this vintage.*

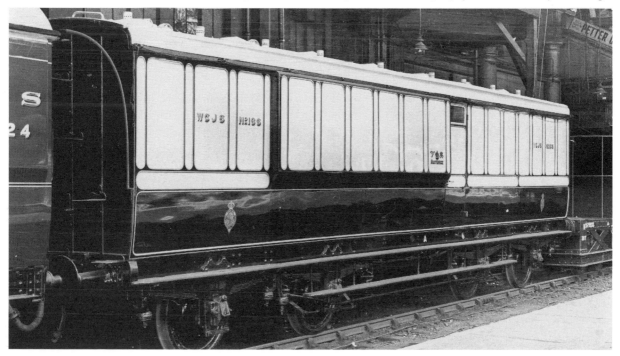

Above *No railway in the British Isles was more intimately connected with the mail service than the Chester & Holyhead. This lovely portrait from the 1850s shows the Menai tubular bridge, with Telford's suspension bridge in the distance. The train is hauled by a single with a haystack firebox. (Authors' Collection)*

Below *A 'Prince of Wales', possibly Billy Ward's No 2275 Edith Cavell of Rugby, heads the down Irish Mail through Colwyn Bay in about 1922, a far cry from the 'single' in the previous illustration.*

The glamour attached to the Royal Mail service, and the working of the Travelling Post Offices, ensured that the mail service has always been well described. However, another service, in which sorting carriages were used, has all but vanished into the mists of antiquity. This was the 5.15 am down 'Newspaper Express' which, despite its name, also carried passengers. Nineteenth-century LNWR public timetables show little variation in time over the decades. Specimen timetables from the 1870s, 1880s and 1890s reveal the same 5.15 am departure time. Arrival at Rugby varied from 7.05 am to 7.07 am. Crewe was reached between 9.05 and 9.13, and Liverpool between 10.25 and 10.30 am.

The 1875 North Western 'Official Guide' gives a graphic account of the 'Down Newspaper' and of its role in daily life. This ranges far beyond the North Western, but is so evocative of Victorian times, that it more than merits inclusion.

CHAPTER VII.

THE NEWSPAPER DEPARTMENT.

WHEN a late speaker rises in the House of Commons to close a debate upon some great question of national interest, he may, in these days, be considered as addressing not only those immediately before him, but also the members of the commonwealth at large. To those who sit within the range of his voice his words, indeed, travel at the rate of about thirteen miles per minute, while to those who are beyond its reach they come, though more slowly, at a speed which years ago would have been deemed incredible. He may have finished speaking at 4 a.m., and on that same morning his speech may be read by the Birmingham manufacturer before starting to unlock his warehouse.

Let us consider how this result is attained. While the honourable member is addressing the House a dozen pens in the reporters gallery are busy taking down his words. Paragraph after paragraph is flashed along the wire, let us say, to the *Times* office, to be set up by the compositor. At the last moment the result of the division is added, the impatient steam-engine is set to work, the printing-machine is fed with its daily rations of paper, and copy after copy of the *Times* of that day is thrown off. Then, about this time, to him who on a winter's morning stands in Printing House Square, appears one of the many strange sights of the nineteenth century. By the light of the gas-lamps the street is seen to be full of vans bearing the name, *W. H. Smith and Son*, or *London and North-Western Railway*. Amongst these, but near to the office door, is gathered a little crowd of men belonging to the coal-whipper and costermonger class; and not far off stands the impassive form of the London policeman. These men and these vehicles are waiting impatiently for the hour of publishing. The vans are backed up to the door, and the men's eyes are frequently bent upon the lighted windows of the office, through which may be seen "faint glimpses of the *inner* world." Presently they catch sight of the first bale of copies, borne on the shoulders of one of the employés, who passes by the window toward the door, and then all is stir and bustle.

Bale upon bale is brought forth and placed by these street-porters in the vans which have been waiting to receive them. If the spectator chance to have anything of an official look about him he will, perhaps, find himself regarded as one sent from 186, Strand, to see that no bale goes astray, or is left behind, and may hear frequent remarks that "all will be right this morning, anyhow."

As the vans are filled they drive off and others take their place, for by 5.15 a.m. all newspapers for the midland and north-western districts of the country must be at Euston. For this reason, and also because they are the most important customers, Messrs. Smith and Son's vans are first served, though any bookseller or stationer may send his parcels by the same train, provided they arrive at Euston in time.

Although we have as yet spoken only of the *Times* office, the reader will do well to remember that the same kind of scene is being enacted at all the various offices of the great London papers, and that a little before 5 a.m. every day a steady stream of Messrs. Smith and Son's vans is setting in towards Euston. Let us now turn to this station. Here the 5.15 a.m. train is waiting, and attached to it are three vehicles, known as "Messrs. Smith and Son's Newspaper Vans." Externally they have no particularly interesting features, but upon looking into the interior we perceive a table extending the length of one side of the van, upon this lie a number of ready-directed wrappers, while others are arranged on little shelves immediately above. Within we also find four or five of Messrs. Smith and Son's employés, waiting

for the arrival of the newspapers to begin their work of counting and wrapping up. As the street vans come in they are unloaded, and in an incredibly short space of time the bundles and bales are all transferred to the railway vans; the train starts, the men at the same time begin their work, and the interior of the van assumes the appearance shown in our illustration (fig 27).

One of the London and North-Western Company's servants accompanies the newspaper van, and as the bundles are made up he receives them from the packers, weighs them, and notes down the weight and every particular, so that the carriage may be fairly charged to Messrs. Smith and Son.

As in the case of letter-bags by the mail, so by the newspaper train the bundles for the nearest places are first made up and are ready for delivery directly at the station. As the 7.15 a.m. Irish and Scotch mail overtakes the 5.15 a.m., this latter train does not take the newspapers for Ireland and Scotland, neither does it convey many other bundles to their full destination.

* * *

the newspapers for Birmingham are counted and made up into bundles between Euston and Rugby, where they are put out to be forwarded by fast trains. Those for Manchester and Liverpool are in like manner made up *en route*, and are put out at Stafford (the extreme point to which Messrs. Smith and Son's vans run), and are thence forwarded by the newspaper train to their respective destinations. The newspaper vans then return empty to Euston, to be ready for service next day.

The hour at which newspapers arrive, by the 5.15 a.m. and trains in connection with it, at the various stations at which they are delivered is as follows:—

Euston, departs at	-	-	-	5.15 a.m.
Blisworth, arrives at	-	-	-	6.35 ,,
Rugby	,,	-	-	7.6 ,,
Nuneaton	,,	-	-	7.30 ,,
Tamworth	,,	-	-	7.50 ,,
Stafford	,,	-	-	8.32 ,,
Leamington	,,	-	-	8.45 ,,
Birmingham	,,	-	-	8.20 ,,
Crewe	,,	-	-	9.13 ,,
Manchester	,,	-	-	10.0 ,,
Chester	,,	-	-	10.27 ,,
Liverpool	,,	-	-	10.25 ,,

The newspapers for Ireland and Scotland are despatched by the 7.15 a.m. mail from Euston, and reach—

Dublin at	-	-	-	-	6.20 p.m.
Edinburgh and Glasgow at		-	6.0 ,,

Thus we see how closely connected the members of the House of Commons may be with their respective constituencies, and how science, commercial enterprise, and the wonderful machinery of the railway have been combined to produce this result. The case we have cited indeed will perhaps be looked upon as chiefly interesting to politicians; but it is of course unnecessary to remind our readers that it is not the politician only to whom the early conveyance of news from a central point is a matter of interest or advantage. Suffice it to say that thousands of individuals are benefited by the admirable arrangements we have described the working of above; while few, we fear, consider or inquire how much they are indebted to the London and North-Western Railway Company for the facilities which they afford the public of learning at the earliest hour every occurrence which may be of public interest or for public advantage, not to speak of the many private interests depending upon an early knowledge of what is done in the world.

Above *W.H. Smith sorters at work.*   **Below** *A newspaper waybill of 1897.*

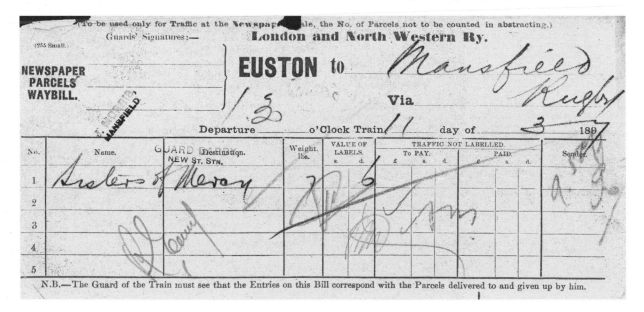

5 Snow!

To the railwayman, snow belongs in one place — on Christmas cards. It has no redeeming features, and in the railwayman's opinion ranks markedly higher in the list of pestilences than most of the plagues visited upon Egypt in the time of Moses. Any railwayman would accept frogs in preference to snow. When it is falling, it obscures visibility, and 'fogsignalmen' have to be called out. Being a fogsignalman is a horrible job under any circumstances, but it is peculiarly revolting in falling snow. Points and signal wires freeze up, and a constant battle must be fought to keep them free, a battle which has more than its fair share of dangers, as the approach of trains is muffled by the blanket of snow, and visibility is likewise reduced. Lines become blocked, and worst of all trains sometimes get trapped in drifts.

'There is a vast amount of back-breaking shovel work needed to try to get the lines clear.' (F.M. Binns)

Snow ploughs have to be run, but there is also a vast amount of back-breaking shovel work needed to try to get the lines cleared. When it has gone, there may well be flooding and washouts. At the best, there will be plenty of repacking of ballast, and other damage to make good.

One of the most exposed, and therefore vulnerable, sections of the North Western was the Merthyr, Tredegar & Abergavenny line. With gradients as severe as 1 in 34, a 1,400 foot summit and sharp curves, it was a nightmare to work even under ideal conditions. On the afternoon of 31 March 1922, snow began to fall, and North Western men feared the worst. By the following morning, a train was stranded at Dowlais, an engine was snowed up at Nantybwch station, and a coach was off the road at Sirhowy. There were drifts of six feet and more in places. Over the next three pages, we will see how the North Western men spent April Fools Day, 1922.

Above left *A pair of coal tanks, Nos 1201 and 573, sit forlorn and deserted at Dowlais on 1 April 1922, their mission to help a short mixed train abandoned as snow drifts reach buffer beam level. J.M. Dunn, who was at Tredegar shed at the time, has left a vivid account of the appalling state of MT&A locomotives of the period, but even engines in perfect condition would have little chance in these conditions. No 573 was written off following accident damage in 1924. (F.M. Binns)*

Left *The scene just a few yards beyond the train is of equal misery, with the lines buried by snow and freight stock scattered about. On the right an engine crew struggle to clear the line, but the signalman has retreated to the relative comfort of his cabin. J.M. Dunn recalled fighting his way on foot through five and six foot drifts to join a relief expedition, only to have the train derail. (F.M. Binns)*

Above *A third coal tank, No 652, is in an even worse predicament at the head of the train, with the driving wheels and buffer beam all but buried. The train formation, of a single coach, van, open and goods brake, is fascinating. (F.M. Binns)*

Right *The LNWR Rule Book postulated that signalmen should work their points frequently to prevent their jamming; in conditions such as these, it was scarcely practical!*

SIGNALLING IN FOGGY WEATHER. 93

86. During the prevalence of severe frost or falls of snow, the Signals and Points must be frequently worked by the Signalmen when the Sections are clear and no train has been signalled, in order to prevent the frost or snow impeding their free working. Fog-signalmen also must see that nothing interferes with the true working of the Arms or Discs, and Lamps of the Signals for which they are fog-signalling ; that the Signal Arms, Lamp glasses and spectacles are kept clear from snow ; and that the wires work freely over the pulleys. The Fog-signalmen must at once report to the Signalman any defect in the Signals or impediment to their proper working. If no Fog-signalman is employed, the Ganger of the Permanent-way must provide for this duty being performed while the snow or frost, or its effect, continues.

When Undermen are required during the night for the purpose of clearing Points, the Signalman must take steps to have them called out as promptly as possible, so as to prevent the Points becoming blocked and unworkable.

6 The Junction

The smooth and efficient operation of the railway system is dependent upon not just one or two people or places, but upon every cog in a vast machine working well. However, some cogs *are* more important than others, and perhaps the key factor in effective railway operations is that the major termini and junctions should be well laid out and operated, for it is there that the traffic is heaviest, and delays most likely. Even today, with the Intercity, HST and block train concepts, this holds true, but in the past, when trains combined and split, through coaches were legion, horse-boxes, carriage trucks and strengthening coaches abounded, and when freight trains were not block rakes, but were formed of individual wagons for a score or more destinations, it was even more crucial. The LNWR recognized this need very early on, and its reputation for punctuality and dependability — which was what the public cared about — sprang from this. The fate of the LNWR rested in the hands of the men running those crucial stations; Euston, Rugby,

Birmingham (New St), Crewe, Chester, Liverpool, Lime St, Manchester Exchange, Preston and the joint station at Carlisle.

In exploring the manner in which the North Western was worked, we cannot neglect those stations, but rather than cover them all in outline, we will look at one in depth, for the lessons of one apply to all. Crewe is the most celebrated junction on the LNWR, perhaps in the world, but with only six routes, one being the North Staffordshire, it comes behind Carlisle, Preston and Rugby, all with seven lines. Carlisle, though important, was a joint station, boasting just one LNWR route. At Preston, three of the routes were LYR, leaving Rugby, with its six North Western routes and one Midland, as the premier LNWR junction. It is also one which the authors are particularly familiar with, and which is less well documented than other great North Western stations.

Three routes converged at the London end of the station, the main line from Euston, via Kilsby

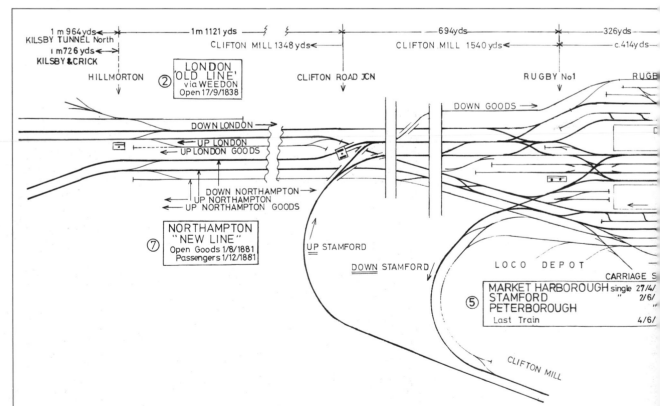

tunnel, the later 'Loop' line via Northampton, and the cross-country line from Peterborough and Stamford. Four routes diverged north and west. Oldest was the L&B line to Birmingham; then came the Midland line to Leicester. This was followed by the Trent Valley Railway which shortened the distance between London and the North; finally, there was the Leamington branch. All of the North Western lines, including the Leamington branch, carried express services, though the latter was primarily as a diversionary route. The Midland, though eclipsed as a passenger line, handled a heavy coal traffic.

A comprehensive system of flyovers arose at the south end in the 1880s, obviating conflict between up and down Northampton and main line trains. Reference to the plan will also reveal that goods from Peterborough and Northampton could reach the down goods line without interfering with the main lines. Paradoxically, there was no such progress at the north end of the station until the 1960s! Here the greatest inconvenience was the crossing on the level of the up Birmingham and down Trent Valley lines at Rugby No 7 box. Trains from Leamington fouled both the Birmingham and Trent Valley

but, mercifully, were less frequent than the 'Brummagems'. Nearer the station, the Midland lines also crossed on the level, and a down empty coal to Leicester blocked every running line!

The Great Central's London Extension, which opened in 1899, crossed the station on a lattice girder near No 1 box. The North Western claimed that this would make it difficult for enginemen to sight signals on the existing gantry, and a new double-deck 44-arm gantry was erected at GCR expense, perhaps the most famous signal in the world! It will be described in detail later. There was no connection of any sort between the LNWR and GCR.

The passenger station was in the form of a gigantic 'H', with two bays, Nos 7 and 8 (and two coach sidings) at the south, and four bays at the north, Nos 3 and 4 leading on to the Leicester line whilst 5 and 6 were used for Leamington, Birmingham and Trent Valley services. Short sidings adjoined the northbound (No 1) and southbound (No 2) platforms. They were used for sundry coaching vehicles and provided a home for the up and down pilots, which provided cover for engine failures, as well as shunting. Beyond the station canopy on each side were

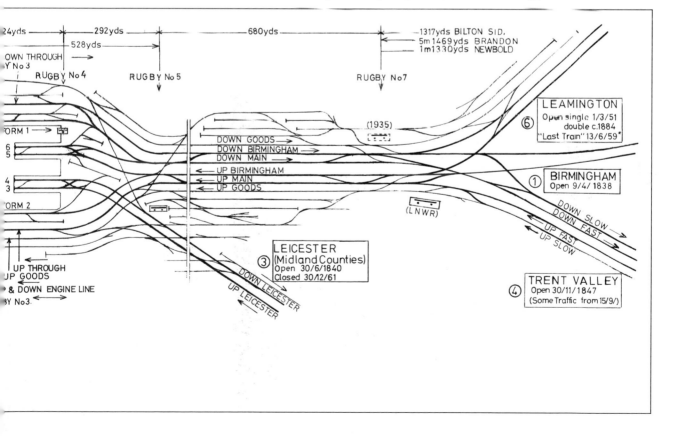

the through lines and, flanking these, the goods lines. Finally, on the up side was the 'up and down' loco line, which provided a communication between the yards at the north end of the station and the shed at the south. Scissors crossovers between the platform and through lines gave added flexibility, as two trains, each of about eight coaches, could use the platform at the same time. They were not used intensively, but in the early 'thirties one of the authors regularly travelled from the north end of platform 2 over the scissors *en route* to Bletchley and Cambridge, as a milk/parcels train occupied the southern portion of the platform.

The original Rugby station, built for the opening of the L&B, was in the vicinity of the later No 7 box. When the Midland Counties line from Leicester opened in 1840, this was replaced by a new station just south of the convergence of the Leicester and Birmingham routes. This was totally inadequate by the late 1860s, but was not replaced until 1885-86 when the new 'island' station was brought into use in two main stages, the down side in July 1885, and the up side the following April. When the Northampton loop had opened in 1881, a temporary level junction was installed, but this was swept away during the comprehensive remodelling of the station.

Following its completion in 1886, the station was little altered until LMS days, when the old

No 7 box, which was on the slope of the embankment, and was suffering from subsidence, was replaced by a new LMS box on the opposite side. Naturally, this was fitted with a new LMS 4½ in frame. No 5 box also needed a new frame, but as there was no convenient site for a new box, the new frame had to be installed in the existing cabin, facing the old frame. One of the authors saw this remarkable sight. There was very little space for the signalman, let alone the fitters, as parts of both frames had to be in use simultaneously. The closer spacing of the LMS frame enabled more levers to be fitted in, and Rugby No 6 and Rugby Midland boxes, both very small, were abolished. The next major change came in 1939 with the introduction of two, three and

Service uniforms remind us of how important the railways were to national life at the time of the First World War portrait of the southern half of the northbound platform at Rugby. The large station sign below the clock and the clear REFRESHMENT ROOMS board remind us that the North Western was decades ahead of BR's design panel with its use of lower case notices which are incomprehensible at any distance. The train indicator board, part of which is visible on the extreme left, is another godsend to passengers. One board pointing at right angles refers to a Coventry and Birmingham train; another, lower board directs passengers to Nuneaton, Stafford, Crewe and the North. The edge of one of the train dials, which indicated departure time, just peeps into the picture. Rugby No 2 box, and a part of the scissors crossover, appear on the right of the view. (Rugby Library Collection)

Above *The approach to Rugby from the south was heralded by Hillmorton Sidings signal box, a tall three storey structure between the Northampton and London lines, some two miles south of Rugby; note that the Northampton line is already several feet higher than the main line. In the down direction, a nest of sidings was established on the main line for holding as well as marshalling trains when Rugby itself was congested, or for empty coals awaiting a path on to the Leicester line. In the up direction, goods loops extended as far as Hillmorton Sidings, the up main goods ending in a sand-drag, as a run-away would otherwise have swept away the cabin! The sidings enjoyed an 'Indian summer' as a main depot during electrification work, but are now lifted. In the background are the 820-foot high masts of the Rugby wireless station, which were being installed in 1924 when one of the authors first travelled through Rugby en route to the Wembley Exhibition. By the time a down train reached Hillmorton, its route through Rugby station had already been determined, and had this not been the case, delays would have been endemic.* (Dr R.P. Hendry)

Below *The LMS signalling arrangements for Hillmorton Sidings.*

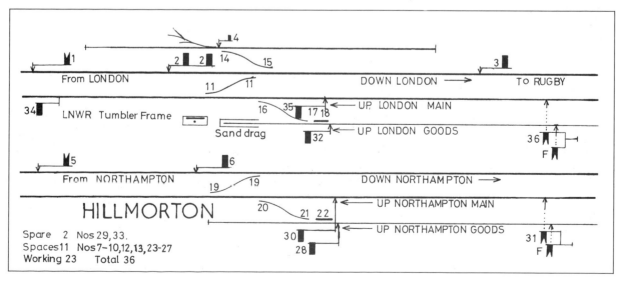

mostly four-aspect colour light signals, largely in the old locations, and worked from the existing boxes, except for Clifton Road Junction, which was abolished. This system, which was in essence nothing more than a peripheral updating of the LNWR signalling system of the 1880s, survived until the installation of power signalling in 1964, preparatory to the electrification of the West Coast Main Line!

Nowadays, mechanical signalling is a dying art, and the majority of main lines are worked from power boxes which can control hundreds of track miles. In North Western days this was not feasible, and large mechanical signal boxes were essential. As the distances at which a signalman could work points or signals were limited, and Board of Trade rules were even more restrictive, so any sizeable station required more than one box. The inter-working between these boxes was very complex, and gave particular interest to any mechanical signalling installation. Just prior to the first World War, the LNWR introduced a Control system, which was expanded

Above *Prior to the remodelling of the southern approaches to Rugby, the Stamford line entered Rugby station via a level junction at the south end of the platform. Plans for remodelling the Stamford and Northampton junctions were deposited with the town and county clerks late in 1881. Two lines were proposed. Railway No 1 started at Clifton Mill station, the first station on the Stamford line, and after burrowing through a shoulder of ground in a 32-foot cutting, swept across low ground on a 45-foot embankment, crossing over the canal on one short bridge, and over the trivial Clifton Brook on a curved 13-arch viaduct, before crossing over the up lines, and dropping into Rugby station on a 606-yard viaduct. Railway No 2, which was to commence near Hillmorton Sidings, and rise on a 730-yard viaduct before crossing over the up London, was to keep down Northampton trains clear of the up main line. The new line from Clifton Mill to Clifton Road Junction opened on 20 September 1885. Here we see a scene some 70 years later, as 'Black Five', No 44711 crosses the Clifton Brook viaduct with a four-coach express from Peterborough. (Authors' Collection)*

by the LMS and BR, but until the First War train regulation was entirely in the hands of the signalmen, and even after the Control system came in, it could only issue broad instructions, and detailed regulation remained with the signalman.

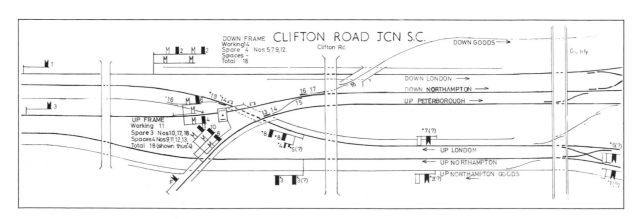

Above *Clifton Road Junction was an incredible box. It was built at right angles to and above the down Northampton line, supported on brick abutments, the Northampton line itself being on a brick arched viaduct at this point. Immediately beyond the cabin, the down Northampton was carried over the up London by a single-span lattice girder. The access stairs ran down the sloping top of the abutment, and then down the side of the North-ampton viaduct to finish by the up London; signalmen had little warning of London trains bursting out from under the North-ants bridge when going on or off duty! The box was fitted with two separate lever frames, each of 18 levers, running not the 'length' of the box, but across the ends. They were called the 'up' and 'down' frames. This was confusing, for the down frame worked the up line from Stamford, and its junction with the down Northampton. This paradox arose because L&B and LNWR practice was to call a branch train approaching a main line an up service, irrespective of the direction the branch faced! LMS*

'4F' 0-6-0 No 4514 is therefore running via crossover 14/15 of the down frame from the up Stamford to the down North-ampton, and is routed to run via crossover 17 to the down goods. The date is 25 May 1939, and within a few months Clifton Road Junction box will have been swept away as a part of LMS modernization work. The co-acting signals 'off' beyond the first wagon in the train are up frame No 3, for an up Northampton train.

Below *A 'Precursor' on an up London express bursts out from under the down Northampton flyover about 1904. In the fore-ground is the down London line with its tall co-acting signals. In front of the 'Precursor' is the facing crossover on to the up London goods, and next to the goods is the viaduct carrying the down Northampton. Note the prominent ringed signals on the secondary route, and the height of North Western running sig-nals, which could often by 60 feet above ground level.*

Above left *Rugby No 1 cabin in the last weeks of its life in July 1964. The cabin, which dated from 1884, possessed 181 levers until 1939 and the abolition of Clifton Road Junction, when four more levers, A,B,C and D, were added next to lever No 1 to work the junction. It was one of the first large boxes built to LNWR standard designs after the company ceased using Saxby equipment.*

Left *Looking south from No 1 cabin as a Standard Class '5' approaches the station with a non-stop excursion from the down London to the down through. To the left are the up Northampton goods, up Northampton and up London. In the centre, the down Northampton and 'up' Stamford drop down from the flyover. Beyond the train is the down goods.*

In a modern power box, the signalmen have a broad view of all train movements over a large area. They can plan ahead from information visible on the panel, but in mechanical days the signalmen had to use intuition and experience as much as information available to them. That they did so with conspicuous success was a tribute to them and to the soundness of the system, for with modern electronics decades in the future, nothing else was possible.

Above *Rugby No 1, (185 levers) one of the largest mechanical boxes in the British Isles, was worked by two men, one handling 'down' traffic, levers 1-67, and the other 'up' routes. As previously mentioned, up and down were confused by the peculiarities of the Stamford line, with an up Peterborough train travelling in the same direction as all other down trains! The unequal distribution of work between up and down men meant that they usually changed ends each week. In any two-man box certain problems arise. Moves have to take place between the up and down sides, and these, although controlled from a single box, are much closer in nature to a shunt move between two boxes. Interlocking of signals prevents conflicting moves, whilst facing point locks (FPLs) prevent a signalman returning a point until a train has passed clear. Ordinarily an FPL lever is next to the lever it locks, but in Rugby No 1 box, points 54 were locked by FPL 91, as the move required action by both men. The size of Rugby No 1 box is apparent from this view, although we do not actually see levers 1-14 at all! The signalman, who is working the 'down' end of the frame, is reaching out to one of the single needle Fletcher block instruments. The normal Fletcher instrument signalled both up and down trains from one box to the next, but as up and down were worked by separate men in No 1 box, half-instruments were necessary. This gave the amusing, and somewhat confusing, situation that the signalman at Clifton Road Junction, for example, signalled to one man for up trains at No 1 box, and to a different man for down trains. He therefore had to have two bell tappers, one to each man!*

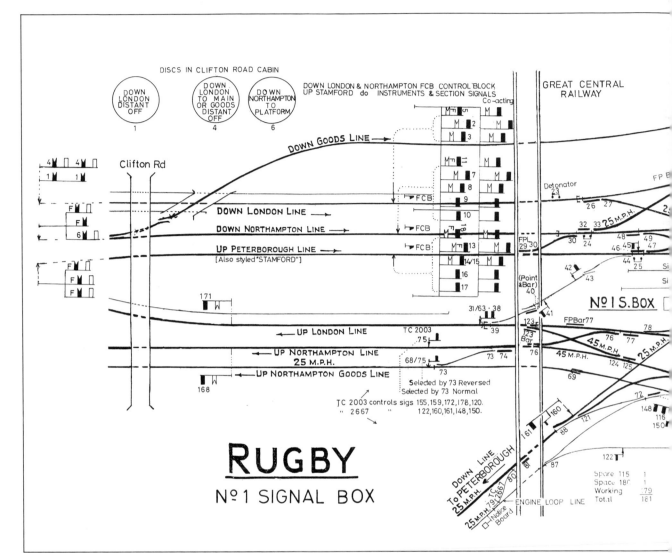

DISCS IN CLIFTON ROAD CABIN

DOWN LONDON & NORTHAMPTON FCB CONTROL BLOCK
UP STAMFORD do INSTRUMENTS & SECTION SIGNALS

GREAT CENTRAL RAILWAY

DOWN GOODS LINE

Clifton Rd

DOWN LONDON LINE

DOWN NORTHAMPTON LINE

UP PETERBOROUGH LINE
[Also styled "STAMFORD"]

No I S.BOX

UP LONDON LINE   TC 2003

UP NORTHAMPTON LINE
25 M.P.H.

UP NORTHAMPTON GOODS LINE

Selected by 73 Reversed
Selected by 73 Normal

TC 2003 controls sigs 155,159,172,178,120.
" 2667 "   122,160,161,148,150.

RUGBY
No1 SIGNAL BOX

Spare 115   1
Space 180   1
Working   179
Total   181

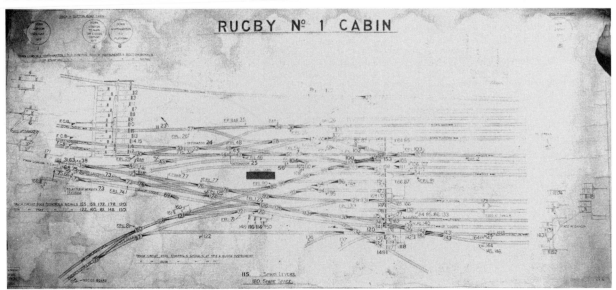

RUGBY No 1 CABIN

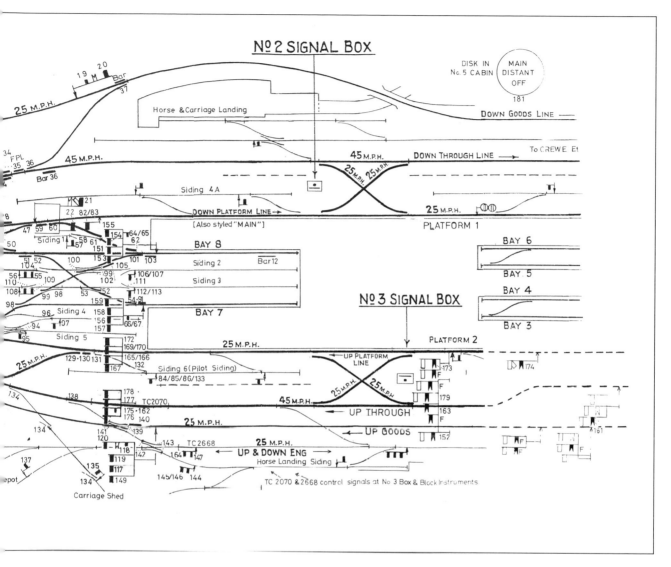

Above *This signalling plan is prepared from the photograph, reproduced opposite, of the signal box diagram which was removed from Rugby No 1 box when colour light signals were brought into use in June 1939.*

The original diagram is characteristic of late LNWR/early LMS practice. Extra detail has been added, for example the position of the GCR overbridge. Signals belonging to No 1 are shown solid, and those of other boxes 'open'. Comparison between an 1895 scale plan and this diagram, which remained current up to 1939, show minimal changes; for example, points 121 are shown in 1895 as coming directly off the down Peterborough, rather than off the connection between the Peterborough and the goods lines. The blades must have been moved a few feet! The most significant change was the demise of the Loco Shed box just south of the GCR bridge.

In the northbound direction, No 1 box offered direct to No 4 box on the down goods, or to No 2 box on the passenger lines. Southbound, No 1 accepted trains from No 3 box, except when that was switched out, when trains were offered direct from No 5. Latterly No 3 box lost control of the 'up and down engine line'. Peterborough departures were offered to Clifton Mill, but until Clifton Road Junction was abolished, this box intervened for arrivals from Peterborough. On the main and Northampton lines, Clifton Road Junction and Hillmorton Sidings were the adjoining boxes.

There were many unusual features. In the down direction, there were eight distants, five being fixed. Distant No 1, London line to through line, was normal, but distant No 4 applied equally to a train routed through the station via the down goods or the down platform. It told the driver he had a clear run, but not where to — he had to know that from the train he was running, not an easy exercise with a parcels train, for example, which could take either route!

In the up direction, distant 181 was a murderous lever to work, as the signal was 1,100 yards away, with an awkward wire run, a multi-slotted arm, and a face disc to work as well. Lever 180 did not exist, and a footrest was provided there to help the signalman in pulling this fearsome signal.

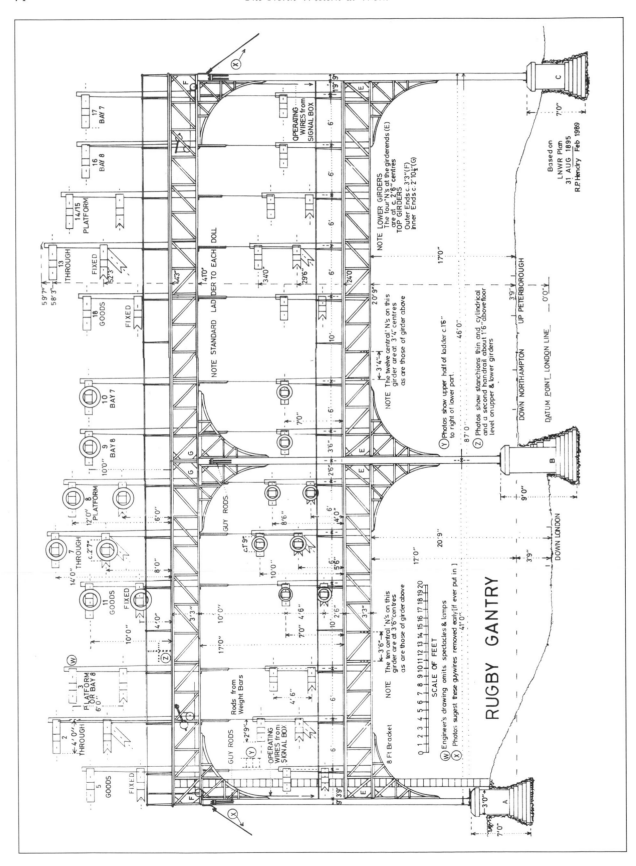

RUGBY GANTRY

Based on
LNWR Plan
31 AUG 1895
R.P. Hendry Feb 1989

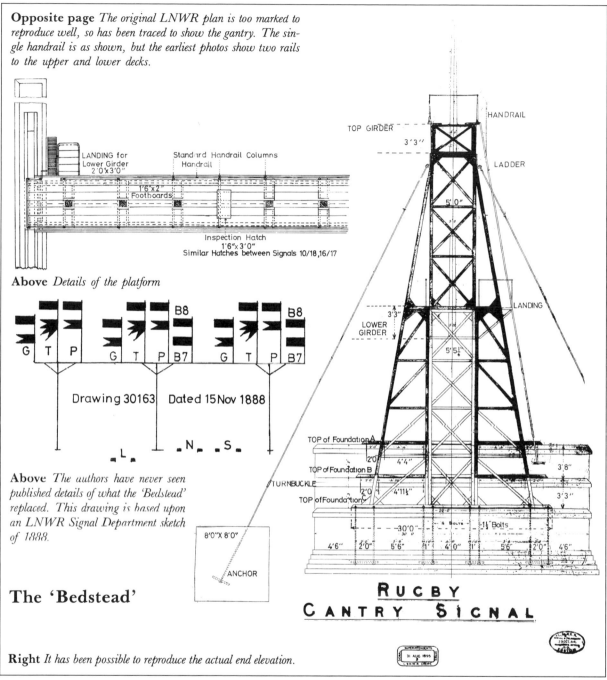

Opposite page *The original LNWR plan is too marked to reproduce well, so has been traced to show the gantry. The single handrail is as shown, but the earliest photos show two rails to the upper and lower decks.*

LANDING for Lower Girder 2'0"x3'0"

Standard Handrail Columns
Handrail

1'6"x2" Footboards

Inspection Hatch 1'6"x3'0"
Similar Hatches between Signals 10/18, 16/17

Above *Details of the platform*

G T P
G T P B7 B8
G T P B7 B8

Drawing 30163 Dated 15 Nov 1888

L N S

Above *The authors have never seen published details of what the 'Bedstead' replaced. This drawing is based upon an LNWR Signal Department sketch of 1888.*

The 'Bedstead'

HANDRAIL
TOP GIRDER
3'3"
LADDER
5'0"
LANDING
3'3"
LOWER GIRDER
5'5¼"

TOP of Foundation A
2'0" 4'4"
TOP of Foundation B
2'0" 4'11½"
TOP of Foundation
3'8"
3'3"

TURNBUCKLE

8'0"X 8'0"
ANCHOR

30'0"
4'6" 2'0" 5'6" 4'0" 5'6" 2'0" 4'6"

RUGBY CANTRY SIGNAL

31 AUG 1895

Right *It has been possible to reproduce the actual end elevation.*

For many years, the Chief Signal Fitter at Rugby was the late Frank Renshaw MBE, a charming man with great sense of humour and a dedication to all things North Western. 'Contempt' is grossly inadequate to describe his opinion of the Midland. It was always said that when Frank retired they would have to re-signal Rugby, as no one else knew it well enough to maintain it adequately, and, true enough, when Frank did approach retirement they did replace all the signalling, and threw in a power box and electrification as well! One of Frank's early comments to one of the authors, delivered in a broad Rugbeian accent, was that he was responsible for 'a fiire' for three months after any work he had done. It seemed hard to blame him for fires, but after a time it became apparent that he was refering to *failures*! Frank was not often blamed, even though the equipment was 50 years old by then.

Left *A celebrated engine and a celebrated signal! No 25673 Lusitania awaits the 'boards' off the down Northampton in 1939 in the last days of the gantry's existence, as Frank Renshaw looks down from the upper deck.*

Above *An S.W.A. Newton photo of the gantry during the construction of the GCR London Extension.* (Warwickshire County Libraries Collection)

Rugby possessed several signal gantries, but the 'Bedstead', as the giant 44-arm double-decker was commonly known, was always the 'Rugby Gantry'. It was 87 feet across the girders, and commonly said to be 60 feet from the down London rail head to the top of the finials — in fact it was 59ft 7in. Owing to the lie of the land, its three bases were at different heights, adding to the complexity of the structure. The upper arms were 4 feet long, excluding spectacle plates, and the lower arms just 2ft 6ins. It is often described as a 'standard' North Western gantry, only on a massive scale. In fact, it was nothing of the sort. It used standard parts, but its size and structural requirements meant that they were used in non-standard ways. The upper deck was the more typical, with its standard-sized arms, and the vertical columns stopping at the lower angle iron of the latticework. The operating wires were taken first to the upper deck, and thence along the lattice, below the flooring, to the cranks and counterweights by the upper signal posts or 'dolls'. In addition, a further set of connections hung down to the lower row of arms (see the drawings on pages 74-75).

For obvious structural reasons, the main vertical columns do not stop short at the lower deck latticework, but continue upwards, so that the end box of the lattice does not conform to the classic rules of lattice construction. Quite simply, a lattice span is always divided into a number of equal-length sections, with the diagonals reversing direction at the mid-point of the span. If there are an uneven number of spans, there is an 'X' box instead of an 'N'. The angle of the diagonals in any span is always the same. Inspection of the scale plan shows that the end lattice is not at the same angle on the lower deck, although it is on the upper deck. The reason is the heavy vertical column, and the diagonal and gusset plate are accordingly displaced. The widths of the two spans also differ, and whist this is unusual in a lattice structure, it is quite proper. As a result, the length to be divided up, and therefore the size of the 'N'-units on the two spans, differs (by about 2in). On a normal LNWR gantry, the end support consists of a pair of uprights supported by horizontals and 'X'-bracing. With a double-decker, this would have been unstable, and added main members create an 'A' section. Heavy guy-wires in the same plane as the 'A' frames give still greater stability, but in the plans reproduced overleaf, which are traced from the LNWR official plans, further wires running at right angles are depicted. If these were ever fitted they were soon removed.

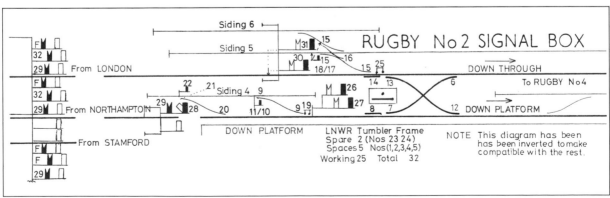

RUGBY No 2 SIGNAL BOX

Siding 6

Siding 5

Siding 4

From LONDON

From NORTHAMPTON

From STAMFORD

DOWN THROUGH

To RUGBY No4

DOWN PLATFORM

DOWN PLATFORM

LNWR Tumbler Frame
Spare 2 (Nos 23 24)
Spaces 5 Nos (1,2,3,4,5)
Working 25 Total 32

NOTE This diagram has been
has been inverted to make
compatible with the rest.

Left *Rugby No 2 box with its Webb frame, LNWR Fletcher block instruments and LMS illuminated diagram.*

Above *The Fletcher block instruments in No 3 box were rare single needle instruments, as explained under No 1 box. The second from the left is a 'permissive' block.*

Rugby Nos 2 and 3 boxes

Owing to Board of Trade rules restricting the distance at which points could be worked on passenger lines, 'midway' cabins were common at large stations in mechanical signalling days. They were usually quite small, working only a few connections, and often only handled trains in one direction. Sometimes they were a part of the station buildings, as at Nottingham. Often they adjoined the mid-point of the platforms, as at Rugby, where No 2 box controlled the down platform and through lines, and No 3 the up side. Both boxes dated from the 1880s, and survived until 1964, the only modernization being LMS track circuit diagrams and the cut-down levers of the colour light signals to warn the signalmen that these were an 'easy' pull.

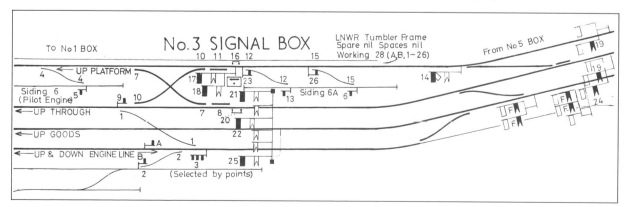

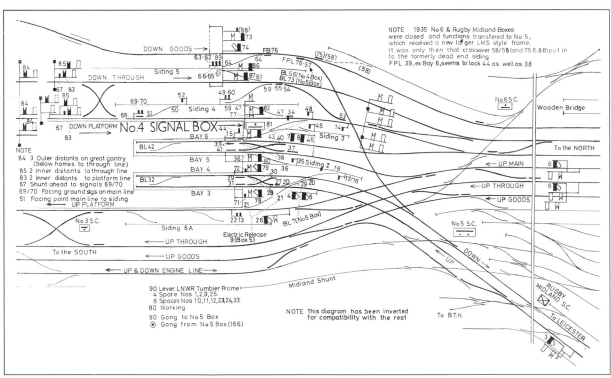

NOTE   1935 No 6 & Rugby Midland Boxes
were closed and functions transfered to No 5,
which received a new larger LMS style frame.
It was only then that crossover 58/58(and 75 & 88)put in
to the formerly dead end siding.
FPL 39, ex Bay 6,seems to lock 44 as well as 38

DOWN GOODS

FB 76
FPL 76·57
BL 56(No 4 Box)
BL 73 (No5 Box)

DOWN THROUGH
Siding 5

Siding 4

No.4 SIGNAL BOX
DOWN PLATFORM
BAY 6

Siding 3

No 6 S.C.
Wooden Bridge

To the NORTH

UP MAIN

BL 42
BAY 5
BL 32
BAY 4
BAY 3

Siding 2

UP THROUGH
UP GOODS

BL 7(No5 Box)

No 5 S.C.

No 3 S.C.
Siding 6A
Electric Release
9(Box 5)

UP PLATFORM

UP THROUGH
To the SOUTH
UP GOODS

UP & DOWN ENGINE LINE

NOTE
84 3 Outer distants on great gantry
      (below homes to through line)
85 2 Inner distants to through line
83 2 Inner distants   to platform line
67 Shunt ahead to signals 69/70
69/70 Facing ground sigs on main line
51 Facing point main line to siding

RUGBY
MIDLAND S.C.
To LEICESTER

Midland Shunt

90 Lever LNWR Tumbler Frame
4 Spare Nos 1,2,9,25
6 Spaces Nos 10,11,12,23,24,33
80 Working

90 Gong to No 5 Box
⊙ Gong from No 5 Box (166)

NOTE This diagram has been inverted
for compatibility with the rest

To B.T.H.

Above left *When Stanier 'Jubilee', No 5597* Barbados *was photographed passing No 4 box with a special on the down through in 1938, the station had altered little since North Western days. No 5597 is signalled on to the down through west of the station, rather than via the little-used 25 mph crossover on to the down main which formed a continuation of the platform line. From left to right, the tracks comprise the down main, down pilot siding, down through, the dead-ended 'Down Independent' and the down goods.*

Above *As well as recording the scene from beyond the Birmingham end of the up main platform/bay 3, this 1950s scene depicts an interesting shunt movement. To the left of the train, and partly hidden by the LMS tubular post splitting signal into 5 and 6 bays, is the LMS-built water treatment plant. To the right of the train is No 5 box and the large bracket signal adjoining it. The two tracks curving across the view from lower left and passing to the right of No 5 box are the tracks into the Leicester bays, the only platform lines accessible from the Leicester line. As with bays 5 and 6, a scissors crossover at the country end of the bays enabled trains to arrive at/depart from either platform, and a second LMS tubular post signal controls incoming moves over the scissors. These splitting signals on passenger lines with the arms mounted above one another followed early signalling practice, and were indeed replacements for similar LNWR*

signals, although normal practice by this time was to provide a splitting bracket signal, as the Board of Trade felt that this was clearer for drivers. On the far right, and surrounded by LMS signals, is a five-arm timber LNWR bracket, which controls set-back movements from the up goods line. The celebrated 'Wooden Bridge' which crossed over the station throat and provided a wonderful vantage point for enthusiasts is visible beyond No 5 box.

The Stanier '8F', No 48255, and her fitted cattle train reveal some of the problems of working a station such as this. She has come in from the north with an up cattle, and her stock must be worked into the cattle dock on the down side. No direct running connection existed from the up lines to the down yard. The signalman at No 5 box could have routed the train on to the up goods line, and then set back (using the five-arm LNWR signal previously noted) into the down yard via the long shunting lead crossing all lines. This is the obvious move, but would block the up and down Leicester, up and down goods, up and down through, up and down main and down goods line No 2, or all nine running lines at this point. Instead of that, he has allowed the cattle train to approach bay 5, and then set back via the up main to the down yard. In this way, the shunt still obstructs all down lines, but keeps the Leicester lines free, and all up roads save for the up main. It is a very neat piece of traffic regulation.

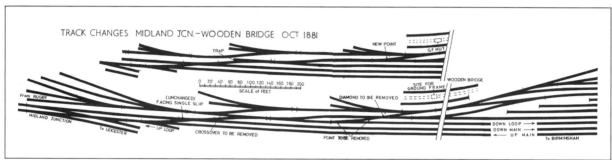

TRACK CHANGES MIDLAND JCN.–WOODEN BRIDGE OCT 1881

NEW POINT

G.F. HUT

TRAP

SCALE of FEET
0 20 40 60 80 100 120 140 160 180 200

SITE FOR
GROUND FRAME

WOODEN BRIDGE

From RUGBY

(UNCHANGED)
FACING SINGLE SLIP

DIAMOND TO BE REMOVED

MIDLAND JUNCTION

To LEICESTER

← UP LOOP

CROSSOVER TO BE REMOVED

POINT TO BE REMOVED

DOWN LOOP →
DOWN MAIN →
← UP MAIN

To BIRMINGHAM

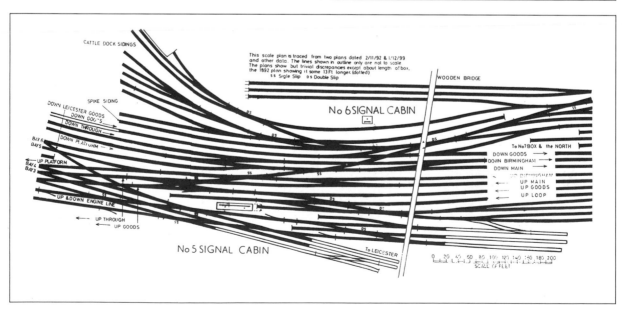

CATTLE DOCK SIDINGS

This scale plan is traced from two plans dated 2/11/92 & 1/12/99
and other data. The lines shown in outline only are not to scale
The plans show but trivial discrepancies except about length of box,
the 1892 plan showing it some 13Ft longer. (dotted)
ss Sigle Slip   ds Double Slip

WOODEN BRIDGE

No 6 SIGNAL CABIN

SPIKE SIDING

DOWN LEICESTER GOODS
DOWN GOODS
DOWN THROUGH
DOWN PLATFORM

BAY 6
BAY 5

UP PLATFORM

BAY 4
BAY 3

To No 7 BOX & the NORTH

DOWN GOODS →
DOWN BIRMINGHAM →
DOWN MAIN →

UP BIRMINGHAM
← UP MAIN
← UP GOODS
UP LOOP

UP & DOWN ENGINE LINE

UP THROUGH
UP GOODS

No 5 SIGNAL CABIN

To LEICESTER

0 20 40 60 80 100 120 140 160 180 200
SCALE of FEET

Left *This 1881 diagram shows the Midland Junction when direct access to the through passenger lines still existed, something which it is often alleged had vanished much earlier.*

Bottom left *An 1892-93 plan showing Nos 5 and 6 boxes, the latter being removed by the LMS in the 1930s. The layout, however, changed little until the 1960s.*

Below *Looking from the 'Wooden Bridge' and up sorting sidings to the North. The down sorting sidings and gas works dominate the scene, with No 7 box just visible, though surrounded by signals, on the skyline.*

Above left and above *These two plates provide a panorama of Rugby, looking from the 'Wooden Bridge' towards the passenger station prior to the installation of colour lights in 1939. On the left is the large British Thomson-Houston electrical works which dated from LNWR days. The Leicester lines pass between the BTH sidings and No 5 box, the latter being flanked by the headshunts from the up sorting sidings. The trailing lead between the up and down sides is prominent in the left-hand view. In the right-hand view the station occupies the skyline, with the goods yard to the far right. (Authors' Collection, left, and Warwickshire Libraries, right)*

Above *The Trent Valley Junction and Rugby No 7 box in the 1930s, looking towards Birmingham and Stafford. This interesting view recalls the old LNWR box, built on the embankment slope. Normally such a box would be timber built throughout, but the LNWR was reluctant to use timber lower storeys due to rotting. The penalty in this case was that the cabin was too heavy for the formation, and had to be replaced in the 1930s. We are standing between the up Birmingham (on the right) and the down main (on the left) on Newbold Road bridge. The level crossing of these two busy routes a few yards west of No 7 box was one of the biggest snags in smooth regulation of traffic.* (Warwickshire Libraries)

Below *This composite plan shows both the old LNWR box on the up side of the line and, dotted, its LMS successor on the down side. Many of the signals visible in the photo above can be seen in their correct locations on the plan, including the three impressive gantries. The new box dated from 1935, and was fitted with a standard LMS frame rather than a reconditioned LNWR Webb frame, but until the installation of colour lights four years later the North Western character remained.*

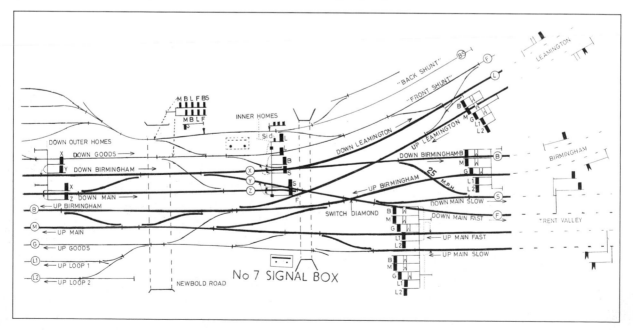

Above *A Johnson '2F', No 58171, heads a long rake of empty chalk wagons from the Leamington line, and has just crossed over the down Trent to make for the up goods lines beyond New-bold Road bridge. As with the down Leicester freights, these moves blocked all main running lines, though in this case the down Leamington remained free. The view is taken from the LMS-built No 7 box, the sidings to the left serving the English Electric works. Chalk trains for the Rugby Portland Cement works at Bilton were a common sight.*

Below *Because of the narrow angle of crossing of the Birmingham and Trent lines, and the need for high speeds when the LNWR '2-Hour' Birmingham expresses were introduced, switch diamonds, rather than the usual fixed diamond crossing, were installed between the down main and the up Birmingham. Although not a point, the switch diamonds, which were very rare in pre-Grouping days, have to be set for the correct road. We are looking towards Rugby station from the down Trent, with the switch diamonds set for the up Birmingham.*

Having studied the signalling at Rugby, we can now see how it was used. For those unfamiliar with the block system, a line is divided into 'block sections' between adjacent signal boxes. Box A 'Calls attention' (1 beat on the 'block bell'), then offers the train to box B, using different codes for the various types of train. If B can accept, he repeats the code to A, and turns the commutator on his block instrument to 'Line clear', which operates a needle on A's instrument, and a repeating needle on his own. When the train leaves, A sends 'Entering section' (2 beats). B repeats this, and turns to 'Train on line'. B then offers the train to the next box, C. When it passes him, he sends 'Entering section' to C and, once he has seen the tail lamp, 'Out of section' to A, returning the needle to vertical. On passenger lines, only one train is permitted in section, but on freight lines, under 'permissive working', further trains can be admitted.

This worked for most of the railway network, but at junctions a signalman must know not just what type of train it is, eg an express or coal, but *where it is going*. Some 7-12 miles short of the junction, the driver whistles at a designated signal box to indicate the route he wants. On hearing this, the signalman does not give the usual 2-beat 'Train entering section' (TES), but a special code to the next box. On receiving the special entering section code, the signalman does not offer the train forward on the usual code, but uses the route code. For example, a coal train is a 4-1; route codes were 4-1-2, 4-1-4 and 4-1-5. This route code is passed from box to box until

it reaches the junction box, whose signalman is thus aware of the train's destination. In the days before advanced electronics, this was essential if non-stop workings were to be correctly routed at junctions, for if the train did not whistle until the junction, it would have to come to a stand until the route was set.

In many places signal boxes are so close together that instead of offering the train forward when 'Entering section' is received from the previous box, it is necessary to offer the train forward as soon as it is offered (block regulation 3b). From Birmingham, the whistle point for Rugby was Coventry No 1, but the next two boxes were at very short intervals, and would offer the train forward when it was offered to them. The block regulations coped with this situation, for under Regulation 3c another code existed, 'Train approaching'. As with 'Entering section', route codes existed for this also, so that where block sections were short, the driver would whistle at box A, who would use a route TES to B. This box would either pass the TES on, or use a route 'Train approaching', so that the route message rapidly got far enough ahead of the train for the signalman to use the route code.

At Coventry, trains running through Rugby without stopping gave 3 whistles for the old line via Weedon, 4 for the Market Harborough line and 5 for the 'new' line via Northampton. On the 'Trent', the whistle point was Shilton No 1 box, with 2 for the old line, and 3 for the 'new' line. In the down direction, trains gave 2 whistles at Welton for the 'Trent', and 3 for the Birming-

Signal box	Distance from last box		Distance from Welton		Whistle code
	miles	yards	miles	yards	
Welton	—	—	—	—	2 Trent; 3 B'ham*
Kilsby Tunnel S	0	1,758	0	1,758	
Kilsby Tunnel N	2	956	3	954	
Hillmorton Sidings	1	964	5	158	4 empty mineral to MR.
Clifton Road Jcn	1	1,121	6	1,579	
Rugby No 1		694	7	213	
Rugby No 2		326	7	539	
Rugby No 4		324	7	863	4 train to MR.
Rugby No 5		292	7	1,175	
Rugby No 7		680	8	95	
Newbold	1	1,330	9	1,425	

*4 whistles were sometimes used for non-stop to the Leamington line.
Rugby No 3 box only signalled up trains (see diagram).

ham. The same codes were used at Long Buckby on the Northampton line.

It is often stated that a 'distant' signal indicates that the next signal is on or off. It does not; a distant signal when off indicates that *all* the relevant signals at a specific box are off, so the driver can expect a clear run for some distance. At busy junctions such as Rugby, boxes can be very close together, as the table on page 86 reveals.

As stop signals are normally a minimum of 440 yards apart, the usual provision for distants would be meaningless. The driver *must* know what his road is for some distance if he is to run hard. Frank Renshaw explained the system in LNWR days to one of the authors. Clifton Road Junction would offer the train to Rugby No 1, who would *not* accept, but offer it to No 2. He in turn would offer to No 4, and so on to Newbold. If Newbold accepted, No 7 then repeated the code back to No 5 without 'Call attention', and 5 did likewise to 4, all the way back to Clifton Road Junction, who cleared all his signals, including the distant. The driver, on seeing the distant, knew he had a clear path through Rugby.

This was cumbersome, for if a shunt move was taking place at No 7 box, for example, No 1 could not accept a train, as No 7 would not. The rules changed in the 'thirties, probably upon the introduction of multiple aspect colour light signalling (MAS) in 1939. The red/single yellow/double yellow/green sequence ensured adequate braking distance for a driver. The signalman could accept trains normally, and once he had 'Line clear' from the next box, he could pull *all* his signals. Unlike the two-position semaphore signal, with its stop or go options, with MAS colour light would only give a green if the following signal displayed double yellow or green. The 'clear through Rugby yard' concept was thus replaced by an adequate braking distance message, which was the object of the exercise.

Mention was made of 'permissive working' on freight lines. Here the block instruments are modified, and apart from a 'Line clear' 'Train on line' needle, have a counter, which goes up to 9 in LNWR equipment. When a second train is accepted, the commutator is given another turn, advancing the number, and when it is clear of the section, turned back, reducing the number. The goods lines at Rugby were worked under permissive regulations. At complex passenger stations, where platform lines are signalled by

a number of boxes, the usual block regulations, which require that the line is clear for ¼ mile beyond the first stop signal worked by the box before he can accept a train, would make operation all but impossible. A 'permissive' system is used, called 'station yard working'. From their training, drivers know that they must enter any section worked under station yard regulations with extreme caution, ready to stop short of another train. At Rugby, the up and down platform lines and the four bays, Nos 3-6, at the Birmingham end were under station yard working. These bays were worked by two boxes, Nos 4 and 5; as the London end bays were controlled solely by No 1, no such facility was needed there. When the line was not clear to accept a train under normal rules, but a signalman was prepared to accept under station yard working, he did not return the usual train code, but 4-3, and the signalman in rear then brought the train almost to a stand at his home signal, before letting it proceed.

The block system had evolved piecemeal, with hazardous locations such as Kilsby Tunnel being equipped early on. Route codes also evolved piecemeal, but as these were only used by a handful of experienced signalmen, there was not the same need to establish a uniform code throughout a given system. A standard code did evolve, the A, B and C route codes, but these were supplemented or replaced locally. Instead of the usual route codes at Rugby for down expresses, a non-stop 'Trent' was 4-4-4, whilst a Birmingham was 4-4-4-2. Readers familiar with the Royal Train code of 4-4-4 may be puzzled, and Frank Renshaw suggested being on hand when a Royal Train was offered! The block regulations postulate that beats are to be made slowly and distinctly, with pauses marked. Experienced signalmen actually worked very fast indeed, and a non-stop 'Trent' sounded like 12 bells, and it was only with practice that one could detect the momentary pause between the fourth and fifth beats and eighth and ninth beats. A Birmingham sounded like 12-1-1. A Royal Train, by contrast, was given by the book, very slowly, with marked pauses.

Special bell codes such as these were not listed in the block regulations or appendices, but only in the box instructions. Many are now lost, and the authors would welcome information upon such codes for other major stations so that they are preserved for posterity.

7 'Conciliation'

To anyone born in the latter half of the twentieth century, with inflation as a seemingly natural fact of life, it is almost inconceivable that prices and wages remained constant not merely for years, but for decades, in past centuries. There were spells of inflation, such as our own, but they were often short-lived and at other times prices actually fell. War, plague and events such as the South Sea Bubble in the eighteenth century, or the Railway Mania of the 1840s, were the times when prices were liable to rise, but these were exceptions, not the rule.

For much of the nineteenth century prices were relatively stable, and indeed fell almost continuously throughout the last quarter of the century! Between 1877 and 1899, the workman's food bill was cut by one-third, and for some items, such as flour or sugar, the price was halved. This was in part due to the opening up of the American prairies and other 'new' countries and, in the case of minerals, the new low-cost mines. Hours were long and wages low, but with the cost of living static or falling, the infant trade unions devoted much of their attention towards a reduction in hours. In this there was steady progress from the 1870s onwards.

From the turn of the century the pattern changed, and there was a slow but steady inflation. Between 1900 and 1907, the retail index of the principal items of workmen's food rose by 7 per cent. To modern eyes, used to 7 per cent or more in a single year, this seems barely noticeable, but in an era when static or falling prices had been the rule, the impact was devastating. The railway unions, which were slowly becoming more organized, became ever more insistent in their demands for higher wages to meet the increased cost of living. Unrest during 1907 came to a head in the autumn, and under the auspices of the Liberal president of the Board of Trade, Lloyd George, a conciliation scheme was arranged between six of the leading railway companies, including the LNWR, and the Amalgamated Society of Railway Servants. The agreement, of 6 November 1907, committed the principal companies and the ASRS to conciliation meetings before sectional boards, followed by a central board, and if agreement was still not

possible, to an agreed independent arbitrator, who, to avoid bias, was not to be connected with either side of the railway industry. Each of the leading companies was to establish its own structure, and on the LNWR, discussions began within days of the agreement being signed.

The employees' side of the sectional conciliation boards was formed from representatives elected by the staff. The grades to be covered by the process were divided into seven sections, A to G, whilst the area served by the Company, and certain joint lines, was split into six electoral districts on 30 December 1907. The Company's side of each sectional board consisted of the appropriate Directors and officers. W.E. Thornhill was a Senior Divisional Engineer of the North Western in the years up to the First World War, and his personal copy of the Conciliation arrangements procedure records that the first elections took place in April 1908 for a three-year term of office.

The first formal programme had been put to George Whale, the Chief Mechanical Engineer, as early as February 1908, but it was not until after the sectional and central boards had been formed that real progress was possible. However, agreement could not be reached through either board, and both sides went to arbitration before Sir Edward Fry GCB PC. C.E. Grasemann, the Outdoor Goods Manager at Euston, represented the Company, whilst the staff selected Richard Bell MP JP, Secretary of the Amalgamated Society of Railway Servants. Bell, who combined his work as Secretary of the Union with the duties of an MP, had vivid memories of his own youth as a brakesman in the days when brakesmen and guards rode outside!

The arbitration hearings began on 9 December 1908, and over the eight days of the hearings Grasemann and Bell were to conduct a good-natured but stimulating duel, the two men probing one another's case and studying the evidence advanced by one side, and then the other. It is this cross-examination which makes the evidence so valuable, for mis-statements by either side were sure to be challenged. When some of the early witnesses called by Richard Bell overstated their case, Grasemann was able to reply with a mass of facts to prove his point. Bell obviously felt that his witnesses had let him down, and must have spoken firmly to his men, as accuracy improved thereafter. Conversely, when a senior North Western officer made a statement which was disputed by the men, he agreed to check up, and readily admitted his error the following morning, even giving the date of the official circular which confirmed the men's contention!

At times there was high comedy, and we shall discover one North Western employee justifying higher wages for Manchester staff on the grounds that country folk were uncivilized and could dig for potatoes! C.E. Grasemann found himself in an equally amusing predicament in revealing the human face of North Western management. Nowadays we tend to see Victorian or Edwardian managers as autocratic and humourless, but we must see them in the context of the day. The story is told of F.W. Webb, the CME, tipping a

For decades, North Western enginemen had been used to Ramsbottom or Webb 2-4-0s, such as No 1220 Belted Will, *a Webb 'Improved Precedent' seen entering Coventry with a down express in 1911. Suddenly the small boilers and tall chimneys of the Webb era were replaced by the much more powerful, and coal-hungry, Whale engines. Rising prices and bigger engines spelled trouble!*

porter, and jocularly asking the man if he knew it was against the rules to accept tips from a passenger. The porter, it is said, responded at once that he knew of the rule, but as the tip was from a fellow railway servant, it was all right in this case! The story may or may not be true — it certainly deserves to be, but, quite understandably, there is no documentary corroboration. The authors are inclined to believe it is true, for Grasemann was to admit quite readily in the official hearing that he would tip a North Western porter, to Richard Bell's amusement. Indeed, Grasemann went much further; he said the rule was not sensible, and that in his opinion the Company should replace it by one forbidding the soliciting of tips.

Celebrated names appeared at the enquiry. Charles John Bowen Cooke, then Running Superintendent at Crewe, gave evidence. They were crucial days, for it had seemed for some time that A.R. Trevithick, the Chief Indoor Assistant and effective second-in-command in the Locomotive Department, would succeed George Whale, but Bowen Cooke's evidence was to so impress the North Western Board that he was to receive the top job, with Trevithick becoming Waggon Superintendent at Earlestown in due course. Herbert Ashcombe Walker appeared as District Superintendent at Euston. He too dis-

The grades represented by each Board are given below :—

BOARD "A."	BOARD "B."	BOARD "C."	BOARD
WHITE Nomination and Voting Papers.	RED Nomination and Voting Papers.	GREEN Nomination and Voting Papers.	GREY Nomination
LOCO. DEPT.	SIGNALMEN AND POINTSMEN.	BREAKSMEN AND SHUNTERS.	GUARDS AND COACHING STAFF. &c.
Loco. Engine Drivers	Gatekeepers (excluding Women)	Breaksmen (including those in Waggon Department)	Coaching Shunters
Loco. Engine Firemen	Ground Pointsmen	Pilot Breaksmen	Coach Workers
Loco. Engine Cleaners (including all in these grades in and out of the Works, and in the Carriage, P. Way, and Waggon Departments) and	Pointsmen	Pilotmen	Conductors
	Porter Signalmen	Porter Breaksmen	Corridor Attendants
	Signalmen	Shunters—Goods and Traffic (including those in the Carriage, Loco., P. Way, P. Way Stores, Waggon, and General Stores Departments)	Guards
	Signal Lads		Lamp Lads
	Telephone Lads		Lamp Men
	Train Boys		Motor Conductors
	Train Recorders		Parcels Porters
	In Signal Boxes.		
LOCO. OUT-DOOR STAFF, *i.e.* :—		*Traffic Foremen Shunters	Pilot Guards
Coal Tippers		Tariff Guards	*Platform Policemen
Cranemen (Hydraulic)		Tariff Men	Point Cleaners
Cranemen (Steam)		Transhipmen	Point Oilers
Hoist Attendants			Porter Guards
Pointsmen			Porter Shunters (Coaching)
Pulleymen			Porters (Adult)
			Porters (Junior)
*LABOURERS IN LOCO. SHEDS. *i.e.* :—			Shunt-horse Drivers (Coaching)
*Washers Out			Telephone Lads (other than in Signal Boxes)
*Fuelmen			Ticket Collectors and Examiners
*Steam Raisers			Train Reporters
*Break Blockers			
*Storesmen			
*Tube Cleaners			
*Toolmen			
*Shed Turners			

These grades were admitted by agreement at the Central Conciliation Board on October 8th and 28th, 1908.

tinguished himself, and progress to Assistant to the Superintendent of the Line followed shortly. By 1910, he had become Southern Division Goods Manager, and on 1 January 1912 took over as General Manager of the London & South Western Railway, and later of the Southern Railway.

The seven chapters which follow explore the mountain of information put before Sir Edward Fry. Evidence was often given in the form of lengthy answers, and we have allowed the witnesses, whether Bowen Cooke or a platelayer or greaser, to use their own words. On occasion, where there was a quick-fire question and answer

"D."	BOARD "E"	BOARD "F."	BOARD "G."
and Voting Papers.	BLUE Nomination and Voting Papers.	PINK Nomination and Voting Papers.	YELLOW Nomination and Voting Papers.
	PERMANENT WAY DEPT.	GOODS STAFF.	CARTAGE STAFF.
CARRIAGE DEPT. OUT-DOOR STAFF.	Assistants to P. Way Inspectors	Bookers	Book Carriers
	Ballast Flagmen	Callers-off	Busmen
Couplers	Ballast Guards	Capstan Lads	Bus Drivers
Electric Light Men	Relaying and Ballast Gangs	Capstan Men	Bus Conductors
Examiners	Platelayers	Checkers	Carmen
Footwarmer Attendants	Timekeepers on P. Way Staff	Crane Attendants	Cart Boys
Gas Fillers		Deliverers	Cart Drivers
Gas Fitters	ELECTRICAL AND SIGNAL DEPT.	Gasmen	Carters
Lampmen		Hookers-on	Chain Boys
Oilers	Chargemen	Iron Counters	Chain Men
Washers and Cleaners (excluding Women)	Chargemen Assistants	Labellers	Draymen
	Fitters' Assistants	Loaders	Grooms
WAGGON DEPT. OUT-DOOR STAFF.	Labourers (Electrical Section)	Number-takers	Horsekeepers
	Labourers (Signal Section)	Porters (Adult)	Lurrymen
Examiners	Labourers (Telegraph Section)	Porters (Junior)	Parcels Van Drivers
Greasers	Linemen	Receivers	Stablemen
	Linemen Assistants	Scalesmen	Van Lads
GENERAL STORES DEPT.	Point Oilers	Searchers	Van Men
		Sheeters	Van Setters
Stores Train Attendants		Shippers	Waggoners
		Shunt Horse Drivers (Goods)	
		Slate Counters	
		Slip Boys	
		Timber Loaders	
		Timber Measurers	
		Van Washers	
		Waggon Berthers	
		Warehousemen	
		Weighers	
		Winchmen	
		Yardsmen	

session, we have linked a series of answers to preserve the continuity. We have drawn particular attention to this in the evidence of W.H. Williams, Southern Division Engineer, for in academic theory we should introduce ellipses, thus . . ., or author's square brackets []. To do so, in many passages, would interfere with the natural flow of the evidence. However, where witnesses are quoted, we have never introduced facts which the witness did not give or agree to, without making the addition clear. Given the caution and respect which Grasemann and Bell developed for one another over the hearing, and the way in which exaggeration or error was

Representative of the new breed of engine was the 19-inch goods, of which No 705 is an example. Her 1,985 sq ft of heating surface was approaching twice that of a 17-inch coal engine, a 'Cauliflower' or a 'DX'. Heavier trains meant more work for drivers, firemen and guards. In the pages to follow we will discover their feelings. (Authors' Collection)

picked up instantly, it seems clear that the testimony offered by the North Western men, from top to bottom, represents a uniquely detailed and accurate insight into not just working conditions, but also attitudes of the men and management of an Edwardian railway at its prime.

The conciliation proceedings before Sir Edward Fry were bound and published, but in common with the whole of the conciliation process, the print runs were so small that the information seems to have escaped the attention of railway historians to all intents and purposes. Perhaps this is none too surprising. We have already referred to W.E. Thornhill, the North Western Divisional Engineer at Crewe. His personal copy of the rules and procedures, with his name blocked in gold, helps to explain this. Rule 27 provided that whilst any item was before any conciliation board or the arbitrator, there was to be no press comment. The newshawks of today would scarcely appreciate that!

The LNWR was to appoint a secretary to the conciliation board, whose duty was to keep an official minute book which had to be approved by both sides. He was to supply copies of the proceedings to members of the Company's side of each sectional board, and a sufficient supply of copies for the men's side also. The latter ranged from 7 to 11, and the Company's teams were equally small. If an issue could not be resolved before one of the sectional boards, it passed to the central board, which comprised a handful of senior North Western officers and Directors, and 14 representatives from the men, two from each sectional board. Circulation was once again limited to members of the central board, and rule 24 went on to add 'That reports of the proceedings at Conciliation Board meetings shall only be distributed in the manner set forth in the foregoing clauses and shall not be obtainable by the remainder of the employees.'

With a circulation so limited, it is doubtful if more than 20 or 30 people ever read the full story, and with the passage of a lifetime it is understandable that the events of eight decades ago and more are all but lost in the mists of time. We will go back to a December day in 1908, when Sir Edward Fry met eight LNWR officers, 14 of its employees and Richard Bell of the ASRS. The North Western officers included C.E. Grasemann, Outdoor Goods Manager, Euston, C.J.B. Cooke, Running Superintendent at Crewe, W.H. Williams, Divisional Engineer, Watford, J.G. Humphreys, District Goods Manager, Birmingham, and the brilliant and likeable Tom Shaw, then District Goods Manager at Liverpool, but soon to be promoted to Grasemann's job (as the latter moved up the tree), but to be dead at the age of 38. There was Cumberland Lowndes, District Superintendent at Manchester, Herbert Walker, the 'Super' at Euston, and J.D. Brown, Secretary of the Company's side of the conciliation board.

8 The Locomen

Sir Edward Fry looked across the table; facing him was a small group of London & North Western officers, and about twice as many of the company's staff. He cleared his throat 'Gentlemen, the first point which I think requires our attention is the question as to who are to attend and appear before me today and throughout the enquiry'. J.D. Brown, the Secretary of the Company's side, explained that the Southern Division Outdoor Goods Manager, C.E. Grasemann, would represent the Company. Herbert Ellison, a fireman at Preston, and the Secretary of the men's side, announced that they had invited Richard Bell, secretary of the Amalgamated Society of Railway Servants, to represent them, as *their* representative rather than a representative of the union. Sir Edward, aware of his lack of detailed knowledge of railway procedure, asked both sides how they felt over his being assisted by an independent assessor. Grasemann suggested that if the assessor was a serving railway official of any company, it might appear biased, and that the officers had talked it over with the men earlier that day, and added 'we rather came to the conclusion that we should prefer, if you were agreeable, for you to settle it by yourself.'

With the procedural matters cleared up within a few minutes, Sir Edward asked for written contracts or notices covering conditions of employment and rates of pay. Grasemann replied, 'I may say that there is nothing of the kind on the North Western Railway with the exception of the Locomotive Department. In all the other departments it is a matter of practice, but in the Locomotive Department the terms of employment have been issued to the staff in printed documents, and I think Mr Cooke has one here which he can give you.' It is a fascinating thought that as late as 1908 the LNWR, the largest railway company in the British Isles, conducted most of its employment matters on custom and practice, rather than with written terms. It helps explain why a written record of the conditions of employment prior to 1908 is unknown!

Richard Bell opened the case for the men, a task which was to be confused by the existence of two parallel, but differing, sets of demands, both of which it was necessary to work through.

The main points that he outlined, and which were to crop up regularly in the enquiry, were the higher cost of living, the larger locomotives, and hence the longer trains, leading to heavier physical work and more mental strain, higher speeds, and the accelerated pace of railway life in general. As Bell was not ready to present his detailed case on the opening day, Bowen Cooke was the first, and indeed only, witness to be called that day. The 17 appearances he made during the enquiry were to be eclipsed by Herbert Walker alone.

North Western enginemen were paid by time, trip or mileage, and Cooke had to explain this very carefully to the arbitrator. 'The wages of engine drivers and firemen on the London & North Western Railway may be calculated on any one of three bases; firstly by mileage trip rate; secondly, by time trip rate; and thirdly, by ordinary time. The mileage trip rates are for the express passenger service, 150 miles equivalent to a day of ten hours. For the through goods service, 120 miles equivalent to a day of ten hours. Time trip rates are based on the actual time occupied in working a particular train averaged for a number of journeys, with 10 per cent added to the average time occupied as a margin of profit to the driver and fireman. Ordinary time is the payment according to the actual hours the driver or fireman is on duty. The actual payment in each case is based on days of ten hours at fixed rates of pay according to the class of train worked.'

Sir Edward wished to know why mileage and time trip rates were converted into notional ten-hour days; 'because it is the easier way in calculating the men's work in making out the pay sheet; and all the wages whether time or trip, are all taken in hours. The driver's day is based on a ten-hour day'. A driver could work on a mixture of the methods in a week. On Monday and Tuesday, he might be on express work, and once he had done his 150 miles, that was equal to ten hours' duty for pay purposes, even though it would not take ten hours. On Wednesday and Thursday he might be on actual time. This would not necessarily be ten hours; on one day it might be 8½ hours, on the next day it could be 11

hours. This would give him 19½ hours. On the remaining two days he might be on trip time rates, in which average time plus ten per cent was the deemed time for the job. If he was on a job which averaged 6 hours plus 10 per cent and finished in 5½ hours, the pay was for the nominal time, not the shorter hours worked. If, however, he was a few minutes over the time, he was still only paid for the nominal time, although a mechanism did exist for extra payments where trips were badly held up.

At this time, the North Western 'Conditions of Service' dated back to 1872, or the start of the Webb era. With prices generally static or declining for most of that period, there had been little need to change wages, though there had been some movement in 1889, a further concession in 1897 to mark the Queen's Diamond Jubilee, and other adjustments in 1900. These were all piecemeal measures, however, and the most significant changes had been in the reduction of hours, which had been virtually unlimited in 1872, when 16-hour shifts were common, but had been progressively reduced to a nominal ten-hour day, with a maximum of 12 hours' duty, by the turn of the century. Bowen Cooke looked back to the early days of the North Western. 'In the past many engines were not fitted with cabs, and the men with much longer hours of duty had no protection from the weather, and when the rails had to be sanded, the fireman had to clamber out on the buffer plank or frame of the engine and put sand down by hand whilst clinging to the handrail. In those days of exposure and long hours, men worked coal trains which might take a great number of hours to get to their destination without having relief, whereas now they are always

relieved after being on 12 hours. Then, again, there are certain duties, such as packing the glands, washing out boilers, raking out ashpans and smoke boxes, and turning engines to some extent, which have been taken off the drivers, and in certain cases of long hours, like the one between Liverpool and London, the men when they get up here step off their engine, and it is taken charge of by relievers, and they simply have to step on again to go back.

'Although railway development in all its branches has brought forward the necessity for building engines of higher capacity, and stronger engines, that has rather had the effect of lessening than increasing the strains on the men working them. Every recent improvement in locomotive construction on the London & North Western Railway within the last few years has been to effect improvements in the engine, and to really give the men a machine with fewer complications and working parts, and one capable more easily of performing its work than its predecessor. It is less than ten years that the larger engines have been put on the road. We admit that the weight of trains has increased, but a locomotive not strong enough to satisfactorily perform its duty does to some extent throw a strain on the driver, and the fault may lie with the engine rather than be due to the lack of skill on his part or that of a fireman. That may be exemplified by taking the work of the "Precursor" tank engine which has been recently put on the road, and which works the heavy local trains between Euston and Watford, and Sutton Coldfield and Birmingham, and other places. When we have had heavier trains put on that road with the smaller engines, there was continual complaint of loss of time, and the men were reproved for loss of time, but they really had a smaller engine than was capable of fulfilling its work. Now they have a larger engine on those particular trains, and, as a matter of fact, we never hear anything about complaints. The driver and fireman have a machine easily able to do the work, and they are never in trouble. I say that of my own knowledge, having to ride with these engines, and to deal with all questions of the working of trains myself. Within the last six years, we have put on the line 315 of the larger type of engine, and those are all employed on working the heavier trains whether they are goods or express passenger, or local passenger. The lighter types of engine are still kept on the lighter trains which have practically not altered within the last few years. In many cases passenger trains have been acclerated, but that acceleration has not put any undue hardship on the driver or fireman, and they really get through their work in a shorter time than they did before.'

Bowen Cooke resolutely opposed any argument of increased mental strain upon the drivers through the larger engines or faster schedules, and introduced some fascinating details about standing time and short working. 'In my ex-perience I get no complaints of men who make 60 hours and upwards, although sometimes when trade is bad by a falling off at one place, I may get men working under 60 hours, and I have often had complaints on that head, but never one for working over 60 hours. The class of work in the Locomotive Department is very carefully considered when arranging the men's duties, and it is rather difficult to apply a constituted day, and number of hours, to men who are working on the trip system, because their hours vary according to their class of work. The more important the latter the more favourable is the trip system, and the less hours work per week and the higher the pay. With regard to the men paid on the average time trip system, it must be remembered that the work on the footplate cannot be compared with any other grade. A workman in a factory is supposed to be continuously at work from the time he starts till he finishes, whereas a driver, although we admit he is responsible for the care of his engine, is only actually employed during the time his engine is on the move, and a great part of the time for which he is drawing pay his engine is standing waiting for the next train. With regard to the amount of time standing, I have the figures of time working and stand-

ing during the 12 months ending December 31st, 1907. Taking the passenger working, the total time that engines were out was 2,563,549 hours; the stationary time, included in the time out, was 946,804 hours, and the percentage was 36.93 per cent. With the goods working, the time out was 3,950,060 hours; stationary, included in time out, 1,235,902 hours, and the percentage 31.29 per cent. It will, therefore, be seen that with passenger engine drivers and firemen, out of the whole of the time they have been out on the line and drawing full wages, they have actually been standing over one-third of the time, and with goods engine drivers and firemen, they have been standing nearly one-third of the time.'

One of the principal reasons advanced in favour of shorter hours in Bell's opening speech had been the higher coal consumption of the new Whale locomotives — he spoke of up to 7 tons in a shift. When Bowen Cooke gave evidence, he readily admitted that the work had increased with the newer engines, observing, 'I might take as an example perhaps the longest run that we do, that is from Liverpool to London and back; that is done in say 8 hours. Suppose the man had a very heavy train in each direction. He would shift, say 8 tons. That is an outside estimate. That means that he would have to shift at the rate of one ton per hour for the time he was on. Now a fuelman has to throw the coal out of the wagon on to a tender which is where the coal is handled,

and he will shovel as much as 20 tons in a day's work of ten hours. The fireman, who has a double trip between Liverpool and London, taking that as an example, for the amount of coal that he moves would be paid, I think it works out, at the rate of 1 shilling and 5 pence per ton, whereas a fuelman moves 20 tons for his day's work at the rate of 3d per ton.'

Cooke's case had been well put, and emphasized management's view that the firemen were much better off than the fuelmen, but to a fireman that was not the issue at all. The first witness to be called by Richard Bell was Herbert Ellison, a fireman at Preston, and the Secretary of the men's side of the conciliation board. Ellison had joined the LNWR as a number-taker in the Mineral Department in 1895, and after just under two years' service, had transferred to the Locomotive Department as a cleaner, with a wage of 8 shillings a week. By 1908 Ellison was rated as a cleaner and extra fireman, having done very little cleaning in the past three or four years. He had progressed up the ladder from firing shunting engines and local freights to main line freights and passenger services, but, at his own request, had been put back to firing shunting

A group of cleaners, firemen, drivers and shed staff gather around No 28 Prometheus. *It would take many years progressing through the ranks before some of the younger men would handle a top link passenger engine.*

Above *The first step on the ladder was firing a shunting engine, almost certainly a 'Special Tank', at some sheds called a 'Grando'. No 3593 is seen at Crewe South in about 1921.* (J.N. Maskelyne)

Below *The next stage was firing a freight engine, often a 'DX', such as No 2022, or a 17-inch coal engine, on short trip work.*

Local or cross-country passenger work followed. This 1911 portrait of Coventry is believed to show No 655, a Webb 5ft 6in tank on a through Nottingham–Leicester–Nuneaton–Coventry –Leamington working, due into Leamington at midday. The solitary LNWR six-wheeler, which is rather upstaged by the Midland clerestory stock, is probably to provide some second class accommodation on LNWR metals. (H.J. Stretton Ward)

engines, so as to concentrate on his work for the conciliation board. During his spell on main line work, he had regularly fired to Carlisle, and also to Liverpool, Crewe and Manchester, and once on a London turn. His wages on this work had been 3s 9d per day. Promotion, when it came, would be to registered fireman, when he would receive the 3s 9d rate as a minimum, as he had dropped to 3s 6d on reverting to shunting duties. Ellison estimated they might use two or three tons of coal between Preston and Carlisle on the newer engines, and observed that after a trip that he was 'ready for bed'. He was happy with the mileage system, but disliked the time trip. He revealed that 'In many cases, we, as firemen, assist the breaksmen to get along the line hold-

ing points... where you get a breaksman who is not thoroughly acquainted with the siding in which we are working — there may be a curve round the siding — and the guard cannot so well turn the points, so we assist so as to be able to do it in the trip time.' This was of course contrary to the rule book, which provided that the driver was only to move the engine when the fireman was on board.

The next witness, Albert Bellamy, was a much more talented speaker than Ellison. He was already a Justice of the Peace in Stockport, and was both Chairman of the men's side of the conciliation board, and an influential figure in the Amalgamated Society of Railway Servants. He was later to become President of the NUR. Bellamy had been with the LNWR for about 23 years by 1908, and had started as a cleaner. After 5 or 6 years as a cleaner, during which time he was taking home 11 to 14 shillings, he progressed to cleaner and extra fireman. This would be about 1890 or 1891, at which time he was earning 3 shillings a day, when on firing work. Bellamy recalled the increase of 6d to commemorate the 1897 Jubilee; 'I believe it was in Her Majesty's Diamond Jubilee year when the Directors granted it'. Bellamy progressed through the firing links to become fireman and extra driver about 1900, and a regular driver five years later. He explained the fine gradation in the North Western system; 'A man can be a fireman and extra driver; that is, he is a fireman marked on the sheet as a fireman, and liable to be called out for driving duties. Then the next stage is what is called an extra driver marked on the sheet as an Extra Driver, subject to be called out at any time required. Then you become a full registered driver.'

Sir Edward Fry asked Bellamy about his wages, which in Bellamy's case were slightly lower than the two guineas (42 shillings) a week which his grade would have allowed. Bellamy was careful to explain the reason: 'I wanted you to allow me to make this statement, that since during these last two years I have had frequently to

be released from my duties, so that my record during these last two years is not a reliable one.' Bellamy explained he was a magistrate and was regularly released from duty, and in reply to Fry's comment that the Company was not a very bad master, commented, 'Well, if we had to depend on these gentlemen round the Board we might get on very well, I think, but we do not always meet them. There is a buffer in between'. Speaking of his work, Bellamy observed, 'I think the strain is heavier, compare with 10 or 12 years ago. The loads have increased since I have been on the railway. The engines are of a larger type, and the haulage capacity of the engines is greater. A heavier and a longer train is more difficult to manipulate even with the larger engines. In working a long goods train over various gradients one has to be careful to manipulate the train, because you have a train on two or three gradients. You have one portion hanging down and the other portion the other way, and in many cases where there are varying gradients the trains are considerably more difficult to manipulate to avoid a break-loose.'

Bellamy was asked by Grasemann to name locations where trains were on several gradients, and responded, 'Well, across the Black Brook

The ultimate accolade was express passenger work, and the crew of No 1301 Teutonic *pose proudly with their steed, after the tailrods had been removed and the front end cut back. The ten 'Teutonic' 2-2-2-0s were the most successful of the Webb passenger compounds, but all had gone by July 1907.*

branch at St Helens; in one or two places across the line from Heckmondwike Junction to Farnley Junction, from Denton Junction to Stalybridge, from Stalybridge to Diggle. Those are just from memory. I do not say a passenger train will run on three gradients. I am speaking of the heavy goods trains. Loads have increased; from Manchester to Leeds they have increased. The load when I commenced was, I think, 35 or 34. I believe that was the load for one engine, and now with a larger class of engine we take 60.' An exchange between Richard Bell and Albert Bellamy indicated how fair both men were willing to be. Bell took up the increased loads on the Leeds run, and asked if 'the increased brake power on the engine has been equal to the additional weight'. Bellamy immediately responded, 'Yes, from the time when I first started', making it clear that there was no suggestion of lower safety standards, but of harder effort.

Sir Edward Fry then asked Bell if he were to make a dividing line for pay purposes between the newer Whale engines and the older classes, how could he do so. Bell felt the list of engines provided by the Company might help, with Fry asking if the amount of coal carried was a useful criterion. Bell suggested haulage capacity was more useful, and the arbitrator turned to Bellamy, still giving evidence, and asked, 'Can you say what the horse power of these large new engines is?' It is to Bellamy's credit, that given an opportunity to strike first blow, he responded, 'No, I think Mr Cooke, who is an expert engin-

Webb had started the move to larger engines with his 'Jubilee' and 'Alfred the Great' 4-4-0s. No 1929 Polyphemus *was built as a 'Jubilee' in 1900, but was one of the first engines to receive a Belpaire boiler in 1904. For their time, they were quite large engines.*

eer, can say'. Bowen Cooke took up the question: 'It is a very difficult thing to estimate the strength of a locomotive by horse power, and it is not generally taken in that way, because an engine starting from rest, and moving a train away, say out of Euston, up an incline of 1 in 70, may develop anything between 500 and 1,000 horse power. Then when it gets on the road and is going quickly, although there is just as much work got out of the engine, it is getting it in a different sort of way. We, as a rule, estimate the power of an engine by its tractive force.' Cooke agreed to provide some yardstick for Fry to consider.

Grasemann, aware of the slow erosion of railway profits during his progress up the North Western hierarchy, revealed that even in 1908 he and his fellow officers were deeply concerned at long-term implications. 'Our working expenses have gone up from about 52 per cent of the gross receipts, say 20 years ago, to 64 and 65 per cent now, and although, as Mr Bell said, the tendency of traffic has been to increase during the last few years, this year has been phenomenally bad. Most of the Railway Companies had a big drop in the dividend for the first half of the year, and taking our own case alone up to the week ending the 6th December, we show a decrease of

£347,000 in the gross receipts for this half year compared with last year. Of course, tonnage moved is not exactly in proportion to the receipts, because in many cases we are making lower rates and the same applies to the fares. We are doing quite as much work now as we did in the past, but we do not get paid as much for it. There is water competition, motor lorries — which account for our losing a great deal of goods traffic and even mineral traffic. Therefore to compete with those other forms of transit, we have to reduce our rates. In the same way as regards passenger fares, what with motor cars and electric tramways, and motor omnibuses and so on, the receipts of the railways for passenger traffic have gone down especially in the big towns. Some of the suburban traffic has gone away, so that in order to compete we have to reduce the fares for a smaller number of people, and there is never any means of increasing the rates without very costly litigation before the Railway Commissioners.'

Grasemann felt that a railway job was well thought of, and revealed that applications for employment were then running at 3,000 per month (with 600 in the Locomotive Department alone), but that average recruitment was just 172 staff per month. Nowadays job mobility is highly praised, but in Edwardian times management and staff alike preferred permanence, and Grase-

Though the North Western men might grumble at their wages, Privilege Ticket rights were one of the fringe benefits. The Loco Department PT order differed from other departments!

mann spoke with pride of the North Western record. More than a quarter of the wages staff had been in the service of the company for 20 years and upwards, and a similar number for between 10 and 20 years. Over 4,000 men had served over 30 years, and 720 had been with the LWR for 40 or more years, or for two-thirds of the Company's existence at the time! Grasemann warmed to the theme. 'At the half-yearly meeting, in 1907, the North Western chairman made a reference to Liverpool, which was taken as being typical because it is one of the biggest places on our line, and there is considerable other employment there. At that time there were no less than 21 instances of three generations, 21 grandfathers, fathers and sons, and 286 cases of two generations, all working for the North Western. We have one family where there are 11 close relatives whose aggregate service numbers 178 years. We will take the one man, whom I know personally. He is a goods agent at a small station. He has two uncles in the service, three brothers, four cousins and a son, and they occupy such different positions as porter, horsekeeper, goods agent, checker, signalman, station master, clerk, parcels porter, two more clerks and an office youth. The longest service of any one of these men is 32 years, and the shortest is two years.'

On the morning of the third day of the enquiry, Bowen Cooke handed in a list of modern classes of engine. 'The first is the "Precursor" type, which is the standard express passenger engine; the "Experiment" is a slightly heavier engine used chiefly for working north over the heavy gradients between Preston and Carlisle; the "Precursor" tank type is for the heavy local passenger trains. Then the next are the heavy eight wheel coupled goods engines, the latest type for heavy goods trains. There are 315 of those. Then there are 67 eight-wheeled coupled coal engines, really an old type of engine which has been rebuilt with a large boiler.' Fry intervened to say this was not quite what he wanted; knowing the present large types was no advantage, as these would eventually be replaced. What he wanted was some way of identifying the large engines. 'I am struck with the fact that the firemen on the engines must have a greater amount of work than the men on the old engines. I want to be able to draw a distinction between the two classes. I do not say I shall do it...'

Bowen Cooke agreed to think further on some suitable guidelines, and in the meanwhile gave some representative figures on coal consumption, using the crack London turns as an example. 'We have for many years worked the down corridor train, the Scotch train, to Crewe and back again. The same diagram working, as we call it, has been in force for a great number of years. I have taken what the consumption on that train was ten years ago. It was 49 lbs per mile. The consumption at the present time is 54 lbs per mile, or an increase of about 10 per cent. That works out to about 14 cwt [just under three-quarters of a ton] more for the fireman to put on in the double run from here to Crewe and back.' Sir Edward's lack of knowledge of railways now became apparent — with the 49-54 lbs per mile figures, he asked if 50 lbs per mile would be a suitable guideline? Bowen Cooke hurriedly explained that the train has a great deal to do with it, we might have one of the modern engines working a comparatively light train, and not burning 50 lbs, or anything like it, per mile, or we might have a very heavy train, exceeding the 50 lbs per mile, with the same class of engine.' With Fry aware that engines could burn differing quantities of coal, Cooke continued, 'We gauge the capability of the driver to some extent by the amount of coal that he burns. Every month, the total coal consumed by every man is got out. In a group of men working together the man who consumes the least coal is put on the top of the list. It might have a little tendency in the opposite direction.' Fry, confused as to what sort of guideline he could rely upon, responded anxiously, 'You are beginning to convince me that it is impossible to draw the line. Will you think it over?'

One amusing tactical battle deserves recalling. On the important long-distance services, the men were paid on the mileage basis. 120 miles for goods and 150 for passenger work for a ten-hour 'day'. The men sought a reduction in the goods mileage to 100, with a North Western counter-claim! Grasemann put the North Western case for passenger and freight trains; 'The present mileage for passenger trains is 150 miles on the basis of a ten hour day. . ., the actual running time is very often not more than three hours, and Mr Bell, I think, admitted afterwards that the gross time would only be about five hours, so that practically, ten hours' pay is being given for five

hours' work. The scale has been in force for a very long time, and our express trains have increased their speed by, I think, it is 28 per cent. We think that the proposal to allow 180 miles for a day's work of ten hours, which would enable the driver as a rule to complete his work in under six hours, is liberal. As regards the goods, we are only asking for an increase from 120 miles to 130 miles.' Bowen Cooke was asked to give some figures. 'I took out express goods trains between Crewe and London. In August 1898, the express goods was 11 hours 15 minutes; and the average for such a train at the present time is 9 hours 8 minutes. Down express goods averaged in 1898 10 hours 36 minutes, whilst in 1906, it was 8 hours 21 minutes.'

Shrewdly, Sir Edward Fry enquired of Grasemann; 'This point was never mooted until the other side moved in the opposite direction, was it'? Grasemann admitted it was a tactical ploy, 'No, it was not: as I explained yesterday, in the past we have been quite contented to pay rather more than what we thought it was worth, especially as most of these trains on the mileage basis are given to the best drivers, who have been in the service the longest time, and are at the top of the tree.'

There was to be one final exchange before the enquiry moved on to other grades. The North Western proposals provided for cleaners, that 'The locomotive foreman to be free to modify the amended scale as local conditions and circumstances may warrant'. Bellamy, with his early comment that it would be easy to get on with the gentlemen round the table, but there 'was a buffer in between', had revealed a respect for top management, but a suspicion of some of the shed foremen, and with a railway the size of the North Western, it was inevitable that there would be good and poor foremen, men who could inspire respect even though strict, and those who could only rule by fear. Richard Bell chose his words carefully; 'What I fear is this, that at every locomotive shed of the North Western system there might be a local foreman of a different temperament. There would be a large number of people with power to modify, and if there is to be modification it should be somebody above the locomotive foreman of the shed. . . [or] we should have no proper system at all. If there is any modification necessary, some superior official should have the power, such as the Divisional Superin-

The 19-inch goods, with their long low splashers, continuous running plate and high pitched boilers must have seemed gigantic engines at first. The low platforms, as here at Leamington in 1911, further emphasized the size of these ill-named engines, for they were in truth excellent mixed traffic machines. (H.J. Stretton Ward)

tendent, or the head of the Department.' Fry had asked Bell if a right of appeal from the foreman's decision would suffice, but Bell responded, 'a direct appeal to a higher official would to some extent modify it, but at the same time we know an individual is very often afraid to put forward any appeal; he would rather suffer the grievance'.

Sir Edward Fry invited Grasemann's comments. Grasemann, though pointing out that this might not be within the terms of the enquiry, had appreciated Bell's concern, and turned to Bowen Cooke, saying, 'We will take out this clause entirely if you like, "The locomotive foreman to be free. . ." You do not mind that being struck out, do you, Mr Cooke?' Cooke, also, had sensed Bell's anxiety, and immediately responded, 'No, I quite agree.' On this pleasant note of give and take, the locomen's enquiry concluded, save for a further appearance by Bowen Cooke, over 'large' locomotives.

'It appears to me that if we are going to draw a dividing line, the best plan will be to take the heating surface, that is the inside surface of the tubes and firebox plates coming into contact with the flames of the fire. I have brought a diagram of a boiler. I have prepared statements showing all our different types of passenger and goods engines. Of course the larger the heating surface the greater the steam generating power of the boiler, and the greater the amount of coal consumed, provided always that the engine is work-

ing up to its full capacity. A large engine working
a light train will burn less coal than a smaller
one working a heavy train. However, we must
concede that we have built these larger engines
entirely with a view to working bigger loads, and,
therefore, I think it is only fair, to arrive at the
conclusion you wish to arrive at, to take the size
of the boiler, because the larger boilers with the
larger heating surface have been made with a
view to working heavier loads. I have thought
this out from other ways besides the heating surface. There is the grate area for one thing, but
engineers differ a good deal in their practice with
regard to the relative size of the grate area or
its value for steam producing purposes, but I
think it is generally conceded by locomotive
engineers that the heating surface of the boiler
is the prime factor in its steam generating power,
and therefore in the coal consumed. I do not see
how any possible change could affect it.'

Bowen Cooke explained how the older engines
had a heating surface from 1,000 to 1,500 square
feet, and that the newer types were around 2,000
square feet. He suggested that the dividing line
for passenger and freight engines be 2,000 square
feet, though advocating that 19-inch goods, or
'Experiment Goods' as he referred to them, at
1,985 square feet, be included in the large engine
category. Under Bowen Cooke's proposals, the
'Precursors' and 'Experiments' would come into
the large category, as would the large-boilered
0-8-0s, but the whole of the Webb engines,
including the small-boilered 0-8-0s, and the
'Precursor' tanks (1,939 square feet) would not.
Richard Bell accepted Cooke's basic ideas,
merely pointing out that the older eight-coupled
engines which had now been fitted with steam
brakes were hauling increased loads too. It was

a shrewd point, and Bowen Cooke had himself
conceded that engines above 1,500 square feet
were practically a new type.

In his award, in February 1909, Sir Edward
Fry struck a series of compromises, conceding
points where there was strong feeling and a
genuine grievance, and discarding others. The
long-standing grievance of multiple bookings on
in a single day was removed, except for trip working, and nine hours' rest laid down as a minimum except in emergency. Fry had considered
Cooke's suggestion of 2,000 square feet, and his
ready admission that the old engines were around
1,500 square feet, and opted for an increase of
1/6d per week to firemen working on engines
with over 1,500 square feet heating surface. This
brought the 'Precursor' tanks into the fold, along
with all but the smallest of the Webb eight-
coupled types. Paradoxically, it also caught the
final 40 Webb 'Alfred the Great' 4-4-0s, though
not the slightly smaller 'Jubilees'! A London
allowance was granted, with the Company having the right to raise rents to the men who had
cheap housing — the benefit was spread to all,
not some, and Bell's anxiety over the foreman's
discretion concerning cleaners' wages was
respected. Foremen were permitted to raise rates
if labour shortages necessitated it, but could not
go below the established scale. It was a very neat
solution.

Perhaps the greatest beneficiary was Bowen
Cooke; his skilled presentation of the evidence,
and ability to reach sensible compromises with
Bell, had impressed the Board. His path to the
top, when George Whale retired in 1909, was
assured. For that reason alone, the discussions
at Euston in the cold grey days of December 1908
assume a unique significance.

9 The Signalmen

On the third day of the enquiry, 11 December 1908, Richard Bell opened the case for the signalmen. He gave a lucid account of what a box was like: 'It has so many levers, varying from perhaps 10 to 150, according to the importance of the place; sometimes operated by one man, sometimes by two men, and some cabins will be operated by three men at the same time, with a certain division of levers for the three men. Then they have the block instruments, that is the telegraphic code communications between the cabin in the rear and the cabin in advance for signalling the train forward and receiving signals of trains from the rear. These codes have to be entered in a train register book. Sometimes a lad is provided for recording the whole of these movements, and sometimes it has to be done by the signalman. They frequently have a number of telephones to communicate either with the station or with the shunting yard. Some have gates where there are level crossings. Those are operated from the signal cabins, and they are locked. All that is in addition to the signals which are for controlling the trains. I am afraid this is going to be our most difficult task, because nearly every signal cabin differs in some degree from the others. I am not in possession of the points of view or whatever the company have to guide them in differentiating between what should constitute an eight-hours cabin, a ten-hours cabin, or a 12-hours cabin. It also carries with it that the eight-hours cabin is usually the highest paid.

'The men feel, and I feel also, in connection with many cabins that I know, that eight hours should be the maximum that the men should be called upon to work. In an eight-hour cabin, the man does not leave the box from the time he enters it till the time he signs off duty. The 12-hour man would be in the cabin continuously, but he would not be so busily occupied as the man in the eight-hour cabin. There would be no set time for him to take his meal, he would have to take it when he could get it. The eight-hour cabin is, of course, already eight hours, and my arguments do not apply; I was merely describing it. The ten-hour cabin is next to the eight-hour cabin, and in many cabins equally as busy, but they have not been fortunate enough to be

reduced to eight hours. I must anticipate Mr Grasemann bringing this up against me that on some little branch line, where they have perhaps only got eight or ten trains a day, to ask that the signalman employed in them should only be engaged eight hours might be unreasonable. I admit that there is a big difference between the cabin on the small branch line, but they are so very few in comparison that it is an easy matter to arrange some little differentiation between those and the others that we are asking should have eight hours. I do maintain that it should apply to all cabins on main lines where there is busy traffic, and on branch lines in industrial centres, where continuously, and throughout the whole of the day, we find that men are constantly occupied; there may not be important through express passenger trains, but nevertheless there is heavy mineral traffic.'

So far, things had gone well for Richard Bell. His witnesses had been accurate, and the evidence they had given to him to present had been reliable. Sadly, this was about to change. Bell had been given some details about Wednesbury Junction signal box, at which two men did ten-hour shifts, with a reliefman filling in for the remaining four hours. According to Bell's information, on a sample day the box had handled 116 trains, 1,028 lever movements, 3,437 bell signals, and 996 entries in the train register book. The arbitrator asked Bell if he could prove the facts, at which point Grasemann offered to accept *most* of them, though he obviously had some reservations. Richard Bell called his first witness, a signalman at the North Western station at Morecambe. This was a 19-hour box, the early man doing ten hours in the cabin, and the second man coming on an hour early to oil points. The box was open on Sundays as a split shift. Bell asked how many trains were handled at the box. 'An average of about 55 in the winter time, and in the summer time about 100'. As the witness was speaking, Grasemann hurriedly checked the working time book, and when he rose to cross-examine, asked for confirmation as to the summer figure. 'On the average about 100'. Mildly, he pointed out the figures in the working book, only to be told that another signalman had ex-

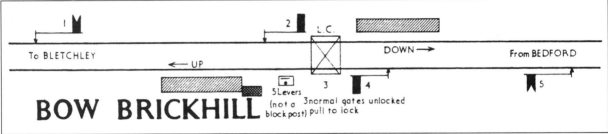

In the arbitration hearings, mention was made of quiet branch lines with just a few trains. Signalling could be very basic, as at Bow Brickhill, a railcar halt on the Bletchley–Bedford branch. An 8-foot square signal hut housed five levers. It was not even a block post, merely a crossing keeper's cabin. We are looking towards Bletchley in 1967.

tracted the information from the train register book. The arbitrator clearly had doubts.

Grasemann called Cumberland Lowndes to give evidence. Lowndes had been District Superintendent at Birmingham for five years, and was familiar with Wednesbury Junction box. Lowndes had considerable doubts about the 3,437 bell signals per day, and pointed out that a bell message varied from the one beat of 'Call attention' to many strokes, for example 3-5-5. He invited Richard Bell to explain whether they had counted individual bell strokes or messages. Bell, who realized how vital it was to retain the trust of the arbitrator, was clearly worried, and offered to clear things up in due course. The following day, Sir Edward Fry took the point up with Richard Bell, as to bell strokes or messages.

Bell replied, 'I certainly have been wrongly impressed, I do not say wrongly informed, with regard to the bell signals; if the number of rings is given as six, it is put as six. I certainly should not have put that forward myself. It represents the strokes, so that when a man gives six, it counts as six. What I want to put in is, that it should count as one, because it is one operation.'

By this time, the signalling section had become a nightmare for Bell, for he had been tripped up twice already! In his opening remarks he had distinguished between ten-hour boxes on busy lines, which he felt should be reduced to eight hours, and boxes on minor lines, but his witnesses had completely let him down. Grasemann must obviously have felt that Bell had been poorly supported, and remarked, 'I think he was a little unfortunate in the boxes he selected, ten-hour boxes, as being indicative of the sort of boxes to which the eight-hour days ought to apply. In the one instance there were only 116 trains in the 24 hours; in the other case there were 42 trains a day, and apparently Mr Bell, himself, has modified his ideas on the subject, because just now he asked Mr Walker whether he did not think that with 150 trains a day it would be a suitable box to alter from ten to eight hours.'

In the programme Bell had been asked to present, a demand appeared that Christmas Day and Good Friday should be treated as Sundays for pay purposes. Grasemann realized that Bell had once more been placed in a ridiculous predicament, and explained 'A man does not get paid for Sunday duty unless he works, but he gets paid for Christmas Day and Good Friday if he does not work. Therefore, if we are to take this literally, we should be quite prepared to agree to it, and only pay those men who work on Christmas Day and Good Friday as if it were Sunday, and not pay those who do not work. If that is your meaning, I am quite willing to agree.' After Sir Edward observed that the men were asking for less than they got, Bell responded wearily, 'I am not responsible for the paragraph

The Birkenhead Docks are an improbable location for an LNWR signal cabin, but through the joint GWR/LNWR Birkenhead Railway, the North Western gained access to the dock system. This cabin, virtually at the end of Joint metals, controlled four routes, connected by a double scissors junction on incredible curves within yards of the box. When the Docks were in their prime, there was constant freight and shunting activity.

going down here... If I were responsible for some of these paragraphs, neither you nor I would have the trouble that we seem to be having with them.'

The final blow came a few days later, by which time Grasemann and Walker had checked the actual figures for Morecambe, Grasemann commenting, 'It may, of course, have been a mistake... [The Witness] said the average number of trains dealt with at Morecambe was 55 daily in the winter and 100 in the summer. We have got out the actual number of trains dealt with during the 12 months ending the 30th November last, and during the five summer months, May to September, the average number of trains in a day was 64.7, and not 100. During the seven winter months, the average number was 47½, not 55. Only on three occasions during the seven winter months did the number of trains reach 55; that was the maximum, and only on one occasion during the five summer months did the number of trains reach 100. That was on the 8th August. We have included all light engines and so on as trains.'

With the men's case in ruins, through overstatement and inconsistencies, Bell was forced to rely upon the evidence offered by Herbert Walker and Cumberland Lowndes. In public his only

comment was, 'I have absolutely no responsibility whatever for the drawing up of this programme. Though I have been obliged to advocate it, I am not responsible for the drafting of it.' One wonders what he may have said in private to the men, for thereafter the accuracy of the evidence improved markedly.

Herbert Walker was invited to give evidence, and presented a table (reproduced below) which split the boxes into the various categories. Wages and hours varied from the 22 shillings per week of 9-12 hour country boxes, to the six men working Euston station box, two per shift, who drew 36 shillings a week.

a relief man for four hours. The maximum rates of pay range from 22s to 36s a week. That is the maximum rate of pay at the boxes, but the rates vary from 20s upwards, 83 per cent of the signalmen employed at the present time are in receipt of the maximum for the boxes at which they work. In addition to the regular signalmen, we also employ 190 porter signalmen, who regularly work some part of the day. They work to a roster and have regular employment. They do their work under the best conditions. They are always in the box and are not exposed to the temperature, high or low, that the case may be, that the men working on the ground are. One man

NUMBER OF SIGNALMEN ON THE L. & N. W. SYSTEM WORKING SIGNAL BOXES RATED AT A MAXIMUM OF :—

	22/-	23/-	24/-	25/-	25/6	26/-	27/-	28/-	28/6	29/-	30/-	31/-	32/-	34/-	36/-	Total No. of men.	No. of Signal boxes.
8 hours men	...	...	9	7	...	90	18	249	6	28	332	60	194	39	6	1,038	309
Over 8 hours and not exceeding 9 hours	...	...	...	...	...	15	...	16	...	4	3	...	3	...	...	41	18
,, 9 10 ,,	121	45	539	71	1	371	18	57	...	...	1	...	...	...	...	1,224	583
,, 10 11 ,,	7	...	9	...	...	1	...	...	...	...	...	...	...	...	...	17	14
,, 11 12 ,,	126	5	60	...	...	2	...	...	...	...	...	...	...	...	...	193	142
TOTAL	254	50	617	78	1	479	36	322	6	32	336	60	197	39	6	2,513	1,066

'There are 1,066 signal boxes, at which there are employed 2,513 regular signalmen. There are 309 boxes at eight hours and 1,038 men. Then we get a few of what I may call nine-hour boxes. There are only 18 with 41 men employed. These are generally boxes that are open for 18 hours or less, 17 hours in some cases, and we employ the men for 8½ or 9 hours. Then the next is a big lot which practically forms more than half the boxes and not quite half the number of men. There are 583 signal boxes and 1,224 men. Those are the nine to ten hour boxes. The next are the 10 to 11 hour boxes, generally open somewhere between 20 and 22 hours. There are only 14 of them, and 17 men working at them. So it follows that most of them are only open for one shift. There are 142 of the 12-hour boxes and 193 men, so that there again, we get a large number of boxes that are open for up to 12 hours.

'At the eight-hour boxes, we can get three men for a shift of 24 hours. The ten-hour boxes are either worked by two shifts of men, or if they are open the whole of the 24 hours by two men and

in a junction box was there till he was 72. There are many other such cases of men working in signal boxes until they are long past 65.'

Herbert Walker was referring to Wednesbury Junction box, and another North Western district officer, Cumberland Lowndes, painted a fascinating portrait of the working of that box. 'Wednesbury Junction is a signal cabin at Bescot on the line between Walsall and Dudley; there is a junction there. There is the main route from Dudley to Walsall, and a goods curve from Wednesbury Junction to Bescot yard. No regular passenger trains are timed over it. There are about 116 trains in the 24 hours.' Lowndes, who was in charge of the Birmingham district for five years, continued: 'When I went to Birmingham, the man who was in charge of this cabin was about 70 years of age. He had then about 48 years of service, and he remained in the box until he reached the age of 72, retiring in July 1904. To the best of my belief, another man named Code is there now. He was there when I gave up charge of the District to go to Manchester. He had been a foreman of brakesmen at Bescot Junction, until it was absolutely necessary to remove him as he was a cripple. I think one of his legs was a wooden one, at any rate it was an artificial one, so I saw him, and I wanted to show him consideration as to what sort of a post he would like. He said he thought the best thing would be a signalman at some such box as Wednesbury Junction, where his artificial limb would not be put to any undue strain. By a little contriving, we were able to give him this particular box, which was a ten-hour box. He had a few weeks training, I should think three or four, and was doing satisfactorily.'

Something which Herbert Walker took a justifiable pride in was the safety record, not just of the LNWR, but of all the railway companies, and looking at the Board of Trade accident returns in the early 1900s, he worked out that the number of accidents attributable to signalmen, of which there were 28,000 in the British Isles, worked out at ten per annum. Walker explained it drily: 'A serious accident would occur, on average, in the life of a signalman, if he lived so long, once in 2,800 years.' Herbert Walker warmed to his theme. 'I was alluding to the abnormal length of life that a signalman would have to live before, under the ordinary conditions, he would have caused an accident which would endanger the lives of the men or passengers. Now, I should like to give you, what in our opinion, is the cause of this exceptional freedom from accidents. For many years past the company has been spending many thousands of pounds in improving the working of the signalboxes, so that today we have got what we consider a perfect system of interlocking, that is to say it is out of the power of a signalman to have off signals for conflicting operations.

'You have heard a good deal about the working of the 12-hour boxes. The number of trains dealt with by each man in each turn of duty on average throughout the system in the boxes in which the men work 12 hours, is 25, practically one train every half hour. For working purposes, the line is divided into districts, with a District Superintendent in charge. One of his duties is in relation to the working of the signal boxes, and he is responsible whenever the work at any box is increased, if he considers it advisable, to recommend that the hours shall be reduced from either 12 to ten, or ten to eight, as the case may be. We have a certain number of inspectors who

report to us continually; we are always in touch with them, and we get to know very well, if not from personal observation, what the state of the work in each box is. During the last 12 years, the hours have been reduced at no less than 293 boxes out of the 1,066. There is no general system of classification of boxes on the London & North Western, and each box is dealt with on its merits. This is why I allude to the District Officers being responsible.'

Herbert Walker was a forceful opponent of any rigid classification system, rejecting the numbers of levers or number of trains as the sole criterion. He explained, 'We deal with it on broad lines, whether it is a junction having important connections, having running loops etc. We do not deal with it necessarily on the number of trains at all. A mechanical arrangement would be quite impossible.'

Sunday duty attracted Walker's attention. 'It is the Company's regulation that every signalman shall have one Sunday off in every two, but I must qualify that by saying that when a man is on Saturday night duty, finishing on Sunday morning, we consider that part of his week's work, not as a part of the Sunday duty. He has every other Sunday or an equivalent. He may work two Sundays consecutively and then he would get two Sundays off. You may take it that the ten-hour men and the 12-hour men always get their alternate week off. It does not necessarily follow with regard to the eight-hour man. Whenever the man goes on duty on a Sunday, he is paid at the ordinary rate of pay. Now a rather peculiar circumstance comes in. We allow the men in the eight-hour boxes at their own request, to work 12 hours on Sunday so as to enable them to get long periods off at weekends, 48 or 56 hours off one Sunday in every three. I have got instances where the men were working eight hours on Sunday, and they asked to be put on to 12 hours, because it enables them to have a long weekend, from 2 o'clock on the Saturday to 2 o'clock on the Monday. If they had to work eight hours, it means that the men would have to go on duty at 6 o'clock on the Monday morning. It applies generally in all the eight-hour boxes that on Sundays the men work 12 hours, and that is an arrangement the Company has made at the men's own request. From an analysis of the trains on Sunday, I find that the average number of trains is 30 per cent of what it is on weekdays. When the men work 12 hours they get a day and a half's pay because they work 12 hours instead of eight, and in many cases, we bring a ten-hour man into an eight-hour box on a Sunday, and he also gets a day and a half's pay.

'I have been Superintendent, or Assistant Superintendent now for, I think it is 14 years; I have never had a complaint from a man doing Sunday duty, but I can quote numerous instances where a man who does not get Sunday duty has asked for it.'

The average North Western signalman usually started as a boy porter or labourer, the only exception being, as Herbert Walker commented, 'If we took a man from another line who had worked as a signalman, we might take him on as a signalman, but in general rarely. The men nearly all start with us as juniors, or as adult porters, either in the coaching or goods departments, or as permanent way labourers. In order that we can be satisfied that they are men that can be relied upon, we never start a man training until he has been with us for six months. Say a lad comes into the service as a junior. In the course of time he reaches the age of 21. After that age we say he is capable of being trained as a relief signalman, to take up the work at boxes in case of an emergency. The men are always very willing to train as relief signalmen and earn an extra half-a-crown [2/6d] which we pay them every week. Then they are always willing to leave that to take up a regular signalman's position. Never mind how small it may be, it is something. By that means a lad starting as a junior porter in the service works his way up to the higher rank of signalman. The usual training is three to four weeks.'

Although Herbert Walker was Superintendent of one of the busiest and most complex divisions on the North Western, signalmen were still personally vetted by him. After their training, they were examined by an inspector 'who has to first satisfy himself that the man is thoroughly com-petent in working the box. He is then sent up to me to be examined, and I put the man through a general examination as to his fitness and knowledge of the rules. I have been examining signalmen for the last 14 years, and I may safely say that on average, I do not reject one man in a year.'

In the early 1900s, bonus payments averaged 3 shillings a week over the basic pay, or between £2 and £6 per man per year. Herbert Walker explained: 'The bonus or part of it is liable to be withheld in cases where the men commit an irregularity or cause a mishap, but the company in 1907 paid over £7,000 for bonuses, and that worked out at an average of 1 shilling per man, so with that and Sunday duty, and the extra pay working temporarily in superior positions, the men receive on average 3 shillings a week more. If every man had received his full bonus, they would have received an extra three farthings a week per man. Seniority would tell in a case of promotion. If I had a vacancy and two or three names were put before me, I should, everything else being equal, give it to the man with the longest service. 36 shillings a week is only given in one box, the big box at Euston, where there are six head men, the blue ribbon of signalmen. 39 men get 34 shillings. These are generally the men in the big boxes like Crewe, Birmingham, Liverpool, Manchester, and very important boxes outside London. During the last 12 years, at 344 boxes, that is one-third of the total, the rates have been permanently increased.'

Men frequently started at ten-hour boxes, and were promoted to more important eight-hour boxes. Promotion from 12-hour to ten-hour boxes was much rarer; 'the 12-hour boxes are generally worked by old men, men that we do not want to get rid of, and that we put into the 12-hour boxes. It is not often that they come out of the 12-hour boxes into the ten-hour, because they are not fit for it.'

10 Breaksmen and Shunters

Conciliation Board C covered shunters and breaksmen, the latter an archaic term, long since dropped by most railway companies, but retained by the North Western for its goods guards. Sometimes the company used the antiquated 'breaksmen' spelling, on other occasions it called them 'brakesmen'! In 1908, the LNWR employed 1,659 regular breaksmen, whose nominal rates of pay varied from 23 shillings to 32/6d. There were a further 820 porter-breaksmen whose basic pay commenced at 23 shillings. In either case, their actual pay was very different, as we shall see.

William Ellison was a long-serving North Western breaksman, and had joined the company about 1880, having previously worked as a miner at Moss Hall Colliery, where he had been earning up to 6 shillings a day, but with the colliery on short time, averaging about 5½ days per fortnight, he had turned to the railway for steady employment. Unlike many men, who served an 'apprenticeship' as a porter, he commenced right away as a breaksman working from Springs Branch, Wigan. There was a notional ten-hour standard day, but shifts of 16 or even 18 hours were not uncommon, as freights were held waiting a path. As a result of union pressure, Parliament passed legislation in 1893 limiting railwaymen's work to 12 hours. At first, Ellison was an extra breaksman, which meant that, as in his mining days, he might work short hours; one week, a couple of years after he joined the railway, he took home just 7 shillings for his week's work. This was exceptional, and after he became a regular breaksman in the late 1890s, he seldom drew less than full pay. Apart from looking after the train whilst running, and shunting at way stations, the breaksman had to prepare their journals, one of which had to be sent to the office of each District Superintendent, through whose territory they ran. On a through run, this could sometimes mean three or four districts. Ellison recalled a tightening up compared to his early days; 'The company are more strict in regard to the rules being carried out. There was a time in my period of being a breaksman when they were not strict as to giving journals, and I have seen cases where men did not give journals at all for so long as three months at a stretch.'

Ellison explained his duties after booking on: 'The breaksman, when he arrives at his train, is responsible for the trimming of his lamps, and he has to get his shunting pole, and his other traps. He wants his fog signals and his flags and his handlamp, and he has to get them and take them to the train and trim the lamps and clean up the van if it is dirty, and then he has to go up the train and couple it up.'

The basic style of LNWR brake vans had been set by the 1870s, and despite a move from 10 to 20 tonners, showed little change up to the Grouping. This van, No 280723, is a late example, but typifies the breed. (H.J. Stretton Ward)

With many of the long-distance trains, the marshalling was done before the breaksman arrived, but the wise breaksman always checked it. 'He is responsible every day to see that everything is safe in connection with the train on both sides and lift the brakes up, and then give instructions to the driver where the next stop is.' With the advent of the eight-coupled engines, higher boiler pressures and other improvements, train lengths had increased from the 1890s, and Ellison commented that 'the load in our district, even for the lowest type of engine, has been increased. At that time [ie, about 1888] the loading for the DX engine, that is the lowest type at present in use, was 30 mineral; now it is 35. The loading for the coal engine was 35, and now it is 40. The loading for an 18-inch cylinder was 32, and now it is 42. And we have a bigger class of engine introduced, which takes, according to the district in which it runs, from 50 to 60 wagons of minerals. To marshal 60 wagons will take more work than to marshal 35 or 40. There is a greater tendency in the running of a long train to break loose than there would be with a shorter train. There is a great deal further to go to put an odd wagon off near the engine with a longer train.'

A breaksman's duties depended on the turn to which he was assigned, for with a long-distance freight there would be little intermediate work. On a short trip it was a very different matter, and Ellison's railway slang caused some confusion to the arbitrator when talking of short runs. 'Generally speaking, we should not be anything like half the time in the brake van, simply because the whole of the journeys that I work, I should say more than two-thirds of the time is spent on the floor.' To the arbitrators plaintive question, 'On the floor of what?', Ellison responded that 'the floor' meant the ground, walking up and down the train and shunting.

Bill Hepden was another long-serving breaksman, commencing at Crewe in November 1891. He recalled that there were about 40 regular men at Crewe, 40 extra breaksmen and up to 100 emergency breaksmen. The regular men had the diagrammed trains, whilst the extra men tended to work most of their time. Hepden echoed Ellison's comments about loads increasing from around 35 to 60, adding that 'we have goods trains going out of Crewe now that take 70 wagons.' His chief criticism was that despite the extra walking at way stations with the longer trains, no additional time had been allowed for shunting, and that one had to hurry a great deal more, or 'get your friend the fireman to help you to do it'. As this was against the rules, Hepden was reticent on persuading the fireman to do breaksmen's work. Hepden gave an account of a specific train, the 5.40 am Crewe to Northwich freight. He booked on half an hour before departure, and left Crewe with 60 wagons. 'I had to go to Sandbach and detach a few there, and then on to Middlewich and detach about 20 and attach 20 more, and then on to Northwich to detach all, to dispose of my train, and then I had to take 48 or 49 to Middlewich and put them on the siding and shunt them in the yard. I got back to Middlewich somewhere about 8.40 am. Then I had to go to Sandbach and put off about 28 or 30, and attach about four or five, and take them back to Crewe. I was due back at Crewe at 1.40 pm, but I arrived there at 2.20 and finished my day at 3.45 pm. During that time I had never opened my basket because I had not an opportunity, nor had I made my journals out. I had done on that train 10 hours and 35 minutes.' Although one thinks of railway freight as being limited on a Saturday, it was in fact a *Saturday* turn that Hepden was describing. An idea of the congestion at Crewe yard is given by the delay between reaching Crewe and his booking off. He explained that, 'for some time, possibly it might be 20 minutes, I stood behind another train waiting to draw up. I had wagons for three or four different sidings on the up side, three at any rate. I had to knock those off, take my train to Basford Hall Junction on the South Sorting Sidings, and wait my turn to put my wagons in. From going on to the up side to the time I got to the sorting sidings, I stood behind another train, which was North Stafford empty waggons; I may have stood there possibly 20 minutes.'

In the opening of this chapter, the breaksmen's nominal rates were quoted, 23 shillings to 32/6d, but in practice virtually all work was done on the trip system, which had been introduced to the LNWR in 1876. Other companies had used the trip system, but the North Western's dedication to it was unique. Herbert Walker explained his company's policy: 'The trip rate system is identical with the workshop policy of paying for work turned out on piecework instead of by time. That is, a fixed payment is made for each journey with the object of inducing the men

*The driver of this class 'C1' 0-8-0, No 1875, awaits the breaks-
man's signal to get a heavy coal from Toton under way from
Leicester Midland in about 1920. The train stretches far into
the distance. The normal limit for the eight-coupled engines was
825-900 tons, but in a few cases over 1,000 tons was permitted.* (Henry L. Salmon)

to finish the trip expeditiously. The basis upon
which trip rates are made is as follows. We first
of all take the timetable of the train. We will say
an empty wagon train has to run from Willesden to Rugby. We take the timetable and we add
to that half-an-hour for the man booking on and
looking round his train, and half-an-hour at the
end of the journey for disposing of his train. We
then, in accordance with our knowledge of the
average running of his this train, add on so much
for eventualities in the running. Then we get at
the maximum time, we will say it is ten hours.
We then decide by which men and at what rate
of pay that train shall be worked. If we find it
shall be worked generally by 30 shilling men we
put down the trip at 5 shillings.

'I shall show you later on that as a result the
trains are worked in shorter times when the trip
rate is allowed. The trip rates have been continu
ally revised and altered. One of the duties of my
staff clerks and my inspectors who are in charge
of the working of the breaksmen is to keep me
constantly advised of all cases where it is found
that on an average the trip that we have allowed

does not pay the men. In all such cases we increase the trip rate. There are other cases, of
course, where they report to me that we are paying too much, and that the train is getting
through on an average better than we expected
it would. We accordingly reduce it, but in getting out this trip time, I may say that our main
object is to give the men a day's pay. We do that
as far as we possibly can, and very often in cases
where we know the timetable time plus the allowance will not exceed nine hours, we nearly always
give a man a trip of ten hours, or 5 shillings for
30 shilling men.

'If a train meets with any exceptional delays,
or if there is a bad fog, or if there is an accident
or anything like that, the men have an opportunity of applying in those cases to be paid for the
time made instead of for the trip. We get many
such applications in the course of a year, and they
are all dealt with personally by the District Superintendent, and wherever we consider that the circumstances justify the case, we pay the men for
the time instead of on the trip. The trip system
has been in operation since 1876, and apart from
[the breaksmen] we have never had any general
application — and I have enquired of nearly all
the chief officers who know anything about it —
for its abolition. Of course, in such a complicated
system as the London & North Western Railway,
and with such a large number of trip rates in

existence based on the average working of the trains under all sorts of conditions, it is inevitable that the whole of the rates cannot, in fairness to the other interests involved, be made in the men's favour. As in every other grade of life, the men must take the good with the bad, and that the good does predominate to an enormous extent is proved by the fact that during the past year it is estimated that the Company paid under the trip system over £10,000 more than they would have paid had the men received wages for the hours actually worked at their booked rates of pay, that is to say the men received a bonus of 8 per cent as a recompense for getting through their work expeditiously. Although that sum is largely gain to the men, we do not look upon it as any loss to us, because we are satisfied that under the trip system, the trains get along better and engines get to the sheds in better time.

'I have had an analysis prepared of all the regular train and trips in order to find out what amount of manual labour is done by the breaksmen. For the purpose of this return, the actual work is taken to include half-an-hour to examine and couple up the train prior to its starting, all time occupied in shunting en route, and half-an-hour for disposing of the train after arriving at its destination. For the remainder of the time the breaksman is in his van, and although he is on duty, it cannot be said it is of a very strenuous nature. It appears that on 27 per cent of the regular trains the men were engaged in actual manual work for less than a quarter of the actual total time on duty. The rest of the time he is observing the signals, and when the signals are at danger, he has to assist the driver in stopping the train by means of his hand brake. With 36 per cent of the trains, the work takes up from one quarter to one half of their time, that is, from two-and-a-half to five hours in the case of a ten-hour trip. With 33 per cent of the trains, they are engaged from a half to three quarters of their time, and with only 4 per cent of the trains run on the North Western, can a man be said to be hard at work for more than 45 minutes out of every hour on duty.'

Herbert Walker's analysis is a fascinating example of the spirit in which the negotiations were handled. Hepden and Ellison had both commented upon the amount of time 'on the floor', with estimates of half to two-thirds of their time so engaged. Walker's figures confirmed that

in a third of the scheduled trips, the men could be hard at it for half to three-quarters of their time, and in a few cases, even more. Walker estimated that 95 to 98 per cent of all goods train work was paid for on the trip. As enginemen were often paid on a mileage basis, he was also careful to explain that 'mileage' did not come into the calculations at all. Walker explained the fluctuating levels of traffic. 'In the same way as the Locomotive Department, we have a very fluctuating traffic. Therefore we make as many breaksmen regular as we think we can find work for all the year round, but in order to meet the fluctuating demands of our traffic, we train a large number of platform porters and goods porters as porter-breaksmen, and whenever traffic gets heavy and we want a man, we bring these men off the platform or out of the goods shed and they work as breaksmen, and receive the same trip rates as the regular breaksmen. I may say that the average hours made by the men throughout the line is just under 60. The regular men shown on the list nearly all work to a roster, which is put up in the office so that they know day by day what work they will have to do. We have also been referring to a certain number of extra regular breaksmen. Those are regular breaksmen who have not got a roster of fixed duty, but who take on what I may call the normal special trains that are run, and not the extraordinary special trains which are taken by the porter-breaksmen.'

The Arbitrator, Sir Edward Fry, found this somewhat confusing, as he was not sure if there were two or three grades, and was additionally confused by the differing terminology used by Hepden, who had spoken of regular men, extra men and emergency men, and by Herbert

(790—Wagon Label.)

London & North Western Ry. _____ Under Sheet N

From THE RUGBY PORTLAND CEMENT CO.

To *Whitchurch* (*Salop*

Via *Crewe.*

Wagon No. 40776   Date 18/5 189

Consignee *W H Smith & Co*

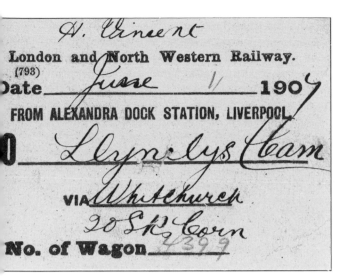

Walker. He asked if there were two or three grades. 'A number of extra breaksmen are always found regular employment, with very few exceptions, as breaksmen, and they are included in the list of regular breaksmen. Practically there are two grades, unless you like to divide the regular grade into those men who have a regular rostered duty and those men who have not.' Walker confirmed that the second tier of 'regular' men, as he termed them, were ordinarily employed as breaksmen, and that it was the porters who took the extra work. The divergence in terms was confusing, particularly as many of the staff referred to the regular unrostered men as extra, and used the term emergency men for the porter breaksmen, which the LWR chose to call 'extra' men. It confused Fry for some minutes, and with the same term being used for different things, it means that today we have to be careful in what we mean by extra breaksmen.

Until recent times, the standard British wagon was four wheeled without any form of automatic braking. The fast block freights of the modern rail scene were non-existent, and Herbert Walker's comments about running times are a salutary reminder of how conditions have changed, 'Take the coal trains from Rugby to London. The time they usually occupy is nine to ten hours with marginal time. Unless we are going to accelerate the speed of those trains very considerably, there is no possible means of getting them through in eight hours, and therefore we should either create intermediate places where we should have to keep a lot of breaksmen, or we should have to split the trip into two at Bletch-

ley.' Walker was commenting on the problems he would face if the eight-hour day was conceded, but in doing so revealed that nine to ten hours was regarded as normal for a coal train to travel 80 miles. The GN & LNW Joint line, which funnelled coal on to the North Western from the Nottinghamshire coalfield to join the main line at Rugby or Northampton, was a similar case. The coals out of the large yard at Colwick took around ten hours to wend their way down the Joint line to the main lines for remanning.

With such protracted journey times, lodging turns were much more common amongst the breaksmen than amongst passenger guards. Richard Bell, for the men, commented that 'as with drivers and firemen, the men are provided with what are called barracks by the company, where they have to put up when they are relieved away from their homes. Of course provision is made for cooking and sleeping, and all the necessary accommodation is provided, but they are made no allowance towards what must of necessity be an additional expense on them of having to provide their food for at least three days away from their homes.' The barracks comprised dormitories, cooking facilities, reading and rest rooms. The LNWR did not pay a lodging allowance when men used the Company barracks, but did pay 2 shillings a night in other cases. Bell asked for a booking-off allowance of 1 shilling for up to 15 hours off duty away from home, and 2 shillings for a longer time.

During the hearings, repeated comment was made as to increasing train lengths, and C.E. Grasemann, as Outdoor Goods Manager, was able to give some of the statistics. 'As Mr Cooke proved today, only 174 really large goods engines have been built out of a total of 1,760, which is 10 per cent. The average loading — not their capacity — is increased from 36 to 50 wagons, but when you add the far larger number of engines, 1,600, whose capacity has only increased in a very slight degree, we find, comparing 1908 with 1905, three years ago, when we first kept these statistics, that the average increase for the whole of the line is only from 36 to 40 wagons, or 11 per cent.'

A remarkable point, which Bowen Cooke had made, was that of the total time on trains, a freight engine frequently spent a third of its time standing at stations, refuge sidings or signals.

Breaksmen received ordinary rate for overtime, and time-and-a-half for Sunday duty, although this was much reduced in extent by the early 1900s compared to the 1880s or 1890s. Herbert Walker recalled his younger days on the North Western. 'Many years ago it was a frequent thing for the line to get into almost a state of block every weekend throughout the winter, that is to say, that the accommodation at the different large junctions was not sufficient to take the wagons as fast as they arrived, and it got worse and worse each day, and it generally culminated on the Friday or Saturday. The result was that the whole staff used to work every Sunday. Not only did the breaksmen have to come out to work the main line trains, but it was a common thing to have to go up to the collieries and do all the shunting there on the Sunday practically the same as on the weekday. It was then felt that there might be some justification, when the men had to work just as hard, and perhaps a bit harder, on the Sunday as on the weekday, to give them something extra for it. But within the last 10 or 15 years the company have spent, I may say, millions, in improving the accommodation at all the large junctions, improving the running lines, providing loops and one thing and another, with the result that now the state of things which I have just explained is practically non-existent. The goods yards, where we deal with all the coal traffic and the local goods traffic, have been so increased that we are able to get through the work day by day. The result is that all heavy Sunday work has disappeared, and the trains that are run on Sunday now are the through express goods in connection with which there is very little work to do, and which invariably carry the higher trip rates. In some places the improvement dates as far back as eight or ten years ago; in other cases it only dates back three or four years.' Walker's admission of the extent to which freight traffic had overwhelmed the North Western by the early 1890s is in stark contrast to the usual picture of a railway always supremely equipped to cope with its traffic, and underlines the drastic need for station enlargements, additional running lines and the eight-coupled engines!

Equally as important to North Western freight services as the breaksmen were the shunters. Richard Bell, from his own days working on the railways, was to provide a graphic account of how a busy yard worked, explaining that yards were normally eight-hour, ten-hour or 12-hour yards,

though the latter were usually the minor places. 'Shunting is the most dangerous occupation we have on the railways. It is an operation in which the men are kept at practically the whole of the time. They break up and re-marshal trains, and dispose of them in various ways, particularly in our great yards. Trains, for instance, come in at Crewe from all directions with traffic for all other directions. Nearly the whole of those trains have to be broken up, and I am informed that the number of trucks to be operated in the Crewe yard amounts to as many as 7,000 wagons in the 24 hours. Shunting yards, like signal cabins, vary according to the size of the yard and the situation of the place. If anything there is more rough work in colliery districts and exchange sidings — between one company and another — than anywhere else, inasmuch as one company, leaving their traffic for the other, does not very often trouble to put it into shape. They say 'It is all North Western Traffic', and consequently, when they hand it over to the North Western, they do not trouble to put it in any form for the North Western system. The work is such that it is impossible to stop. The shunters cannot stop to have their meals. They get their meals the best way they can. It very often happens that one train is in the way of another for a few minutes, and they snap their food at those times.

'The men have to continually run about, and they have to jump up and down [on] wagons, and it is a most trying operation. After the end of eight hours' work in a shunting yard, without any relief or any break by which a man could get away for an hour or so, as other artisans have, they become very tired. It has been proved in one or two instances — but not on the North Western — that men have met with accidents because they were too fatigued. I have had my own experience in the shunting yard, and I know that nothing tires a man more, and will make him less on the alert than being overfatigued with this shunting.'

By 1908, the most important LNWR yards were eight-hour yards, but ten-hour and 12-hour yards still existed. Richard Bell continued that 'there may be some odd yards on the North Western that are 12-hour yards. In these, the work would not be anything approximating the importance of the shunting to be done in the ten-hour yards and the eight-hour yards. But the ten-hour yard is invariably busy, and the ten-hour man has little or no time to himself.'

Herbert Walker outlined the position 'Out of a total of 1,118 men, 393 are already eight-hour' men. Then we have 500 ten-hour men, and the others in smaller numbers. In a few cases, we have different hours in the winter than in the summer. Firstly, in the winter the weather is worse, and secondly the traffic is often heavier. Therefore we have shorter hours in some cases in the winter than in the summer. As a rule, it only applies to large yards where in the winter the hours may be eight, and in the summer nine or occasionally ten. The men at 11 and 12 hours are generally employed at the small stations. The whole of their time, as a rule, is not occupied in shunting, but they are paid through the shunters' paybill. They are men engaged about the yard in all odd jobs, or in many cases employed in the goods shed in loading and unloading goods to and from the carts and wagons. When trains call at their station — it may be two trains a day, or it may be a dozen — these men come away from their regular work and they go and assist

Close co-operation between shunters and enginemen was vital, and although the Ramsbottom/Webb 'four-foot shunters' only had a cab access on one side, a step and handrail were fitted on the blind side for the shunter! No 3070 was built in 1872, and survived until 1930.

the breaksmen in detaching and uncoupling wagons. There are very few cases where the men work 11 or 12 hours a day at shunting and nothing else.

'The eight-hour men are all employed in the very busy yards, and that applies generally to the very few men who are rated at nine hours. The ten-hour men are employed at the less important yards, and their work as a rule is not quite so heavy or continuous as the men at the eight-hour yards. The District Officers, by means of their assistants and inspectors and their own observation, have to decide upon the amount of work to be done at the different yards, whether they shall be rated at eight or ten hours for the day. Some yards are much busier in the winter than in summer. The ten-hour men are shown on their roster to have one hour for meals. As regards the eight-hour men, they work with a shunting engine. The shunting engine has to stop at different periods to get coal and water. Shunting engines often stand for a quarter of an hour or 20 minutes while trains are coming into the yard and being disposed of, or while other trains are going out of the yard. There are always two men with an engine, and while that is taking place, while the engine is getting water or coal, or it is standing, one man, sometimes both, goes to have his meal.'

11 Passenger Staff and Examiners

Illustrations of the old time North Western guards, with their frock coats, broad leather belts worn diagonally across the chest and martial bearing, reflect the dignity and pride of the London & North Western Railway as a whole, for it was above all things a dignified railway. Had the company survived, free of the fetters of the LMS and of BR into modern times, one wonders how it would have adapted to the modern age, with its emphasis upon the commonplace. That it would have adapted one is sure, but in doing so it would probably have lost its special magic. We are therefore free of the image of a North Western guard in modern utility uniform, and can dwell instead on polished buttons and buckles.

Although most small boys wanted to be an engine driver, it was the guard who was most in touch with passengers. Cumberland Lowndes, a North Western divisional officer in the early 1900s, spoke of stories handed down to him of the very early days, and of his youth on the railways.

'In the olden days, they sat outside. That was in the time when they and the driver were equally responsible, before the elaboration of the block system, for vigilance upon which depended the sole safety of the train. He loaded the luggage

Two LNWR guards pose for their photograph in about 1920. Herbert Joseph Wilmshurst, on the left, was born in Deal about 1860, but spent many years at Edge Hill and Holyhead, working the 'Irish Mail' regularly. (R.W. Wilmshurst)

on to the roofs of the carriages and he dealt with the parcels at the stations. He had no van, but he had to put them on and off the carriage roofs. It was mostly luggage and not parcels. Their responsibilities then were very onerous, and coming down to the days of my own experience, before the introduction of the vacuum brake, the driver and the guard together were responsible for the application of the chain brake. There was no continuous brake throughout the train that could be applied by the driver, so that the guard was equally responsible with him for controlling the train at all stoppages, not only at the stations, but whenever the signals were at danger. That state of things which lasted until the introduction of the vacuum brake, has now completely changed, and the responsibility which fell upon the guard has disappeared, because the driver applies the brake power throughout all the train from the engine, and the guard is not expected as formerly to keep a constant look-out, and is only called upon to apply the brake power from the van in emergencies, and when the train enters terminal platforms. I may say that the introduction of the vacuum brake on the carriage stock has cost the company £478,000.

'The guards are selected from men already in the service, porters and other junior grades. The method usually adopted is that at big stations we have what are termed porter-guards — we have 36 of them. We also have other porters, a number of them at the large stations, who work short trips, mostly empty carriage trains, for which they are paid a higher rate than their usual pay. In this way men are initiated into the duties of guards gradually and easily, and from them, the most suitable men are picked for promotion when vacancies occur.

'I should say that the guard's post is looked upon as a prize, and we have more competition than in any other grade in my experience. On the other hand, we have hardly any resignations. On the whole line, I find they are less than one a year, the exact number being four in five years. Most of the guards remain as guards until they reach retiring age. 65 is the general age, but if a man's health breaks down, he can retire between 60 and 65 with the advantage of a pension. Before being put in charge of a train, the guard has to obtain knowledge of the section of the line over which he will work, and he is sent over this section under the tuition of a regular

guard. He then has to pass an examination in rules for protecting the line in cases of breakdown, and for taking the initial steps to obtain relief if the train is disabled. He also has to make himself acquainted with the rules for the working of the automatic brake. The men are generally put on short distance trains at first, and they have the opportunity of obtaining experience gradually and easily.

'Guards are allowed three days leave with pay after one years' service in any capacity, four days after five years' service, and after being employed five years as guards they are allowed a week's leave and pay. Taking the line throughout, the cost to the company is over £900 a year for the guards, and is equivalent to an addition to the wages of 7d per man per week. A very good uniform is supplied; the value is £3 12 11d, equivalent to 1/5d per man per week. The guards have three sets of passes, one at Christmas, one at Easter or Whitsuntide, and one for annual leave. From passes lately issued this works out to more than 8d per week per man.

'Out of 2,880 vans we have, 1,800 have already been fitted with warming apparatus, which is a steam heating apparatus (two coils in the large vans), at a cost of £3 12s each; the total cost that the company have gone to for warming the guards vans has been £6,480. For the long distance vans running on the night trains between the north and London we have nearly 400 fitted with a stove for cooking food and boiling tea. I know by experience that the conditions under which they sort their parcels are altogether different for what they were even ten years ago. In the large vans now, we have six incandescent lights. The vans have been painted white and are as brilliantly lit as a room. With regard to parcels, the duty of the guard has been very much lightened, because in 1898, that is ten years ago, all our parcels, that is parcels conveyed from one of the North Western stations to another, have been stamped like a postal letter, so that the whole duty of checking the waybills, which formerly fell upon the guard, has been removed. Instead of the guard having to check the waybill, which is the note with the particulars of where the parcel is from and to, and its weight, with the parcel itself, and tuck it in the string of the parcel, or deal with it by handing it out separately, he now simply gets a parcel handed in with the stamp on it.'

The October 1908 rosters record that there

were 555 regular guards on the North Western, their pay ranging from 22/6d for one of the provincial men to 45/- and 47/6d for 13 men based at Euston for the through 'Scotch' expresses, a duty shared with some of the Caledonian men. Lowndes summed it up thus; 'The London guards secure a very large proportion of the highly paid rates, the pick of the main line work, and if their wages are averaged out, and compared with the guards in the provinces, it will show that the guards in London receive £1 14s 10d a week. That is the average pay of the men stationed in London at Euston and Willesden. In the provinces, the guards receive £1 11s 10d a week, so that the difference in the average is exactly three shillings.'

Sunday duties were a strange paradox at this time, for if a guard was brought on duty on a Sunday, he received a standard day's pay irrespective of time worked. To the man who was on duty three or four hours, this represented a very good overtime rate, but as the average duty worked out at 8 hours 50 minutes, many men felt it was not so attractive. Lowndes explained the very traditional North Western attitude to Sunday working: 'I may say that on Sunday, in my experience, we run nothing for profit. It is the policy of our company not to run any trains for profit on Sunday. We confine ourselves to the trains running for postal requirements, and the early services in the morning and the late services at night, and the work in those trains is kept to a minimum. There are no parcels or letters and not much luggage.' Until about 1906, the men had been paid for hours worked, and Lowndes' explanation of the change has a quaintly paternalistic ring to it: 'It was conceded, if I may so put it, on purely sentimental grounds. We have always looked on the men as members of the family, and in giving this concession, the officers of the company responsible for it knew that there was no ground for giving it in the way of labour performed. It was given on sentimental grounds, pure and simple. Sunday duty is kept down on the North Western to the requirements of the Post Office and the Public... that has always been our policy.'

In 1908, Edwin Yates had worked at Crewe for about 20 years, the first half as a passenger shunter, latterly as a guard. He was one of about 18 guards *stationed* at Crewe, not all of whom *belonged* to the station. Yates explained the distinction

thus: 'There are three guards belonging to London Road, Manchester, but they live at Crewe. Their duties start from Crewe in the morning, so they live at Crewe, but really belong to another division, the Manchester Division. There is another one belonging to the Shrewsbury division, and another to the Chester and Holyhead division. They live at Crewe, but they are paid from those districts.'

There were four passenger links at Crewe, three in No 1 link, and four each in 2, 3, and 4 links, Yates being in the No 3 link. The four men worked a particular roster for a week, and then moved to the next roster, completing the cycle over the four-week period. The duty hours on the four turns were approximately 10½ hours, 9¾ hours, 10 hours and 9½ hours.

William Colcutt was stationed at Lime Street, and had been with the LNWR for around 20 years, part of which was spent as a fish checker at Lime St, before becoming a breaksman. His transfer to the passenger department was unusual. In the early 1900s, the Liverpool guards worked a range of routes, Colcutt's link taking him to Blackpool, Lancaster, Shrewsbury and Manchester, and very occasionally to Euston, on the American Specials. His account of the 6.05 am link makes fascinating reading: 'I start out at 6.05 in the morning. I stop at all stations to Preston. We reach Preston at 7.57. We are due out again at 8.15, to Wigan at 8.51. Out again at 8.58 to St Helens. We are due there at 9.16 am. We start back from St Helens at 9.27, due into Blackpool at 10.50; out again at 11.25, due into Preston at 12.15; out again from Preston at 1.05, due at Leyland at 1.15. Due out from Leyland at 1.45, into Preston at 1.55. From Preston at 3.02 pm to Liverpool at 4.15. On that roster we are marked, if there is a second portion running, to stop behind and work that, and on several occasions I have worked 40 to 50 minutes over the time that we are shown to finish, because on each rostered turn the guard is shown to finish at the actual time of arrival of the train, which is an impossibility.'

Colcutt explained his duties in more detail: 'When you finish with a train you have to see that the train is empty; you have to go through your vans and cupboards. You have to see that there is nothing left in, and when you are handing over the train to another guard, you have to see your own stuff out, and to give him an idea

of what is in the train, because he has not sufficient time to go through it before leaving. At terminal stations, as at Lime Street, or a large
station like Manchester or Euston, where you get
letters with the train marked for the Superintendent to be delivered, you have to go and deliver
them to the Superintendent's office. You frequently have telegraph messages with trains; you
have to take them round to the Telegraph office.
You have insured parcels, to take to the Parcels
office, and get a signature for them. At a station
like Crewe, if you have over half an hour between
the train you are working and the train you take
out, you have to go and get a barrow and put
all your 'insureds' on and take them to the Parcels office and get a signature, or hand them over
to another guard.'

The Liverpool guards started at 25 shillings
a week, working up to 40 shillings. Rates increased automatically to 32/6d, and thereafter
by vacancy into the crack 35 or 40 shillings turns,
which comprised the lodging runs to Euston,
Glasgow and Bristol. They would normally work
three round trips a week, and would incur around
5 shillings in lodging expenses.

The North Western was keen to publicize the quality of its latest
coaching stock. These postcards were two amongst many pub-
lished by the Company.

CORRIDOR OF NEW 57FT CORRIDOR COACH
L & N.W. RAILWAY

NEW CORRIDOR TRAIN.

NEW 57FT CORRIDOR COACH. L & N.W. RAILWAY.

Christopher Hayes was one of a dozen guards working out of Leeds, where there were three links. His comments cast some doubts upon the perfection of LNWR timings. 'On one turn, we start at 12.25, for the 12.35 to Copley Hill, due there at 12.45, but we usually get there about one o'clock. Then we have to walk from Copley Hill to Leeds, which takes half an hour, and we are due out with the 1.42 pm, a stopping train to Manchester, due there at 3.55 pm, but never gets there at that time. We usually arrive at about 4.05 pm. Then we usually have letters for the Superintendent's office or Telegraph office, and Parcels to take into the Parcels office, and then due out with the 5.15 pm to Liverpool. That is what we call a Fast Train, not an Express. We stop at the important stations. We are due into Liverpool at 6.08, and then we have ''values'' [valuable parcels] as a rule, and letters for the Telegraph office, and we have a book to sign on arrival, and sign again on coming off. We are due out at seven o'clock, with a through train from Liverpool. When I have the book signed and my letters delivered, I go straight away round to the train ready for coming back. We are due at Huddersfield at 9.28 pm; we hand the train there over to a Huddersfield man. A train is due in at 9.50 from Stockport, and it is a rough train. We have a lot of stuff to see out. We are due away at 10.00, all stations to Leeds at 10.53 pm. I usually finish from 11.00 to 11.15 pm.'

Hayes started as a guard in the mid-'nineties, earning 25 shillings, and by 1908 had worked up to 35 shillings. Hayes comments at the 1908 arbitration hearing led to a fascinating and good-natured series of exchanges between the arbitrator, Richard Bell for the men, and C.E. Grasemann for the Company.

The arbitrator, Sir Edward Fry, was well aware of tipping, and asked Hayes what he made in a week. 'I would not average 6d a week, not in the trains that I work.' Bell interjected to ask if Hayes was allowed to take tips. 'Not that I know of', came the answer, to show that tips were against the rules. Bell, satisfied that he had made the point, commented, 'As long as the tips are prohibited by the Company, I do not think that the Company can put that forward as part of the men's earnings.' The exchanges then became hilarious:

Grasemann: I would like to remind Mr Bell, as he said that tips are prohibited, and that the Company ought not to put it forward, that we have not by word or deed, made any suggestion with regard to tips. Anything in connection with tips is common knowledge as well to the Arbitrator, who travels by rail, as to myself who, when I travel on the North Western, treat whoever looks after my luggage as well as the ordinary traveller would.

Bell: I am surprised to hear you say that in the face of your rule.

Grasemann: I say it is merely an old rule intended to prevent anyone from asking for tips.

Fry: I am surprised, I confess, to find the rule amongst your rules.

Grasemann: I quite agree that it would be better to have a rule to the effect that they are not allowed to ask for gratuities. That is my personal opinion. But it is the same rule which is in force in other companies, and there are a good many old relics of the past. I have no doubt that this expression of opinion on your part, Sir, will induce the Company to reconsider the question.

Fry: I should think there should not be a rule that is not enforced.

Grasemann: I quite agree with you personally, and I will see that a representation is made in the proper quarter to that effect.

Grasemann was as good as his word, and the rule book was in due course amended as he had desired!

Cumberland Lowndes, the LNWR District Superintendent at Manchester, explained the Company's training system for platform porters, one of the Company's key recruiting grades.

'We have 1,069 adult platform porters and 396 juniors. On the North Western the duties of platform porters are, broadly speaking, those of unskilled labourers, when they are working as porters. The nature of the duties is generally well known, but during a great part of the day — especially in the country — their duty consists of attendance rather than of continuous arduous labour. We have on the North Western Railway developed more particularly during the last 15 years a system by which we train porters in more experienced grades, for which they are given every encouragement to qualify. That has always been so to some extent, but more particularly during the last 15 years. This system prevails all over the line now, and it has a very great and beneficial influence on the career of men entering the service as porters. In fact, as a result of it the porters on this railway are essentially a grade of cadets. I must lay the utmost stress upon this. Our North Western system is that as soon as junior porters are of age, they are encouraged to qualify either as porter-guard, porter-brakesmen, relief-signalman, or shunter, and when they are competent in any of these grades they are used as reliefmen when required, and for this work they receive extra pay. Of the 1,069 adult porters, no less than 740, or 69 per cent, are trained in the duties of higher grades, and receive in addition to their earnings as porters, extra wages, amounting to an average of 3s 3d per man per week. Twelve per cent of the men are over 19 but under 21 years of age, and not therefore eligible for the more responsible duties at present. Eight per cent are not fitted for further training. It is my experience that amongst the porters, there are always some who

display no aptitude for taking up more important duties, and, then again, there are others who for some physical cause, such as shortness, or perhaps of temperament, prove unsuitable for promotion. It has ever been the policy of the company, as far as my experience goes, provided these men are good workers, and honest, to refrain from casting them adrift, and they are given such of the porters' posts, mostly at the small stations, where it is not indispensable that they should be treated as cadets. These men continue as porters, perhaps during the whole of their railway career, until they are old men, and are often the most familiar figures at roadside stations. The prospects of porters on the North Western, because we have developed the cadet system as no other railway has, are altogether different and better than the prospects of unskilled labourers outside the railway service, such as badge porters and agricultural labourers.

'In promoting them to other grades, the District Superintendent, who is responsible for the safe working of the line, makes the choice. The officers of the company and the station masters are responsible for his training and his safety while he is training, and then as he goes on he is gradually educated at the company's expense in the duties of more experienced grades, and in the case of the porter-signalman he is given a retaining fee all the year round, even if he is

Walter John Boston, a porter at Nuneaton in 1900-05. Later he joined the Co-op Bakery, retiring as manager. (Mr & Mrs Lea)

never called on to actually work the box as a responsible signalman, and in all cases when he is called upon to do more experienced work, he is given increased pay. That is a system peculiar to the North Western, by which the porter gets a retaining fee of 2/6d a week.

'In the case of a porter who lives at a station, and does not want to move, I have never known of a case of his being forced to move, but on the other hand, where a man lives at another station to the one he works at, everything is done to assist him, in my experience, to move. Of 396 junior porters, about 300 live at home, and beginning with junior porters, we are most careful to adapt the requirements of the work to the circumstances of the man.'

Junior porters commenced at 11 shillings, rising to 17/6d when they became 'Adult' porters at 19. Lowndes explained that the average age of porters was well under 30 and most men were under 24. The porters, far more than guards, were in an excellent position to secure tips at the

main stations, though less likely to do so in the country districts. Reticence about the extent of 'tips' is as old as tipping itself, but its significance was apparent to every North Western officer, and when asked if porters ever declined promotion, Lowndes remarked wryly: 'Without going any further than Euston, I have heard of several Euston porters who have refused promotion because they find it more advantageous to remain as porters at Euston. This we find at most of our big stations to be no uncommon feature.'

One feature of the porters' duties actually dated back to the dawn of the railway age. Theoretically LNWR porters worked not the six-day week of most grades, but a seven-day week of 12 hours a day, except on lines where no Sunday trains ran. In fact, the men were relieved one Sunday in two, but the notion of seven-day working without extra pay was seemingly confined to just two main line companies by 1908, the LNWR and the Great Northern! Grasemann explained this strange anachronism: 'When railways first started, they had passenger trains on Sundays as well as on other days, and at first the traffic consisted chiefly of passengers, and therefore the platform porters were paid for seven days per week, and they have always continued to be paid on that basis.' Given the early agitation against Sunday trains, Grasemann's explanation, though a cherished concept of North Western official thinking, was not entirely correct. Sir Edward Fry did not think it could be justified, and his 1909 arbitration award fixed the standard week as six days.

Listening to William Horn, a passenger porter at Euston, we gain a more detailed impression of the job. Horn describes the early shift: 'Commencing at 3.45 am in the morning, we [start] on the Up Mail and unload mail bags. After that, one of us is told off to open the District Superintendent's letters, and we do that till eight o'clock. We attend the 8.30 Irish Mail and the passengers. After 8.30, the same man has to go and do a turn at the post office — that is, to relieve the sorting porters who come up on the night trains and have to be ready to go down on the down train in the evening. We are supposed to finish that job before we go away. After that we come up on the front [of the station] and wait on the passengers, or do anything that is required; work empty stock trains to Willesden, and also go shunting, and get any stock orders and that sort of thing that are wanted for the night trains. We book off at 1.30 in the afternoon.

'We get a little bit of breakfast the best way we can, at the station, between the trains, or between the jobs. There is no set time for breakfast, nor any other meals. Euston porters are divided into gangs. There are what are called trip gangs that work empty coaches and do mail bags and shunting and that kind of thing. Taking the platform porters, they come on at six o'clock at night and they go on the milk dock till seven, and sort all the empty milk cans ready to be transferred into the trains to go away in the morning. When they have done that, they go and assist in the parcel post for the 7.30 mail to Ireland. Then they stand on the front and attend to passengers and do mail bags and anything they are called upon to do till 9.00. Then they go back over to the milk dock and sort the empty cans and take loaded churns out till 11.00. They go on the front and attend passengers from 11 o'clock till 12.00, and get their supper from 12.00

for perhaps three-quarters of an hour. They work till 5.30 am.

Horn's basic pay in 1908 was 17/6d as a porter, with the 2/6d retaining fee as a relief signalman, but with trip working and brakesman's duties he was averaging 24/6d. When asked about tips, Horn was decidedly non-committal, which was understandable in the presence of several senior North Western officers! When continuously on platform duties, he agreed he could make 2 shillings or 2/6d in a day, often had to take empty stock to Willesden, and might not make 6d in a couple of days.

Joe Needham, a porter at Buxton, was equally vague over tips. He had started as a porter at Dove Holes, near Buxton, in 1892, earning 11 shillings a week. He moved to Buxton in the late 1890s, where the North Western employed three ordinary porters and a foreman porter. Rosters averaged about 11½ hours, with 1¾ hours for meals. Between trains, Needham served as a general handyman, sweeping the platforms, cleaning buildings and attending to the station lamps, and on the appropriate turn, the signal lamps as well. The rosters overlapped, the early turn running from 5.15 am to 4.30 pm, and the late turn from 9.00 am to 8.30 pm. Needham spent four hours of the late shift in the signal box, where his basic pay rose from 17/6d (plus retaining fee) to 26 shillings. On the subject of tips, Needham felt that the introduction of the 'passengers' luggage in advance' system in the early 1900s had been detrimental; 'They have not been as liberal the last few years as they were formerly.' He added, 'It has been a moderate summer in Buxton; there has been so much wet weather. As a matter of fact, the tips are there, but the porters are not allowed to get at them. They are intercepted by other men, Carriage Department men or any of the casual labourers who can come in and wait on passengers.'

Needham's comments revealed a deep rift between the platform staff and the Carriage Department staff under Charles A. Park. Park, who was responsible for the magnificent LNWR carriage stock, controlled not merely the Wolverton works staff, but 'CD' men up and down the system, but before we look at their jobs, it is interesting to recall Park's own career. His railway career had begun with a five-year pupillage to his father, J.C. Park, Locomotive Superintendent of the North London Railway at Bow. From

1879 to 1882, he worked for Craven Brothers in Manchester, designing heavy machine tools. In 1882, the Locomotive Superintendent of the North Eastern Railway, Edward Fletcher, retired after decades of service, and his successor, Alexander McDonnell, came from the Great Southern & Western Railway of Ireland.

Park joined him to reorganize the workshops and erect the carriage works at York. He became Assistant Locomotive Superintendent of the Southern Division of the NER, and later Superintendent of that Division. In July 1885, he became Assistant Carriage Superintendent of the LNWR, and Superintendent in January 1886. He was to preside over the move from lightweight six-wheelers to the majestic 12-wheelers of the WCJS and American Special Stock. Park's role at Wolverton is well known, but we forget that his men looked after the stock in service. In 1908, there were 1,532 men in the outdoor staff of the Department, of whom 1,208 were washers and cleaners, 189 were examiners, and the remainder included such odd grades as lampmen (19), gas fillers (11), gas fitters (11), couplers (17), electric light men (31), footwarmer attendants (40) and 6 oilers.

Arthur Thorner came from one of the rarest grades, the 19 gas lampmen, of whom six, including Thorner, worked at Euston. He had joined the LNWR as a lampman in July 1889, having previously worked as a lampman for the Great Western. With the spread of electric lighting, his was a dying trade, but with his five colleagues he was responsible for cleaning, servicing and lighting all lamps on trains still fitted with gas illumination and in the case of incoming trains, 'we have to turn out every train that comes in, see that every light is all right, and nothing broken'. The lampmen were divided into three shifts, one night shift from 6.00 pm to 6.00 am, and two day shifts, 6.00 am to 5.30 pm, and 7.00 am to 6.30 pm. The other special grades worked on a similar basis at Euston, and were organized under gang foremen, who were responsible for trains being properly cleaned, coupled, lit and gangways connected up. Cleaners were divided into 'outside' and 'inside' cleaners, and worked to a different shift pattern.

Practices at different stations varied greatly; at Euston, couplers were responsible for dealing with couplings and the gangways, but at Liverpool Lime St, the traffic department men handled this work. The CD men were of course confined to the principal stations, such as Euston, Lime St, Crewe, Manchester and Birmingham, and indeed Euston, with 245 men, and Lime St, with over 100, employed almost a quarter of Charles Park's 'outside' men alone! Away from the principal stations, traffic department men did the necessary work, a curious dichotomy, and scarcely what one would have expected from an invariably logical organization such as the LNWR. The CD men's wages were rather curious also. Generally, on the LNWR, the London staff received rather higher wages than the other towns and cities, but on the CD side, Liverpool Lime St frequently topped the bill. Gas-men at Lime St received 23 shillings, as against 22 shillings at Euston. Examiners were on 27 or 28 shillings as against 25 to 27 shillings, and so on. In some grades, there was quite a spread between starting and top scales at Euston, but the lower wages paid to many Euston men may have originated out of a misunderstanding between the traffic and carriage departments. As this emerged, it added a note of comedy to the normally staid arbitration proceedings.

Richard Bell had argued cogently that the CD wages were too low to support an experienced man with his family, especially in the lower grades. As there were so few in the specialist grades, promotion in the CD section must have been very slow as well, and Bell's argument had much force. C.E. Grasemann, in discussing the London men's position, remarked that 'Mr Bell is entirely wrong in stating that the Carriage Department do not get any opportunities for tips in the same way as the porters. Anyone arriving at Euston by any express trains will see as many Carriage Department men there for certain trains as porters, and the result is that so many of these men, as well as men from one or two other grades, come to meet the train, that complaints that I have often heard about other termini in London as to an insufficiency of porters to meet the passengers with their luggage are unheard of in connection with Euston. As a rule there are three or four porters at every compartment door, but they are not platform porters. Many of them — I might almost say the majority of them — are men from the Carriage Department, who, when they are off duty, before going home, or even after going home, come back, and assist passengers with their luggage.'

Above *Steam billows up towards the train shed as a 'Precursor' stands in platform 1 at Euston, her work done for a few hours. This was the world which was so familiar to Grasemann and Arthur Thorner.* (H.J. Stretton Ward)

Below *Looking along departure platforms 12/13 at Euston in about 1905.*

Grasemann assumed it was off-duty CD men who thronged the platform, but when the District Superintendent, Herbert Walker, was asked his views, his explanation was very different: 'When a train comes into Euston, you will find perhaps 50 or 60 men all ranged up in a line waiting for the train to come to a standstill, and waiting to look after the passengers and their luggage. Out of that 50 or 60, certainly half of them are Carriage Department men, some of whom cannot attend to their duties on that train until the passengers are all out and their luggage is cleared away. Then they have to examine the interior of the carriages and do any uncoupling that there is to do, or any other duties, but for the first five minutes after the train arrives, those men are looking for tips.' Herbert Walker confirmed that apart from the on-duty men waiting to start their train duties, there would be off-duty men supplementing their income as well.

Richard Bell recalled Arthur Thorner, the lampman.

An LNWR 'fat-box' or grease box of 1894. The colloquial name for wagon greasers, and no slighting reference was meant to their waist-line, was 'fatboy'.

Bell: Do you get any opportunities for attending to passengers' luggage?

Thorner: Yes. I get the sack if I go there when I am on duty; that is the opportunity I get. It has been done. More than one man has had the sack for doing it. You are strictly forbidden to wait on passengers while on duty.

Fry: That is the lampmen?

Thorner: All men concerned in the Carriage Department.

Bell: Therefore they go in their own time to attend the train?

Thorner: That is so.

Bell: During the period that they are on duty, they are not allowed to wait upon passengers?

Thorner: No, they are not allowed to; and, more than that, there is a foreman there to see that they do not do it. There is a foreman walking about on the arrival side to see that these men do not wait on the passengers while they are on duty.

Fry: Mr Walker says there are men waiting to do the cleaning of the trains as soon as the passengers are all discharged. They are waiting for the arrival of the train, and until the train is clear they cannot do their work as cleaners. Do you mean to say that these men do not do anything to assist in attending to the passengers with luggage?

Thorner: They dare not do it.

Fry: Is is forbidden, Mr Walker?

Walker: No, it is not forbidden... As long as a man does what it is his duty to do, it is not forbidden.

Fry: Mr Walker must know if it is forbidden by the authorities.

Bell: I do not know whether he would. This is not his department; he has no supervision over it. But this witness of mine is a man actually at work in the grade that we are now considering, and he says that he dare not do it for fear of being dismissed.

The arbitrator decided he had to get to the bottom of this conflict of evidence, and asked Herbert Walker if the CD foreman could attend the following morning to give evidence. As it happened, foreman Lewis was unavailable and Herbert Walker again took the stand.

Grasemann: Will you tell the facts to Sir Edward?

Walker: I made a statement last night to the effect that the Carriage Department men, when on duty, were not prohibited from attending passengers on the arrival side. I find I was wrong. Some time, prior to 1897, apparently an order was issued on the subject, because I find from a letter written by Mr Park to the Carriage Department here on the 5th October 1897, this occurs: 'I have again to call your attention to the rule on this matter which prohibits any of our staff attending to or waiting upon passengers. Complaint is made that this rule is being neglected at several of our stations. Please give this your special attention.' The carriage foreman at Euston tells me that the rule is still in force, so that I can only assume that a large number of men in the Carriage Department that I see attending to passengers on the arrival side are not on duty at the time.

Richard Bell acknowledged Herbert Walker's admission of error courteously. It was a rare case within the LNWR of the left hand not knowing what the right was doing.

'Section D' included not only the guards and coaching staff, and the 'outside' men of the Carriage Department, but the outdoor men of the Wagon Department as well, under the Wagon Superintendent, Mr H.D. Earl. Their inclusion in a section otherwise wholly given over to men dealing with passenger services was one of the foibles of the North Western system. For sake of fidelity to that system, we have covered them here also.

Earl's outdoor staff comprised 208 examiners and 89 greasers. In large centres their work was distinct, but in smaller depots the dividing line was often blurred. William Marriott was an examiner at Netherfield and Colwick, near Nottingham, at the northern extremity of the GN & LNWR Joint line from Welham Junction, near Market Harborough. It was an important route, down which a vast amount of coal traffic flowed. There were four examiners at Colwick, and as there were no greasers or repair men, they had to be jacks-of-all-trades. Marriott explained how the yard worked: 'At Netherfield, the trains back in from the collieries, and they probably bring 30, and some 25 wagons, and they are made up into trains of 42 loads. We have to grease them and examine them as well, and a 42-wagon train in summer time will take you 40 or 45 minutes to examine and grease it properly. You examine the wheels and axles by tapping. We are responsible for the safe running of the wagons to the next place. We have to examine everything, draw gear, buffers, axleboxes and springs, and everything connected with the wagons. We have to do slight repairs to our own wagons, also to oil the axleboxes. At our station we have no greaser, we have to do our own greasing, and in summer time we use up close on two barrels of grease a week, averaging 11 or 12 hundredweight.' There were two 12-hour shifts, day and night, out of which meals were supposed to be allowed, but with the unpredictable movements of extra trains, mealtimes were often lost, and paid in lieu.

The examiners learned to take a lunch-box with them, and grab a snack when opportunity arose, especially on the night shift when freight traffic was at its peak. Handling greasing as well as examining was most unusual on the North Western, as it meant that the men had to go over the train twice, once examining, and then greasing, and this slowed turn-round times. The absence of any wagon shops, where repairs were normally sent, was another rarity. Apart from the routine duty hours, the four examiners took it in turn to cover Sunday nights.

Wagon Department examiners normally commenced as greasers as boys of 15 or 16, when they would be earning 12 shillings a week. A few who showed no aptitude might remain as greasers, but the majority would be promoted to examiner, with wages running from 22 shillings to 32 shillings. If a lad showed promise, he would serve the necessary time as a greaser, and then spend a couple of years in one of the wagon shops, as wagon lifter, smith's striker, or brake repairman. As work at the different stations varied greatly, wagon examiners, in common with other grades, were not on a specified scale, but individual rates were settled by the Wagon Superintendent. Although the work was arduous, and necessitated the men being out in all weathers, resignations were few, only ten in the decade up to 1908.

12 Dustless Tracks

The LNWR was intensely proud of its permanent way, often referring to its smooth riding and dust-free tracks. On 31 December 1913, when the LNWR was at its very zenith, the Company owned, leased, worked or jointly owned 2,062¾ route miles, or 5,770½ miles of track, including sidings. From its Euston headquarters, the Chief Civil Engineer's department, working through the Divisional Engineers, employed around 7,000 men on permanent way duties, of whom 5,000 were regular employees, and the rest in extra gangs. Permanent way maintenance cost £681,718 in 1913, and when the cost of earthworks, bridges, fences, superintendence, buildings, signalling and telegraphs is added in, the department was spending over £1½m annually, or significantly more than the maintenance costs of locomotives, carriages and wagons combined. It was a massive department, yet one which has been persistently neglected by railway historians.

The Divisional Engineers, with their personal inspection saloons, kept a close watch on their multifarious tasks, and William Hugh Williams, Divisional Engineer at Watford for over 20 years from the early 1890s, will tell us in his own words how the department worked. Williams was responsible for the prestige Southern Division main line from Euston to Rugby, and all branches. His neighbours to the north were based at Crewe for the main line, Walsall for the Birmingham area, and Northampton for the tiny Northampton, Nottingham and Peterborough District. All had changed a number of times during his long reign, and his only rival in length of service was C.O. Cotton, of Abergavenny. Towards the end of his long career, an additional office was opened at Camden, to create a tenth divisional officer.

'There are 5,000 regular platelayers. These men are distributed throughout the length and breadth of the North Western system in small gangs, generally containing from four to six men. There are, however, about 50 to 60 gangs with only three men in them, and there are a few with seven to 11 men, but they are quite exceptional. Their work consists principally keeping the rails in good line and level and in tidying up and keeping in order the slopes, fences, drains, hedges and ditches alongside the railway. They also repair the approach roads to stations and bridges where the company are responsible for them. The length of railway which they are responsible for varies from one to perhaps three miles. There may be some a little shorter and some a little longer. These lengths are from time to time, owing to alterations and improvements, varied; that is, some are shortened and some are lengthened. In other instances the length remains the same, but the number of men in the gang is varied. We are continually making such changes. These men are rarely called upon to work away from their lengths, consequently they can spend a greater part of their leisure time at their own homes. They are not called upon to work during heavy rainfalls, except in case of emergency, or when there is something urgent to be done, nor do they lose any pay during wet weather.

'They are provided for their convenience with cabins or huts in which they can cook their food and take shelter in bad weather. They work shorter hours in winter [50½] than in summer [56½], but they receive the same rate of pay the whole year through. In addition to that they have many opportunities of adding to their weekly wage without working excessive overtime or being on duty excessive hours. After 12 months' service they get three days leave with pay. After five years service, they get six days leave with pay. About 20 per cent of them live in cottages provided by the railway company. Generally they enjoy the same privileges with regard to passes and that sort of thing as the other grades.

'Generally the rates of pay are sufficient to attract the requisite number of men into the service. If not, after due consideration of the causes, we have in many instances to offer more money. Amongst the regular men, 159 rates have been raised this last year [1908]; in 1906 there were 15 rates raised; in 1904 none; in 1902 37; in 1900 975. We find it is practically impossible to reduce the rates; we do not attempt it. Resignations vary from 3½ to about 7 per cent per annum, principally from the under-men, but not entirely, but we never have any difficulty in filling the vacancies — as I say we have a very expedient way of dealing with it. About half of the new [regular] men are transferred from the extra gangs. The other half we engage principally in agricultural districts. A considerable part of the work is such that any handy man can perform it satisfactorily straight away. I had the curiosity to go through the character forms received with our men for about three years; that is, information given by the previous employer. I found that about a third of the men did receive more money when they entered our service than they had been receiving. There were quite an equal number who came in for less money, but I would not like to say that they all left their previous service voluntarily. They may have left because the work was finished. I could point out that the men in the extra gangs are always willing and ready to accept a position with the regular gangs at a shilling to 1/6d less wages per week. They look upon it as a promotion with less pay, because of the permanency. Contrasted with agricultural labourers, the employmet is very permanent. I have been

District Engineers enjoyed the privilege of their own private locomotive and carriage. No 742 Spitfire, *a 'Waterloo' of 1893, had only just become* Engineer Liverpool, *replacing a venerable 'Samson' 2-4-0 in 1921, when this view was taken in Edge Hill loco yard.* (J.N. Maskelyne)

several times upbraided by farmers for taking their best men from them.

'Ten years ago, or thereabouts, we did, for the convenience of our men reduce their hours about 2½ per week during the winter months. At that time it was the practice for the men to finish their work at 4 o'clock on Saturday afternoon, but now they leave off at 1 o'clock instead.

'The weight of the rails has increased from 90 to 95 lbs per yard. It took place about two years ago, and consequently a very small section of the line is at the present time laid with 95 lb rails. The extra work involved in the actual lifting of the rail does not put upon the men any additional work worth speaking of. In the case of the extra gangs and the relaying gangs — they are the men that have to handle the rails to a considerable extent — we have increased the gang more in proportion than the weight of the rails has been increased. For instance, it used to be 20 men to a 60 foot rail; that is practically a man to a yard. The present practice of handling a 60 foot rail is to have 22 men, so we have got two extra men to deal with the additional 100 lbs in weight.

'Where you have got cinder ballast, or the old

kind of ballast, after every heavy shower of rain, after every spell of frost, after every change in the weather nearly, you find that your road is more or less disturbed. I am speaking now, not of brand new cinder ballast just put down, but ballast that has been done, say two or three years. Further it is much weaker; the sleepers settle in it more regularly, and the road laid on cinder ballast is affected by heavy traffic to such an extent that we have had to give up using it on our main lines, because we could not keep a good road with it. It is easier to shovel cinders than stone ballast, but when we had the cinder ballast there was about twice as much of it to shift at each operation as compared with the stone ballast. When we had weaker ballast it was piled up almost to the level of the rails in order to make up for its weakness. Gradually as we introduced this stronger ballast, we were able to lower the level of it.

'Where we have got the heavier engines running, we have also got the improved permanent way. The one has kept pace with the other, so that the ultimate result is that the platelayer of today has no more work to do to keep his length in order than he had 10 or 15 years ago. If cinder ballast were used there would be much more work. My own experience is that up to 15 years ago I kept one of my staff told off to simply keep in touch with all complaints, and it used to occupy him about one day a week recording complaints in diagram form to enable me to put my finger quickly on the men at fault. I am glad to say I have not seen that diagram for the last 12 years. I have had no complaint and I put that down entirely to the improved permanent way. I do not get them from drivers or from other departments. We set the inspectors to work, and a large number of the complaints I spoke of as being put in diagram form from me came from my own inspectors.

'I cannot say that we expect less from a man now than we did 15 years ago. The nature of his work has altered. That is, he has not to pack so frequently as formerly, and we expect more attention to small matters of detail which do not necessarily involve more arduous labour. We have now put in more sleepers — 24 to a length which means less packing. The new ballast is more difficult to handle in equal porportions, but it does not have to be handled so often, and you do not have to handle so much of it. It is very

slightly affected by rain. The heavier rails are much less easily displaced by the heavy traffic; generally they are twice the length, which means we have got practically half the number of joints to maintain, and the joint is the troublesome part of the platelayer's work.

'I should say that all the lines that are subjected to heavy and fast traffic are by this time all reballasted. I finished that portion of my district six or seven years ago practically. It is rather curious that during the first three or four months before the stone ballast has time to settle it does cut into the boots a little, but not afterwards, because the interstices get filled with what we call "blowers", that is cinders thrown out from the engines, and it is not so bad to walk on then. Another point about it is that what little trouble is experienced by the men from that source falls almost entirely on the ganger, because he is the man who does practically all the walking. He has to walk his length twice a day. Sometimes that means, say, a four-mile walk on this rough stone, and I do believe that in the case of the gangers, it has made some difference in their footwear, but as to the men who are standing opening out joints, and stepping aside when they have any long walking to do, they can pick their path at the side of the line, and it does not affect the ordinary length-man to any serious extent. When the ballast gets filled up with dirt it is not so porous, and you get it riddled to get the dirt out. This has a rather peculiar effect that it rubs the sharp corners off the rest of the ballast. The question of shovels [which were bought by the men, not the Company] is one that affects the men very differently. A shovel costs on the average about 2 shillings or 2/6d. Its life varies from six months to two years; it all depends upon the vigour of the man using it. With the improved ballast they have not to shovel anything like the same amount, the regular length-men.

'With the exception of certain localities, it is a noticeable fact that we have always a long list of applicants on our books. I have not the slightest trouble about getting men in my own case. There is practically no "standard" wage amongst the platelaying staff. The wages are subject to continual adjustment whenever necessary, but I know of cases where the same rates have been in existence during the whole of my connection with this division, and the men who get them do not want to move. Class for class, if you

An LNWR official postcard depicting permanent way men at work.

except about five individual cases, the men in the London district are paid 3 shillings a week more than the men outside London. I have been very carefully through the whole of the staff lists of the platelayers throughout the whole of the system, and I have only found five rates. I have taken the minimum rate in London, say for an underman, and that is 3 shillings higher than the minimum rate for undermen in a corresponding position anywhere else. I have taken all the third men of the gang, all the fourth men, all the fifth men, and all the sixth men right away through.'

W.H. Williams' remarks about the five rates could be misleading, for his account of the permanent way department was given in evidence to the 1908 wages arbitration hearing, rather than as a continuous address. From evidence advanced elsewhere in the hearings, the five rates did not apply to lowly paid London men, but to five exceptionally highly paid provincial pw men.

In reproducing Williams' account of pw work, the authors have found it preferable to depart from the strictest rules of quotation, in which authors' additions or amendments are by square

bracket, and omissions indicated by ellipses. Williams' remarks were given in evidence, and whilst many of the paragraphs are verbatim, in some cases a series of short answers to questions have been grouped to give the same easy flow as Williams achieved in his longer answers. Very occasionally the subject was 'understood', ie given in the question, and only referred to obliquely in the answer. For clarity we have inserted the subject, but any facts not introduced by Williams, or assented to by him, have been shown in square brackets to indicate an authors' addition. The academic purist may criticize the approach, but we feel that it will be preferable to the majority of readers. The paragraph referring to London rates, etc, is in fact taken from eight separate answers.

The wages of the permanent way men varied considerably, based upon experience, responsibility and the general level of wages in the area. W.H. Williams detailed this in tabular form for 1908. A few concrete examples may bring the table to life. In the rural parts of the Chester & Holyhead line, gangers received 25 shillings; sub-gangers 20/6d; third men 19 shillings; and under-men 18 shillings. The sub-ganger would regularly take charge of the men, whilst the ganger was away on other duties, and if both the ganger and sub-ganger were away, the third man stepped in. They usually received 6d or a shilling more than the other undermen. At Crewe, gangers were on 27 shillings; sub-gangers 20/6d; third men 18/6d; and undermen 18 shillings. It was the custom for many years that when the ganger was away for more than one day, the sub-ganger received gangers' pay, but a very controversial order of November 1908 in the Crewe area reduced the sub-gangers entitlement to 1/6d below whatever the ganger's rate was. W.H. Williams was asked to explain the move, which was to be applied generally.

'It is simply an attempt to regulate the pay to fit the services performed. The ganger's responsibilities are continuous, but when a sub-ganger steps into his place for a few days he does not assume the full extent of the ganger's responsibilities. He cannot do. There are certain returns that have to be made out, certain stock-keeping and the ganger has to look ahead. His interest in his length is not confined to the day, he has to look ahead weeks sometimes. He has to do certain work that does not trouble the sub-ganger for a moment, and if a sub-ganger is taking the duty for a week, and he finds anything disagreeable or troublesome to do — I do not say that he does so — but there is nothing to prevent him putting it off until the regular ganger comes back again. During recent years you will find that there have been changes in the rates of pay, and the fact we have to face now is, that in some instances there is a very considerable difference between the rate of pay of a sub-ganger and the rate of a ganger in the same gang. That difference ranges from about 2/6d to about 9 shillings, and we have often had the fact to face that the sub-ganger may be quite a recent appointment, where the ganger is receiving a much higher rate, so that it is evidently an unequal arrangement that under all circumstances the sub-ganger should get the full rates.

'We have plenty of sub-gangers who have been many years in the appointment. As a rule those who remain long as sub-gangers do so because they are not fully qualified to be made gangers. We frequently find that, after selecting a man with a view to training him as a ganger, when he reaches the position of sub-ganger he loses all further ambition. I have quite recently had to look through my staff and put men back, because I found that my inspectors were introducing men

for promotion that I thought ought not to be brought in and that they were bringing in sub-gangers from one part of the district to be gangers in another. When I inquired into this, I found that the sub-ganger who ought to have been promoted to the job was not fit.'

In describing the regular staff, reference has been made to the extra men. W.H. Williams described their duties in detail: 'At the present time there are about 2,000 of these extra gang-men. Their numbers vary according to the season of the year, and the amount of work which is required to be done. They work under very different conditions from the regular men. To begin with they are not confined to any particular locality or section of line, but they have to travel to and from their work, which may lie on any part of the division to which they are attached. As a rule, they are carried free, and with few exceptions paid the whole time they are travelling to and from their work. They work in much larger gangs than the regular men. Some of the gangs contain as many as 50 men. Their work consists principally of relaying, reballasting, screening ballast, carrying out drainage works, and generally assisting in carrying out new works. They are not called upon to work during bad weather conditions except in case of emergency, or when there is something urgent required to be done, nor as a rule is their pay stopped when, owing to bad weather, they are unable to carry on their work, provided they remain on the job. If they leave the job, of course, their pay is stopped. While they are in the railway company's service they do not work for other people. They may, in harvest time, when they finish their work, go in the fields and assist the farmers.

'When we dispense with their services, as we have to do sometimes during slack times, they are snapped up as a rule by contractors, provided that there is any work suitable for them going on in the district. About 80 per cent of these men have in the past been found more or less regular work throughout the year, excepting at such times at Christmas, Easter, Whitsuntide and August Bank Holiday, when owing to their work being of such a character that it interferes with the traffic, we have to suspend operations for three or four days, sometimes as much as a week. Their work is not interfered with by such circumstances as snow, because they are the men that we fall

IDGE OVER SHIP CANAL NEAR **WARRINGTON**
N.W. RAILWAY

Apart from track, the District Engineers were responsible for thousands of bridges, many of them substantial structures.

back upon when we have snow to deal with. The remaining 20 per cent we cannot offer the same inducement to stay with us, because generally they are engaged for a particular job only, and when that job is finished we dispense with their services. Sometimes we take the same men on three or four times in 12 months. We get, say, a slip or subsidence, and we have to engage 40 to 50 or 100 men as quickly as possible to deal with the matter, and then we dispense with their services.

'The 80 per cent are on our books to all intents and purposes as permanent staff, except this, that the work these men do was, as recently as 25 years ago, all let to contractors, and there is nothing to prevent our letting the same work to contractors again. It is quite apart from the ordinary maintenance. Dealing with the 80 per cent, I should think a fortnight would cover the days these men are unable to work owing to the traffic being too heavy. The remaining 20 per cent are

merely a fluctuating body engaged for special purposes. I may add that these extra men, although they get stopped for a few days at these holiday times, make considerably more than their weekly rate of pay, owing to the special works they have to carry out principally on Sundays. A man might be working for about eight hours on Sunday, but would get 16 hours of pay. He gets time and a half when working, but there is so much of the time taken in travelling, which he is paid rate and a half on Sundays.

'If we had to guarantee these extra men pay, when we could not possibly find them any work, we would have to consider whether or not to revert to the old system of having more of these jobs done by outside contractors, so they would not get all the other advantages attached to the service. Some of the work we would certainly have to deal with in that way, and for other jobs, which would be simple jobs that did not come in contact with the traffic, it would simply mean that we should engage the men for a shorter length of time.

'Annually about ten per cent of these men are

transferred from the 80 per cent to our regular gangs, to permanent employment, and others from the 20 per cent to the 80 per cent. They are always going up.

'Rates for overtime differ. It is an attempt to regulate the payment according to the inconvenience to which you put the individual. We pay time and a quarter between 5.30 and 10.00 at night; time and a half from 10.00 at night to 6.00 in the morning. It is not so much inconvenience to a man to continue his work from half past five for an hour or two, but still we pay him time and a quarter for it; but if that same man had gone home, we will say, after finishing his ordinary work, and you send for him at 10 o'clock to work through the night, we consider that he is put to more inconvenience still, and ought to be paid more for it, and so we give him time and a half.

'Practically the whole of the men work to these hours, with the exception of certain men in tunnels, where, owing to the bad atmospheric conditions, we have cut their hours down to 48 per week, and there are certain of the men who, under emergency and under certain regular working conditions, when they have to alter their duties from day work to alternate night and day work, work the 12-hour turns of duty, but very exceptionally.

'A large number of the extra men travel to their work on the Monday morning and return to their homes on the Saturday, so that the travelling comes in twice, that is going to their work on the Monday and going home on the Saturday. There again with regard to the travelling time we have to adopt different practices. The greater part of the travelling time takes place during what we call working hours. When it takes place outside working hours the man is either paid for the actual time he is travelling or he gets an allowance, a fixed allowance, made to him, or in other districts if he loses time in travelling on a Monday morning he is allowed to work it up during the week between Monday and Saturday, the underlying principle throughout being that provided the man shows an inclination to do his work as he ought to do, he shall not suffer by having to travel.

Thousands upon thousands of buildings provided further work for the District Engineers, for even a minor station possessed a variety of structures. This is Clifton Mill on the Stamford line in 1947. Timber buildings such as these were legion, and all required frequent painting and periodic repairs to timberwork.

'As a general rule, all these men are allowed one shilling a night lodging allowance, in some districts when they are working away from their homes. But in other districts where the men are attached to a depot, that lodging allowance is only paid them when they are working away from their depot; but taking the whole of the districts

throughout I have only come across a few instances where a man is deprived of his lodging allowance both when away from home and when away from the depot.

'After travelling home on the Saturday you will find that on that day they are more intent upon spending their earnings by marketing with their wives; but where the harvest days come in I have known cases where you get a gang of men working in country districts in harvest time. There is nothing else for them to do after they have finished work at half past five. They are practically living in the middle of the cornfields or harvest fields, and they turn to and help the farmer,

and get paid for it. I do not think there is very much of it done, but it is done.'

Williams' observations here are of particular interest, as the LNWR rule book forbade servants of the Company from working for anyone else, and clearly he was ready to turn a blind eye to the non-observance of the rule by the extra men, on account of their fluctuating employment! When asked about it, he could hardly admit that as an officer of the Company he approved of rule breaking, and when asked if the men were bound by the same conditions of service as the men in the other grades to devote the whole of their time to the Company, he replied, 'Well, the whole time while they are on duty'. It is not the first occasion that we have seen senior North Western officers — by their own admission — turning a blind eye to disregard of rules where it would have been harsh to enforce them.

One of the most interesting aspects of Williams' evidence is that with only quite minor contributions from pw staff, his summary of pw duties was accepted as readily by men as by management as a basis for the Wages Arbitration to be settled upon. It must be rare that management's version of working conditions is accepted by the men as a large part of their case, and says much for Williams' standing amongst his pw staff.

Of the other evidence, the most interesting came from John Camp, who joined the LNWR in 1898 as a labourer in one of the extra gangs, but was rapidly brought into one of the regular gangs, and by 1900 had worked up to 25 shillings, and in 1907 became sub-ganger of the Broad Street gang at 26/6d. There were four men in the gang, which covered the North London section as far as Willesden; the ganger drew 32/6d, making him one of the top 20 gangers on the North Western. Much of John Camp's time was taken up at Broad Street goods depot, which, with high land values in London, was a two-level yard, with reception and sorting sidings at the same level as the adjoining North London Railway passenger station, and with the goods depot below these sidings, and reached via wagon hoists. Camp had some amusing exchanges concerning Broad Street yard with C.E. Grasemann, who was of course the LNWR 'Outdoor' Goods Manager.

Grasemann: You work in Broad Street Goods station; the work is not absolutely continuous is it?

Camp: Yes it is continuous; in wet weather we have always a job underneath.

Grasemann: In wet weather you can work undercover? This is not the case for the playelayers working away from a station. In those cases, as soon as it begins to rain they take shelter?

Camp: If it rains sufficiently hard.

Grasemann: Do you mean to tell me that you are really hard at it all the time at Broad Street? I was stationed there for some years before your time, and I used to spend quite half my time going around the station, and I used to see considerable intervals in the actual work while wagons were being shunted and while lifts were being lowered or raised, and while capstan working was going on.

Camp: There are slight times, but most of our jobs we work where we find a vacant space. Take my own case. For the last month we have been on a job with my foreman where we could not stand still a matter of five minutes all day, because we were cleaning out checks [removing debris, straw, manure etc from the flangeways of inset track], and then we have to go and find a place where there is a vacancy, and we sweep it out and take it away and then we go and find another spot.

John Camp's job as a platelayer, retiring to the dark recesses of the lower level of Broad Street goods depot whenever it rained, is scarely typical of the North Western platelayer's life, but provides a delightful postscript to his chief's exceptionally detailed account of his department.

13 The Goods Department

In 1913, the LNWR moved 57½ million tons of freight, more than half of which originated on the system. To handle this avalanche of business, the Company employed an army of goods guards and breaksmen, shunters, goods porters, loaders, checkers, yardsmen and so on. We have explored the duties of some of these men already, but in this chapter we will look at the men handling the freight itself. There were over 30 grades, some with thousands of men in them and others, such as the warehousemen, of whom there were just 67 on the entire system in 1908.

The goods system revolved around the goods shed teams of porter, loader, caller-off and checker. On the bottom rung was the porter, earning 19 to 21 shillings a week, and who would bring goods, usually by barrow, to and from the wagons or road vehicles. Careful stowage of merchandise was vital for a multitude of reasons. Heavy articles could not be loaded on top of crushable ones; fragile articles needed to be protected from transit shocks; items which might leak if tipped up had to be loaded to obviate such risks; and goods which might spoil through leakage or contamination had to be placed well away from such packages. As it was only major centres which would have direct wagon services, transhipping was common, and items which required to be removed from a wagon in the early stages of its journey could not be trapped behind those to come out later on. The job of loading a wagon might best be likened to assembling a three-dimensional jigsaw puzzle without the pieces having a helpful pattern, or necessarily even fitting together perfectly! Some freight moved at Owner's risk, but other items moved at the Company's Risk, so that mistakes could be costly, and at an early date the railways realized that the safe and efficient packing of wagons could not be left to junior porters. A skilled grade of men, known on the North Western as loaders, came into existence. In the early 1900s, a loader earned 19 to 24 shillings a week.

Important though it was to keep the goods safe, and to make efficient use of wagon space, as a poorly-loaded wagon with a small load cost as much to run as a well-laden one, it was equally vital to keep track of the individual consign-ments, and in the first instance, this was the duty of the caller-off, who read out the labels on the goods and their destinations. Again it was a responsible job, for labels were not always well written, and there was the risk of old labels being left on consignments. The caller-off received similar wages to the loader. At the head of the team was the checker, who had the goods invoices before him, and who checked the details of the consignments in the wagon against his paperwork. Checkers received 26 or 27 shillings a week.

At a major depot, such as Curzon St, Birmingham, there could be 30 such teams. Until the early 1900s, there were usually five men in a gang but, with fluctuating levels of traffic, the North Western found it more economical to reorganize the gangs and take on extra men at the depot gates to cover busy days. This was none too popular with the regular men, as the extra men, though frequently employed, were not a part of the gang, nor usually as efficient. The gangs worked a nominal 72-hour week, of which 12 hours were allowed for meal breaks. At some depots, meal breaks for each gang were laid down, but at Curzon St it was at the discretion of the deputy foreman, who would release gangs when he could, ideally for two relief periods of one hour each day. At Curzon St, the LNWR employed around 500 men, about a quarter of whom were in the gangs, the rest being employed on a multitude of other duties, including spare porters.

The Crewe trans-ship shed, with 400 men, was another key point on the LNWR, and opened in February 1901. Harry Kennerdale, who worked there as a caller-off, explained his duties in more detail. When loading wagons, he had to look at all labels and call them out to the checker, then hand the goods to the loader for stowage. When unloading wagons, he received goods from the loader, called out the marks and passed them to the porter. The gangs worked alternate day and night shifts each week with a hand-over at 6.00 am and 6.00 pm. To allow for Sunday working, the hours, although nominally 60-72 were slightly shorter, as the shift going on duty at 6.00 pm on Saturday night knocked off at 3.45 am with 1¾ hours for meals, making eight hours of duty that time. Promotion to caller-off or loader could be quite rapid, and Harry Kennerdale, who started as a porter at 19 shillings a week, had become a caller-off at 23 shillings in under four years. He also participated in the bonus system, which was introduced about 1902.

Thomas Shaw, District Goods Manager at Liverpool in 1908, explained the workings of the bonus system. This was based upon an additional payment to each gang after a specified tonnage had been loaded during their shift. The thresholds varied from depot to depot, and in Harry Kennerdale's case, it worked out at 5/8d per week in 1907-8, though this was unusually high. Of the 5,500 men in the regular gangs, Shaw noted that 2,600, mostly at the large depots, were on the bonus system, and that average payments had been 3/3d per man per week. Shaw's explanation of how the system worked is interesting. 'It has had the effect of shortening the hours and curtailing the overtime. This is one of the most satisfactory features of the bonus system. Prior to its introduction we used to incur a considerable amount of overtime, but now the men put their backs into the work. They are relieved to a great extent of disagreeable supervision by the foreman; they do not have to be urged; they are their own foremen to a great extent, and more than that, they use their heads in the work. They economize their labour in trucking. Instead of a man taking a package down to one of the loading berths, and then another package down to another loading berth, the packages are better grouped, so that they take two to one loading berth and two to another. They do not make so many waste journeys... within the last few weeks at one station where we have 183 men working on the bonus system, the rumour prevailed at that station that the bonus system was going to be abolished. I received a memorial signed by 172 out of the 183 men emphatically protesting against the abolition of the bonus system.'

Problems arose in applying the bonus to smaller depots. District officers such as Thomas Shaw had considerable authority in correcting anomalies, and there was a headquarters officer available to assist the district officers in assessing fair yardsticks.

Shaw's comments about recruitment and promotion are informative: 'The porters are recruited as far as we can from the agricultural labourer class. That is the type of man we prefer to get if we can, with one reservation, that we give preference to ex-soldiers and sailors. From the ranks of the porters we select the men who are shown to be careful, and of good conduct, and we make them loaders and checkers, and we select our capstanmen and shunt horse drivers under the same qualifications. The shunt horse drivers, of course, have had a previous acquaintance with horses... We try as far as we can, to make the staff a permanent one. We prefer to have men who are employed permanently by us, but the work at the goods stations, and particularly in large places, varies very much from one day to another. I may quote Liverpool. I should first of all say that Liverpool is perhaps an extreme case. The work at our large goods stations varies by as much as from 25 to 30 per cent from one day to another. You will have at a large station let us say on Tuesday 600 tons; on Wednesday it may be 800 tons; on Thursday it may drop again to 600 tons, and in order to cope with the variation of traffic, we have to employ a certain margin of extra men who are engaged day by day.

'We employ in the Goods Department a considerable number of boys to act as cart boys, messengers and so forth. When those boys reach the age of 17 or 18, they become rather a problem. They are too old for boys' work, and they are not fit for men's work. My experience tells me that generally speaking a man is not fully grown and not fit for man's work until 21. It is a very exceptional thing if we engage a man less than 21 and start him as a porter, a *very* exceptional thing. As I have said, these youths are rather a problem, and taking my own district I could in many cases, with advantage to the company, on the mere question of money, have dispensed with the services of those youths at the age of 17 or 18. I have no further use for them as boys and they are not fit for men's work, but we have kept them on because we thought they might grow into suitable men, and we felt that it would be hard to turn them adrift. We give a graduating increase of wages up to the age of 21. We do pay off the lads who are clearly not going to grow up into healthy men, but taking my own district, we always give them a very considerable notice they they will have to leave the service. We give them three or four months

LONDON AND NORTH WESTERN RAILWAY.

GOODS DEPARTMENT.

Park Lane and Wapping Station,

LIVERPOOL, *July 15th 1901*

Dear Sir,

I am looking forward to spending a fortnight's holiday in the Island, at the beginning of August, after several years absence, and should be pleased if you could procure me a pass over your system for myself & wife.

I am chief delivery clerk at this Station and handle nearly all the goods &c, traffic that passes through Liverpool

If you could grant me this favor, I should be greatly obliged.

Thanking you in anticipation

I am,

Yours truly

Robt W Gillies

notice. Whenever we think they are likely to develop we keep them. They are put to junior porters' work, covering a variety of grades. To do goods porters' work would be quite exceptional. We fit them into grades such as number-takers, putting labels on wagons, and a variety of things. We have two kinds of number-takers, junior and senior.'

Periodically, it was necessary to put men in higher grades temporarily, and Thomas Shaw explained how this worked, and also the training methods. 'The rule has been laid down that differences of pay should not be given for work lasting less than a week in the higher grade. I am speaking now of the Goods Department of course. In some cases it is given for less than a week, and discretion is left to the district officer. One reason [for the difference with other departments, where the rule was to pay for all work at a higher grade] is that a number of these higher

Left *In pre-Grouping days, the railway companies, great and small, extended free pass facilities to the senior officers of other companies. Passes would be issued to District Officers without hesitation, but the further down the tree, the greater was the need for an individual to put up a convincing reason. Robert Gillies, the Chief Delivery Clerk at Park Lane, Liverpool, wrote to G. H. Wood, the Manager of the Isle of Man Railway, in 1901. He got his pass!*

Below *Goods shed teams spent their working lives amongst opens such as 42375, a standard 10-ton wagon. At some stage, this particular wagon was labelled for coal traffic, and the '10 TONS COAL WAGON' inscription is just visible.*

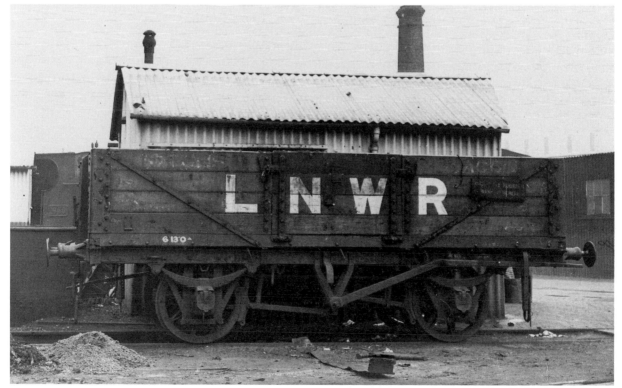

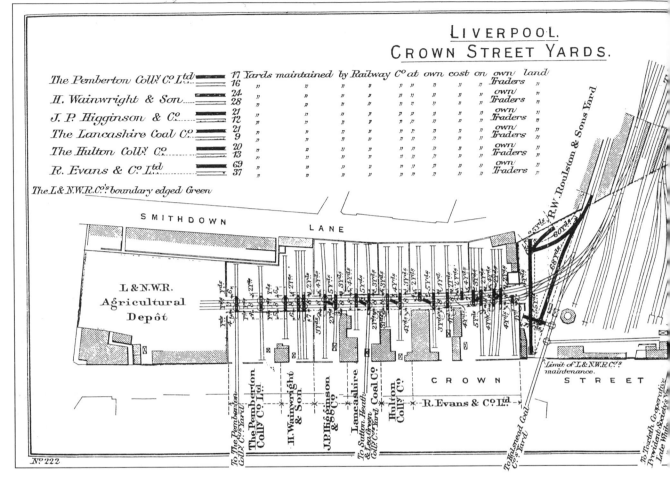

grades are performing work which does not call for skill, but only for care, and they have been given to men of long service and good conduct. Another reason is that we put men to such work as loading and checking, or tallying goods, and so on, in order to give them the experience that is necessary. May I give you an instance of how unfair I think it would be if a man put to higher duty was always given the higher rate of pay. We have a grade called searchers. They are employed in the large goods sheds in looking for missing packages and making inquiries; they are men of considerable experience. We pay them pretty high rates of pay — the maximum for the large towns is 35 shillings. We not infrequently put a porter who is perhaps getting 22 shillings a week to do the work of a searcher to train him, but that man is not so efficient, nor anything like, as the man whose place he takes. He takes a much longer time in his enquiries, and we do not attach the same responsibility to him. The searchers work up from 27/6d to 35 shillings. We

should pay a porter after a week's service, generally 25 shillings. Provided the man is intelligent we put him to that work to allow him to show us what he can do. We take frequent opportunities of testing any likely man to see whether he is intelligent and hard working. If he proves so, we keep our eye on him with a view to promoting him through the other grades ultimately to the position of a foreman. Every reasonable allowance would be made for his inexperience. He would certainly not be held responsible in the same way that we would hold an experienced searcher responsible, provided he showed us that he had tried his best.'

Much of the inwards goods was transferred by the four-man gangs from the wagons straight to the cart bays for loading on the lurries (a railwayman's term for an open horse-drawn cart, also used by permanent way men for their trolley), but other items were stored to await collection. With the ever-present risk of pilferage from items left unattended for some days, warehouse-

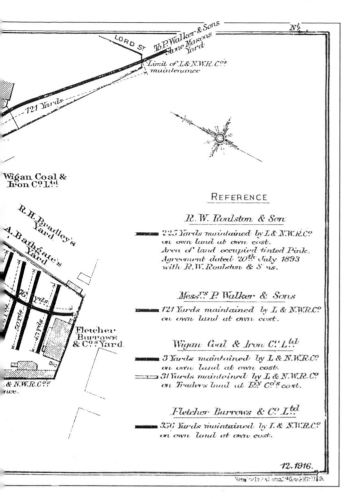

Liverpool Crown Street was one of the most important historical sites on the entire North Western system, for it formed a part of the original Liverpool & Manchester Railway, and predated Lime Street by some years. This plan, reproduced from an official LNWR drawing, comes from the Lancashire District (South of Preston) private sidings book. These diagrams, although not always to scale, are accurate enough for most purposes, and always retain an excellent sense of proportion. On this cramped site between Crown Street and Smithdown Lane, the LNWR squeezed in an agricultural depot, a string of coal depots, connections to other private sidings off the site, including a stone mason's, and a set of general sidings. Comprehensive details are given on maintenance responsibilities. Over 30 wagon turntables existed in this one depot!

men were appointed at larger depots to take charge of stored traffic. In 1908 there were just 67 warehousemen on the whole system, 24 of whom were in Manchester. John Neil, who joined the North Western as a porter at £1 a week in about 1876, was one of them. In his youth, the standard week had been 56½ hours, but in about 1879 the hours were revised to 60 working hours (plus meal times). Neil had joined the LNWR at a time when the cost of living and wage rates were actually declining, due to low-cost grain and meat imports from America and Australia, etc, and within a short while the starting wage for porters had been cut to 19 and then 18 shillings. Although Neil retained his wages, and it was only the newer men who had the lower rates, the ancient grievances was recalled vividly 30 years later. Part of the cuts were made made good in 1889-90, and the balance about 1897. He described his duties as a warehouseman as 'one who takes charge of certain classes of goods subject to his care. He keeps a book of account of

what he receives, and he also keeps an account of what he delivers; he receives checks for anything he has to deliver, and is responsible in case anything goes wrong. He is expected to know what he is doing, and to be left in full charge.' There were seven warehousemen at Liverpool Road depot, Manchester, each having his own secure locked store, and handling one type of traffic — in Neil's case Great Western Railway traffic. The GWR collected its own goods in Manchester, but had an arrangement, as Neil explained: 'The North Western do their storage at Manchester; we store for the Great Western. It is kept separate in a part of the warehouse set aside.'

Except for spare porters sent to help them barrow goods, the warehousemen had no staff of their own, and as goods were only taken to or from the store in business hours, they worked a 6.00 am–6.00 pm turn, with 10½ hours actual duty Monday to Friday, and 7 hours on Saturday. The maximum wage was 27 shillings per week.

In 1908, the Manchester goods staff put forward a wages claim higher than any other goods staff on the North Western, with John Neil as one of their spokesmen. The result was high comedy.

Grasemann: Can you explain why the Manchester programme is on a higher basis than for the rest of the line? Is there anything in the work in Manchester which causes you to ask for a higher maximum rate of pay than for similar workers on all other parts of the line?

Neil: It is not on account of the work.

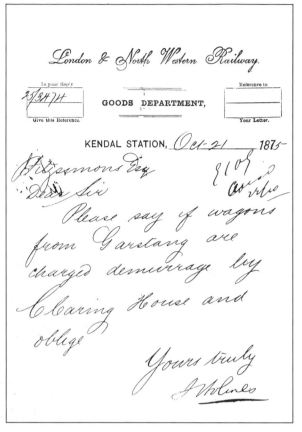

Above *A plaintive cry as to what to do with wagons from the impecunious Garstang & Knott End Railway!*

Right *Apart from general freight, the North Western handled a vast tonnage of coal. Coal yards, such as here at Coundon Road on the Coventry–Nuneaton line, made provision for the coal merchants.*

Below *Propping of wagon doors, for use as shovelling and unloading platforms, led to many accidents, hence this notice.*

Fry:	What is it on account of?
Neil:	It is because we live in a different part of England, where rents are higher and coal is dearer, and everything, of course, applies to a man who lives in a civilized city. His wants are greater than they are in country places where they can spend their time in digging potatoes.
Fry:	Do you mean it is not civilized to live in the country?
Neil:	In some parts it is not civilized.
Fry:	Some of us who live in the country think it is civilized.
Neil:	I do not think they are.

Fry: Is it the superiority of the City of Manchester that requires higher wages?

Neil: Yes.

Grasemann, who must have found it increasingly difficult to keep a straight face during this exchange, enquired mildly, 'We will assume that Manchester is the most civilized place in England. As a Londoner may I claim a certain amount of civilization for the Metropolis? I would like you to compare London with Manchester.' The figures hardly suggested that the cost of living was materially higher in Manchester than other big cities, and during the summing up Sir Edward Fry asked the men's chief negoti-

ator, Richard Bell, if the claim for shorter hours was 'on the ground of superior civilization', Bell, who was an accomplished negotiator, and who realized the absurdity of a claim that most of the North Western men were scarcely civilized, remarked wryly, 'That has something to do with it, I suppose'. We may conclude the story by remarking that in his 1909 wages award, Sir Edward Fry ruled that 72 hours per week, less *three* hours each day, be the standard week for goods staff elsewhere than in Manchester. This went some way to meeting the overall wish for a reduction in hours, but he went on to rule, tongue-in-cheek, 'That the standard hours of a week's work be the same in Manchester as elsewhere on the line'.

Other grades to be found in a large depot included yard loaders, whose job entailed loading heavy goods off the lurries in the open. Usually these would be full wagon loads which required a good deal of handling, such as flour or iron, or commodities such as wet hides, which were too unpleasant to handle inside the depots. Loaders were recruited from porters, and as the work was arduous and exposed to the elements, received up to 27 shillings a week. Sheeters were another group of outdoor workers, whose responsibilities were considerable, as a badly-sheeted wagon could result in water ruining the goods, or a sheet could come loose when a train was in motion and do damage or cause injury. The sheeter, as well as checking that the sheet was properly secured, had to confirm that it was sound, and not liable to leak. On large loads, he might well have to use two sheets. Goods porters, rather than sheeters, handled the less skilled task of removing sheets from incoming wagons. Mostly the work was done outside, though in inclement conditions, where loads might be spoiled within a few minutes, the sheeters were able to work under cover. They earned around 25 shillings. Scalesmen, who were responsible for weighing all traffic tendered for dispatch, were similarly paid. Although a good deal of shunting in a large yard was performed by engine power, the shunt horse and hydraulic capstan played an important role. Depots differed markedly. At Liverpool Road depot, Manchester, all shunting was by engine or hydraulic capstan. At the nearby London Road depot, there were four horse-shunters, two handling pair-horses, the others handling single horses.

Capstan-men, who worked the hydraulic capstans by means of foot treadles (some of which were said to be excessively stiff), had a dirty and unpleasant job, as the ropes, chains and hooks had to be constantly handled and stowed, and in the early days they frequently worked barehanded, until leather gloves were provided by the LNWR. Any form of rope shunting possessed risks, as a rope which broke under tension could pose a lethal threat to anyone nearby. Stringent orders were issued regarding inspection of ropes, etc, and a tackle-repairer was employed at large depots, but accidents still arose. An idea of the importance of capstan shunting may be glimpsed from a North Western analysis of 1908, which listed 94 capstan-men in the Liverpool/Birkenhead area. In the previous two years there had been 17 injuries — thankfully none fatal.

A typical scene at a busy goods depot. Note the hard-wearing granite setts and the capstans.

A LOAD OF MANCHESTER GOODS

14 The Cartage Men

The North Western cartage staff occupied a unique position within the Company, for although they were railwaymen, most of their working hours were spent away from the railway. They had an independence unknown to most railwaymen, yet they were bound by rules and conventions alien to most North Western men, and those rules and conventions could vary dramatically from town to town — indeed, they could be diametrically opposed to one another, and a carter moving from Birmingham to Liverpool or London would find the conventions he had to live by as alien as the roads he would travel. Their wages varied, their hours varied, and even the names they went by varied. In Liverpool, Manchester and Cardiff they were 'carters', yet everywhere else they were 'carmen', 'draymen' or 'lurrymen'. Two-horse men were naturally more senior than one-horse men, and it is perhaps symbolic of this strange facet of railway life that two-horse men in most provincial towns received 25 shillings a week in 1908; 26 shillings in Cardiff, 27 shillings in Manchester and 28 shillings in Liverpool.

Ernie Wale was a carman working out of Curzon St, Birmingham, in the early 1900s. He joined the North Western in July 1889, and became a carman in the mid-'nineties. His working week of 60 hours consisted of five 10½ hour days and 7½ hours on Saturdays. There were two 'shifts' at Curzon Street, the first going on duty at 7.10 am, and the second just half an hour later, at 7.40 am, both finishing at 7.00 pm, the earlier 'shift' having an hour and a half for lunch as against the hour for the second group. Ernie Wale had moved around a fair amount, having transferred from Manchester to Birmingham, with a spell in Sheffield, and had for a time been foreman at Windsor St yard, with a dozen men under him, but had applied in 1906 to revert to a carman with a reduction in wages from 30 to 24 shillings. Partly this was because of shift work which he had to do as foreman, and which was not popular due to his wife's health, and in part through the loss of side earnings — for the carters on some runs were able to supplement their wages with income from the traders. For a railway which officially frowned upon tips, this was

a remarkable situation, but was well known to management. Indeed, when Wale applied to go back to cartage duties, his boss, the Cartage Superintendent Mr Thomas, noted that: 'This was Wale's old lurry and he is confident he could regain the Sansenina Company's meat traffic if he was put on the same lurry again.' Thomas went on to note that Wale expected to get 5 shillings a week extra through the butchers!

At this time, the North Western was employing some 200-250 carmen in Birmingham, mostly one-horse men, as it was usual in the city to employ two men with a two-horse team. The most junior carters received 19 shillings a week, rising to 24 shillings, and on occasion a pair of quite junior men would be entrusted with a two-horse outfit. When working with a one-horse lurry, the carman was usually accompanied by a lad, whose normal position was at the back of the lurry to assist the carman when loading or unloading, and to stand by the horses, to comply with police rules, whilst the carman was absent. Wale recalled that there were a dozen or so carmen at Curzon St who did not have boys, and they were usually employed on 'drop loads' — in other words, a full load going to one trader's premises.

After coming on duty, the carman collected his horse from the horse-keepers and stablemen, put it into the shafts and, after assistance from the goods staff in loading the lurry, aimed to make his first calls about 8.30 am. Any earlier was unpopular with the traders. Distances travelled, and the type of load, would affect the number of trips, but three or four trips in a day was common. The maximum load for a single horse lurry was 1¾ tons. It was usual, though not invariable, for the horses to be returned to the stables for a feed during the day, the men taking their meal break at the same time.

Wale shared the hostility of many older carmen to the new-fangled internal combustion engine, complaining the roads were no longer safe, and he hated the electric cars which had replaced the old steam trams in Birmingham, commenting that 'it is much more detrimental to horseflesh, and there are more of them, and they are in more streets.'

A LOAD OF HOPS.
L & N.W. RAILWAY

Broad Street was an important goods station, and was provided with a wide variety of drays, lurries, carts and vans. This phenomenal load of hops, if not added to by photographic touching in, suggests that both horse and driver had a tiring day ahead of them!

Fred Desbonnet, who commenced as a carman in 1895, worked out of the big LNWR freight depot at Broad Street. Although the standard week for most carmen was 60 hours, working hours averaged 65-70 a week *without* overtime payments. This variable week arose through the large cartage area, and could entail up to a 13-hour day, Desbonnet remarking that 'it is according to the distance a man has to go after completion of his delivery that he puts the other hours in'. In contrast to Curzon St with its two shifts, Broad Street had three general traffic shifts, commencing at 7.30 am, 8.00 am and 9.00 am, and the market shift who came on at any time between midnight and 4.00 am. In the event of exceptionally heavy fish, fruit or meat traffic, some of the general merchandise men might be temporarily assigned to the markets. In contrast to Curzon St, where it was usual for horse and men to return to the stables for their midday meal, this was rare in London. Sometimes the horse would stand in the station yard 'with the bag on', but frequently the break would

be taken in the street or on the dock or wharf.

This totally different working pattern arose through the difference in traffic and other conditions in Birmingham and London. Although the streets of Birmingham were often busy, congestion was far worse in London, particularly for the Broad Street men, who handled much of the work to and from the docks. One problem was the sheer number of railways in London, for with around ten main lines, each of which might well load a van to an important customer, delays were endemic. When the firm's own vans, and outside carters bringing in goods from the docks or markets, were added, queues of 15 or 20 carts waiting to get to the unloading bays were not uncommon at large firms such as Rylands or Morleys. It was 'first come, first served', so that the earlier shifts had the best chance of prompt attention, but even then things could go wrong. Fred Desbonnet, who was often in at 7.00 am rather than the nominal 7.30 start, was sometimes on the road by 7.40, and on occasion could arrive at a warehouse before 8.00 am, and still wait an hour for his turn. In the docks and at the markets it was far worse, and delays at Billingsgate in a single week included 4 hours, 5 hrs 30 mins, 7 hrs 40 mins, 7 hrs 30 mins, 3 hrs 55 mins and an 8 hrs 55 mins record performance!

Whilst side money from the market holders was some compensation, the delays were irksome, as the chances of a ten-hour day vanished with six, seven or eight-hour detentions, as did any prospect of tonnage money. This was a bonus system, in which the carman received 8d per ton after hauling a specific tonnage. At Broad Street, this was usually four or five tons in the day. Congestion was such that Fred Desbonnet seldom earned his bonus. What was particularly annoying was when the day had started well but there had been a long detention on the last round before the tonnage money would begin. The delays and traffic congestion also explained the adoption of the open-ended day; indeed, the North Western defended it as vital given the conditions. Another curious example of local conditions varying was that whilst carmen did not deliver upstairs or downstairs in Birmingham and most provincial towns after about 1900, this persisted in London, and Fred Desbonnet recalled instances of having to take goods to the fourth or fifth floor of the large warehouses. Theoretically it was not a part of their duties, and the most that a refusal would have earned was a mild comment from their boss that they might have obliged the firm concerned, but given the competition in London between the main line companies, it was an accepted practice. Another curious difference between London and Birmingham was that the single-horse load was 1¾ tons in Birmingham, but 2 tons at Broad Street.

John Griffiths was a carman at Manchester, and his remarks provide a fascinating insight into stable arrangements, and virtually unknown working arrangements between the North Western and the Lancashire & Yorkshire. Griffiths had joined the LNWR about 1890 as a goods porter, earning 19 shillings a week. After two years, he became a junior carman at 21 shillings, working up to 25 shillings after four years, at which rate he stuck for more than a decade. Ostlers or stablemen got 21 to 23 shillings a week, and the more responsible horse-keepers about 24 shillings. The horse-keepers spent much of their time dealing with sick animals, and if a carman was not satisfied about his animal when he arrived, he would report to the horse-keeper, who would examine it to see if it was fit for work. Some of the more experienced horse-keepers earned 26 shillings a week. Nowadays we look back on Victorian and Edwardian times as a period of great cruelty to horses, with the van, lurry or dray horses often being worked until they collapsed. Whilst this was true of the smaller carters and sundry merchants who often bought old horses cheaply and worked them to death, surviving accounts suggest that the railway companies were much better. A bedraggled animal, or worse still, one dead in the shafts, was no advert, so the railways tended to buy young animals and break them in. They were expensive, and commonsense demanded reasonable treatment.

Another depot job was that of the van-setter, who led the lurries to the loading stages, would lead them away for collection by the carman, and would not normally go outside the station at all. Most interesting of all were the combine men who collected on behalf of the LNWR and LYR. They usually worked in pairs, one from each company, collecting for both lines, and would meet at an agreed point to trans-ship goods. Sometimes this was a station yard, but quite often a convenient by-street, when the two men might have to shift heavy crates, weighing up to a quarter of a ton. At Manchester London Road there were around 30 combine men, with others at Liverpool Road.

On Merseyside a tradition of horse handling grew up which was quite different from the rest of the country. Instead of carmen or lurrymen, they answered to the name of carters, and many were independent hauliers belonging to the prestigious Master Carters Association, which in the early 1900s represented about four-fifths of the non-railway carters. The railwaymen carved out their own unique terms, which prompted C.E. Grasemann, the LNWR Outdoor Goods Manager, to remark that 'In Liverpool, the Carters are a quite peculiar race, different from anybody else all over the country, I should say from what I have heard and seen. They take a very great pride in their horses and are an exceptionally good body of employees altogether. They have always been in the habit of looking after their own horses, and I do not think a Liverpool carter would like to give that up. It has been in connection with that, that they have had higher wages than anyone else.'

Robert Jones was one of that 'peculiar race'. Unlike most centres, where junior carmen received a lower wage, the Liverpool carters went straight on to the 26 shillings rate the day they started, the only other rate being the 28 shillings of the two-horse men. Although van boys were usual in other towns, Liverpool carters (and horses) scorned such luxuries, and Robert Jones, at the Dock station, spoke of just one lad, who would accompany the carter on any very long runs out of town, or with special loads. The Liverpool men worked a more complex roster than was usual. Jones would commence at 7.00 am one week, working until seven in the evening, and start half an hour later the next week, and so on until he was turning out for a 10.30 am-10.30 pm shift. Overtime — except for stable duty — was paid at 6½d an hour. Grasemann noted in 1908 that of the 180 LNWR carters in Liverpool, less than half had worked overtime, and that had been no more than an hour a week.

The most unusual feature of the Liverpool situation was the stable duties, with the men coming on duty, technically without pay, to tend their horses. To save every man from coming in each Sunday, the men in each stable block would come to an agreement. The usual block at the Dock station held six horses, with four carters attached to it, with four taking it in turns week by week, giving one Sunday on duty in four. The horses needed tending twice — at around 7.30 to 8.30 in the morning, and 3.30 to 4.30 in the afternoon. Jones reckoned it took him around two hours each visit to look after his six horses, and that he in fact came in one Sunday in five. Jones also recalled that there would be seven or so men coming in to the docks on Sundays.

The massive complex of docks on both sides of the river dominated the Mersey scene, and with goods depots on the Wirral and the Lancashire sides, the LNWR was well placed to handle this business, particularly with its network of lines into central Lancashire and the West Midlands. Working in the docks was difficult and, to the inexperienced hand, dangerous.

Apart from the ships' own derricks, sheer-legs and cranes, there were the fixed and movable dockside cranes and, for really heavy lifts, the massive floating cranes. Despite this vast array of crane power, much was still done by hand, for the Mersey Docks & Harbour Board naturally charged for crane power, and many shippers opted to use sweat and brawn instead! This could lead to amusing problems, Robert Jones recalling one involving a three-ton motor vehicle in a crate, which had to be lifted by hand off his lurry. Liverpool carters may have been a tough lot, but they were not that strong, so Jones had to rope in as many other North Western men from his home depot as he could find in the vicinity before they tackled the job! Technically it was not their responsibility, but they knew that sooner or later it would be their turn to wrestle with a 15-foot long crate. With an extensive dock railway system on both sides of the river, there was the risk of an argument in which the cart would come off worst with an engine or wagons, and Jones commented wryly: 'We have to keep a very shrewd lookout for those locomotives.'

The life of a carman or carter, out in all weathers and usually with little more than a leather apron and heavy coat to keep out the rain and cold, was a tough one. They seldom complained of the spartan conditions; indeed, the internal combustion engine or electric tramcar were far more vexatious to them! They were a vital link in railway freight services, but other than for the occasional lurry on a model railway, are all but forgotten by today's enthusiast. The world in which they lived, with its differing rules and conventions, was as unfamiliar to the authors as it will have been to most readers when they commenced this study of life on the LNWR. We hope the reader will find the voyage of discovery as fascinating as we did.

15 Gilbert Claughton — Peacemaker

Railway history and folklore abounds with the stories of inter-company battles in Parliament for traffic and prestige and, on occasion, even physical brawls. This is one aspect of the railway story, but there is another, seldom remembered side to railway history. This was the close co-operation which grew up between the companies through the Railway Clearing House and the Railway Companies' Association. The RCH is the best known, as it was involved in the production of station handbooks, railway maps and so on, some of which have been reprinted for the enthusiast in recent times. The Railway Companies' Association, is, by contrast, a far more shadowy body, yet it was within the RCA, where deadly rivals met in harmony, that matters of common policy were thrashed out. North Western officers played a key role in the affairs of the RCA over the decades, and an account of LNWR involvement would be virtually equivalent to a history of the Association.

However, there is one episode where the LNWR role was so crucial and which relates so closely to the theme of this book, that we may move to the wider world of Britain's railways for a few pages. In November 1907, as we have seen, the principal railways established a conciliation and arbitration system with the amalgamated Society of Railway Servants, and this was the basis of the 1908 hearing before Sir Edward Fry. Other companies established similar structures, which were to last for seven years, but by 1910-11 there was widespread dissatisfaction, partly due to over-ambitious demands by union leaders, and partly through the inherent slowness of the system, coupled with intransigence by some managers. A series of disjointed strikes in the summer of 1911 prompted the four leading unions to seek Board of Trade intervention, and when this failed, an official strike was called on 17 August. Government fears of sympathy action, and pressure upon union leaders and management, resulted in a successful 'armistice' meeting on 19 August, the RCA being represented by the LNWR Chairman, Gilbert Claughton, and the Midland Railway manager, Sir Guy Granet.

A Royal Commission was hurriedly set up to look into the workings of the 1907 conciliation scheme, and after a major debate in the Commons on 22 November 1911, the Board of Trade invited the unions and the RCA to send delegates to a conference. The BOT wrote to Claughton and Granet a few days later, and an emergency meeting of the RCA council was summoned for 1 December, held at the LNWR Westminster office at 35 Parliament Street. Although the Liberal Prime Minister, Herbert Asquith, had said that both sides would have to accept the Royal Commission's findings in principle and substance, some of the RCA council were suspicious, Sir Frederick Banbury of the GNR being very dubious. Colonel A.R.M. Lockwood, a North Western Director and also an MP, was able to allay fears on this ground, ably assisted by a fellow MP, Stuart Wortley, of the Great Central. After a long discussion, in which Gilbert Claughton played a major role, the meeting was agreed to, and on 6 December the RCA Council met once more to appoint a team to represent the railway companies. The list of Council members present at the meeting, railway Chairmen, Directors and General Managers, reads like a 'Who's Who' of leading railway figures of the day, and of those 19 council members, more than a third were to give their names to locomotives, Sir Alexander Henderson and Sam Fay of the GCR; Lord Claud Hamilton of the GER; Sir Frederick Banbury, of the GNR; Viscount Churchill of the GWR; the Earl of Bessborough for the LB & SCR; and Gilbert Claughton and Frank Ree of the LNWR. The LNWR input was even more impressive, for apart from Claughton and Ree, the LNWR solicitor, C. de J. Andrewes was present, together with Herbert Walker, then still with the LNWR but soon to become General Manager of the LSWR, and I.T. Williams, a future General Manager of the North Western!

Lord Claud Hamilton suggested that Claughton and Granet, who had attended the earlier discussions, attend, but as delegates rather than plenipotentiaries, with authority to bind the companies. The Great Northern remained dubious, and Claughton pointed out that the Government was obliged to recognize that the conference could only take place if the report was accepted by both sides. 'If this is not clearly agreed to, I will be the first to break up the conference.' Herbert Walker, who had been involved in the LNWR arbitration hearings in 1908, and in the preliminary meetings in August 1911, was recommended as secretary. Lord Allerton of the GNR felt that two Council members was not sufficient, and that Sir Alexander Henderson, the GCR Chairman, should be present as well. Henderson declined, but added that unless the Great Central was represented by its Manager, Sam Fay, they would withdraw. Considerable doubt existed as to whether the unions would agree to accept the report, but Claughton personally offered to clear up the point before the conference began. The RCA team was finally settled as Gilbert Claughton, Guy Granet, Sam Fay and Herbert Walker.

A fascinating sidelight is that at the time only Granet had received a knighthood; within a few years, all of that quartet would have been so honoured. At the meeting the following day, Claughton raised the question over acceptance and received an assurance. The RCA Council met again the following afternoon, and Gilbert Claughton outlined the events of the morning, which had gone quite well. As many issues involved points of detail, a committee of managers and senior officers was set up to assist Claughton and Granet. Herbert Walker was a natural choice for the committee but, somewhat embarrassingly, his name appeared ahead of his own General Manager, Frank Ree. Within 24 hours, I.T. Williams had been co-opted to the committee, and when it met on the following day, 8 December, this led to the paradox that in a committee representing all the railways of England, Scotland and Wales, over a fifth of those present were North Western men! The LNWR team, of Claughton, Walker, Ree, Williams and the solicitor Andrewes, outnumbered the entire contingents fielded by the Great Northern, Great Central and Great Eastern put together!

The delegates met the union team again, also on 8 December, this time at the Charing Cross Hotel, and most points of detail were thrashed out. Some suspicions remained on both sides, for the unions had initially rejected the report, and then accepted it, whilst the Irish railway companies' action in telegraphing their opposition to any discussions at all had not helped matters either! Employment of casual or extra staff

remained a thorny subject, and as this had been a key issue in the summer dispute, it had to be resolved, although, paradoxically, it was outside the terms of the official Report. Claughton, Granet and Fay had declined to discuss the issue without RCA approval, but were unanimous that some commitment in principle should be given to the unions, as this would help the negotiations. George Armytage, Chairman of the LYR, suggested that the delegates might intimate that some leading companies would agree, but Gilbert Claughton felt a more tangible promise was essential, and suggested that he and his colleagues would agree on behalf of their own companies, and promise to use their good offices with the others. This was agreed by the RCA Council. With that issue out of the way, Claughton, Granet, Fay and Walker met the union team once more, and signed a new agreement. It is indicative of the role played by the LNWR in resolving the railway dispute, that the initial breakthrough was made by Gilbert Claughton of the North Western and Guy Granet, and in the final deal two of the four railway signatories were North Western men, Gilbert Claughton and Herbert Walker. It is also fascinating to recall that the leading member of the ASRS team, Albert Bellamy, has already made his appearance in these pages, and a North Western driver at Stockport. The agreement, of 11 December 1911, restored peace to the railway industry, and as Claughton was to remark the following day at a further RCA Council meeting, the 'good offices' clause had been critical. 'This has given great satisfaction to the Union leaders, and will be of assistance to them in the somewhat difficult position in which they must find themselves. It has also raised hopes which it would be impolitic to disappoint.'

Many years previously, Richard Moon had stressed the sacrosanct nature of the word of a North Western officer, and Claughton went on to remind the RCA council that they would need to consider how the companies should discuss the matter, 'in order that the delegates may have an opportunity of fulfilling the pledge which we have given. I would also ask whether any Companies, whose representatives are present at the meeting, find themselves in a position to agree to the proposed arrangement.'

Claud Hamilton of the Great Eastern agreed immediately, quickly followed by the SECR and

Above Sir Gilbert Claughton — *the engine* — *just ex-works in January 1913 and prior to running her trials or full painting. She has the original square-cornered buffer beams, lamp sockets and no cover for the reversing gear.* (Authors' Collection, from LNWR official print)

Below *Gilbert Claughton — the man. Claughton, whose father had been Bishop of St Albans, served an apprenticeship with Beyer Peacock, became agent to the Earl of Dudley and joined the LNWR Board in 1905. He was Chairman from 1911 until his death in 1921.*

LSWR representatives, whilst Alexander Henderson of the GCR proposed that the matter be put to the General Managers' Conference at the Clearing House, his resolution stating that the GER, SECR, and LSWR had already adopted the arrangements agreed by the LNWR, Midland and GCR! Predictably, it was a North Western man who seconded the resolution, Frank Ree.

George Armytage, chairman of the RCA, moved a vote of thanks to the three delegates and Herbert Walker, and it must have given them particular pleasure that the seconder was Henry Cosmo Bonsor, chairman of the SECR, for less than a fortnight earlier he had been totally opposed to the idea. 'As the one member who had dissented from the decision to accept the invitation of the Board of Trade, I feel a particular pleasure in seconding the resolution. Had I foreseen the ability and success with which the proceedings have been conducted, my dissenting vote might never have been given.'

The 1911 agreement led to the introduction of a modified version of the original conciliation scheme, and extensive discussions took place in the spring and summer of 1912 to get the new schemes and wages in operation. It was to form the basis upon which the LNWR spent the last years of peace, and, indeed, the conciliation system was used with considerable success to cope with the difficult conditions of war, with rapid inflation, shortages of staff, unskilled labour and a host of other problems. In February 1914, Robert Turnbull, who had taken over temporarily as General Manager upon Frank Ree's death in office, issued the collected conditions of service of the LNWR staff. They run to over 140 pages, but a few sample pages reveal what working conditions were like in the last days before war came to the North Western.

A 1

London and North Western Railway.

LOCOMOTIVE DEPARTMENT.

RATES OF WAGES, HOURS OF LABOUR, AND CONDITIONS OF SERVICE OF :—

ENGINE DRIVERS AND FIREMEN.

1. RATES OF WAGES.

The rates of Wages are as follow :—

ENGINE DRIVERS

Will be paid at the rates applicable to the class of work they are regularly appointed to do, as set forth below :—

	Per day of 10 hours.
	s. d.
Main Line Express Passenger Trains	8 0
Main Line Ordinary Passenger Trains	
Local Passenger Trains—Booking-off Jobs	
Main Line Goods, &c., Trains	7 6
Local Goods, &c., Trains—Booking-off Jobs	
Local Passenger Trains	
Local Goods, &c., Trains	
Taking Engines to or from the Works with Break-van attached	7 0
Banking	
Ballasting	6 6
Mixed Goods Shunting and Local Trips specially rated ...	6 6
	6 0
Shunting	
Relievers within Station limits	
Taking Engines to and from the Works	
" Learning the Road "—by Extra Engine Drivers	6 0
Piloting—by Extra Engine Drivers	
Piloting—by qualified Firemen	
Piloting—by Regular Engine Drivers	Staff List Rate.
Shed Turners	36 0 per week of 54 hours.

FIREMEN.

	PER DAY OF 10 HOURS.							
	1st year.	2nd year.	3rd year.	4th year.	5th year.	6th year.	7th year	8th year, and onward.
Firemen's wages, irrespective of class of firing duty, to be	3/9	3/9	4/-	4/-	4/3	4/6	4/6	4/9
When passed as Extra Drivers, as the exigencies of the traffic require, or after 313 days' or occasions Driving Duty	4/9	4/9	4/9	5/- and onward				
When employed on Engines with Heating Surface of more than 1,500 sq. feet	3d. per day of 10 hours in addition to the above rates.							

2. HOURS OF LABOUR.

The standard hours of labour are 10 per day—60 per week. The maximum length of a turn of duty is 12 hours, including meals.

No man will be called upon to book on more than once for one day's work, except in the case of men working on the "Trip" system.

3. GUARANTEED WEEK BASED ON FOUR WEEKS' AVERAGE.

Wages for 60 hours per week, based on a four weeks' average (exclusive of Sunday Duty between 6.0 a.m. and 12.0 midnight, and Sunday Duty Allowance for the time worked between 12.0 midnight Saturday and 6.0 a.m. Sunday, together with any Overtime Allowance for time worked on the hour basis over 60 hours within the wages week) will be paid to all Engine Drivers and Firemen provided they are available for duty throughout the period and that the traffic is not disorganised or in any way disturbed by strikes. Each week to stand by itself as regards overtime.

Where a Driver or Fireman is not available for duty owing to sickness or leave for one or more days in any one week of the four comprising a period, any time short of 180 hours in the other three weeks will be paid him, but if he is not available for one or more days (holidays excepted) in any two weeks of a period, he will be excluded when making up the time for four weeks.

Regular Extra Drivers (*i.e.*, men marked regularly on the Working Sheet in the Extra Link) if short of the guaranteed number of hours for a period, will be paid for such time at not less than the rate of 6/- per day.

4. REST.

The minimum interval for rest between two turns of duty is nine hours, except in case of emergency, which will be decided by the responsible Officer of the Company, and in that case the time worked before the expiration of nine hours will be paid for at the rate of time and a half.

5. METHOD OF PAYMENT.

When on a Mileage basis—

For working Mail and Express Passenger Trains ... ... } 15 miles = 1 hour, 150 = 1 day.

For working Through Goods and Mineral Trains ... ... } 12 miles = 1 hour, 120 = 1 day.

When on a "Trip" basis—

For working Local Passenger and Local Goods or Mineral Trains, and Shunting where specially arranged } An allowance in hours is fixed for the particular service performed.

When on the Hour basis—

For working Local Trips, Banking, Ballasting and Shunting ... ... { The hours actually on duty, including time standing for meals when not relieved from responsibility.

Where the Trip Rate has been sanctioned on the basis of a Train being worked by a small Engine, an extra quarter of an hour will be allowed on the Trip Rate if for any reason it is worked by a large Engine.

6. TIME WORKED OVER TRIP RATE ALLOWANCE.

In all cases where Time occupied on any Trip exceeds the time covered by the Trip Rate by 30 minutes or more, Time in lieu of Trip will be paid. If any man should earn less in a week when working on the Trip system than if paid by Time, he will be paid ordinary Time for the hours worked.

7. DIFFERENCE OF PAY (TEMPORARY DUTY).

(*a*) Regular Engine Drivers rated at less than 8/– per day, and Extra Engine Drivers if called upon to work or assist Main Line Express Passenger Trains ordinarily paid for at 8/– per day will be paid at 7/6 per day.

(*b*) Regular Engine Drivers rated at 7/– per day will be paid at their Staff List Rate when working on higher rated work, except as in (*a*).

(*c*) Regular Engine Drivers rated at less than 7/– per day and Extra Engine Drivers will be paid at the rates applicable to the work assigned to them in each case up to and including 7/– per day, but not above that rate, except as in (*a*).

Regular Drivers **temporarily** assigned to lower rated work than that on which they are ordinarily employed—

If through exigencies of Traffic, or in emergencies	
If on what would otherwise be their Shed day	Will be paid at their Staff List Rate.
If in substitution of Regular work discontinued at Holiday or other times	

Engine Drivers permanently reduced through slackness to a lower rate, will, when **temporarily** engaged in place of regular men upon work which is paid for at their old rate, or a higher one, be paid at their old Staff List Rate.

Extra Engine Drivers working in place of Regular Banking Engine Drivers will be paid at 7/– per day throughout, but when called out for special Banking they will be paid according to the class of duty performed, *i.e.*, 6/– for Shunting and Standing and 7/– for Assisting or Train work.

After a Fireman has been passed to act as an Extra Engine Driver, he will not be paid less for any firing he does than at his Staff List Rate, excepting when put back for neglect of duty or other irregularity, or proving incompetent as a Driver, in which case he will not be paid at a higher rate than 4/9 per day for firing during the time of his reduction, whatever his length of service.

Firemen with more than two years' service as such, temporarily working in the Shed as Cleaners will be paid at the rate of 21/– per week of 54 hours. Firemen with less than two years' service as such, similarly engaged, will be paid at the rate of 20/– per week of 54 hours.

Firemen occupied assisting Drivers or Turners temporarily (*i.e.*, for less than a week) on the Shed, or within the Shed Yard limits, will be paid at their Staff List Rate per day of 10 hours for such work. If they are occupied permanently as Turner's Mates (*i.e.*, for a week or more consecutively), they will be paid at the rate of 20/– or 21/– per week of 54 hours, according to their length of service as Firemen.

Firemen with less than two years' service as such, working in the Shed temporarily for not less than half a day within the wages week in place of higher rated men, will be paid an increased rate of 3/– per week as a maximum, over the Cleaners' Staff List Rate for age, but in no case exceeding the rate of the person in whose place they are temporarily working.

8. TWO RATES OF PAY IN ONE DAY.

Payment will be made at the higher rate when the preponderating hours are worked at that rate.

When the preponderating hours are at the lower rate, payment will be made at the respective rates for the work performed.

9. OVERTIME.

Time worked on the " Hour " basis, over and above 60 hours made within the wages week, exclusive of Sunday Duty, will be paid for at the rate of time and a quarter.

10. SUNDAY DUTY.

For all Time actually on duty on Sundays, *i.e.*, from 12.0 midnight Saturday to 12.0 midnight Sunday, time and a half will be paid. Men working on the "Trip" system whose duties commence on or extend over any portion of a Sunday, will have one-half of the time actually on duty on the Sunday added to the Trip Allowance.

11. CHRISTMAS DAY AND GOOD FRIDAY.

Will be reckoned as Sunday, and the time on duty on these days will be paid for in all respects the same as for Sunday Duty.

12. SPECIAL ALLOWANCES.

Men called out for duty and booked off again owing to their services not being required will be allowed a quarter of a day's pay.

Firemen who have to drop the fires of their Engines on completion of their duty will be allowed 15 minutes extra payment for the work.

13. ANNUAL HOLIDAYS WITH PAY.

Will be granted to Engine Drivers and Firemen between the months of November and October in each year at such times as will suit the work in the various Districts, as follows :—

> With one year's service and under five years' service since appointment as Extra Fireman—three days.
> With five years' service and over since appointment as Extra Fireman—one week.

14. LODGING EXPENSES.

A lodging allowance of 1/– will be paid for the first time of booking off away from home where the Company provide free lodging accommodation. If booked off duty away from home a second time, or for a period exceeding 20 hours, an allowance of 2/6 per man will be paid in addition.

15. HIGH RENT PAYMENT (LONDON DISTRICT).

Engine Drivers and Firemen in the London District will be paid a sum per week in advance of the wages paid to like men in the Country Districts, as follows :—

> Unmarried men ...   . 1/– per week,
> Married men at Willesden   ...   . 2/6   ,,
> ,,   ,, Camden   ...   . 3/–   ,,

provided that this shall not prejudice the right of the Company to advance the rents of Cottages or Houses occupied by the men, or the right of any man to agree with the Company to accept the continuance of his present rent in lieu of the said advance.

16. MARGINAL TIMES FOR PREPARING ENGINES.

The time allowed for preparing Engines for duty prior to the due time of whistling or gonging off the Shed will be—

> For Engines with a heating surface of more than 1,500 sq. ft., 60 minutes
> For all other Engines going out on Train working   45   ,,
> For all Engines for Shunting duties   30   ,,

" In accordance with the Agreement entered into between representatives of the Company and representatives of the Employees in the above grades, dated June 18th, 1912, these conditions of service will come into operation on July 4th, 1912, and continue in force until January 1st, 1915, and thereafter until they are varied, superseded, or nullified by agreement between the Company and the Employees, or by such machinery for settlement of differences as may hereafter be established."

C. J. BOWEN COOKE,

Chief Mechanical Engineer.

CREWE,

(*Revised, July*, 1913.)

A 5
London and North Western Railway.

CARRIAGE DEPARTMENT.

RATES OF WAGES, HOURS OF LABOUR, AND CONDITIONS OF SERVICE OF:—
LOCOMOTIVE MEN IN CARRIAGE DEPARTMENT, WOLVERTON.

	Rate per week of 54 Hours.	
	Minimum	Maximum
Engine Drivers	30/-	32/-
Firemen	22/-	24/-

Engine Cleaners according to age, as follows:—

	s.	d.	
14 to 15 years	7	0	per week
15 to 16 ,, ...	8	0	,,
16 to 17 ,, ...	10	0	,,
17 to 18 ,, ...	12	0	,,
18 to 19 ,, ...	14	0	,,
19 to 20 ,, ...	16	0	,,
20 to 21 ,, ...	18	0	,,
21 and onward	20	0	,,

Men employed temporarily in a higher grade to be paid the minimum rate of the higher grade where such minimum is in excess of their own regular grade.

1. HOURS OF LABOUR.
Engine Drivers and Firemen—
  The standard week is 54 hours.
Cleaners—
  The standard week is 61½ hours.

2. REST.
  Nine hours' rest will be allowed between turns of duty, except in case of emergency, to be decided by the responsible Officer of the Company, and in that case time worked before the expiration of the nine hours will be paid at rate and a half.

3. OVERTIME.
  Will be paid for at the rate of time and a quarter up to 10.0 p.m. and time and a half after 10.0 p.m.

4. SUNDAY DUTY.
Engine Drivers and Firemen—
  Time and a half will be paid for all duty performed between midnight Saturday and midnight Sunday.
Cleaners—
  Rate and a half will be paid for all time worked between midnight Saturday and midnight Sunday, except in cases of men finishing or commencing their week's work on Sunday.

5. GOOD FRIDAY AND CHRISTMAS DAY.
  Time and a half will be paid for all duty performed on Good Friday and Christmas Day.

WOLVERTON,   H. D. EARL,
  February, 1914   *Carriage Superintendent.*

A 6

London and North Western Railway.

WAGGON DEPARTMENT.

RATES OF WAGES, HOURS OF LABOUR, AND CONDITIONS OF SERVICE OF:—

ENGINE DRIVER, FIREMAN, AND CLEANER.

1. RATES OF WAGES.

Engine Driver	35/– per week of 54 hours.
Fireman	24/– ,, ,, ,,
Cleaner	27/– ,, ,, ,,

2. HOURS OF LABOUR.

Engine Driver and Fireman—
The standard week is 54 hours.

Cleaner—
The standard week is 67½ hours.

3. REST.

Nine hours' rest will be allowed between turns of duty, except in case of emergency, to be decided by the responsible Officer of the Company, and in that case the time worked before the expiration of the nine hours will be paid for at rate and half.

4. OVERTIME.

Engine Driver and Fireman—
Time and quarter is allowed up to 10.0 p.m., and time and half afterwards when working continuously after 54 hours have been made within the week.

Cleaner—
Time and quarter is allowed for all time worked over the standard week.

5. SUNDAY DUTY.

Time and half is allowed for all duty performed between midnight Saturday and midnight Sunday.

6. GOOD FRIDAY AND CHRISTMAS DAY.

Time and half is allowed for all duty performed on Good Friday and Christmas Day.

EARLESTOWN,
January, 1914.

A. R. TREVITHICK,
Waggon Superintendent.

D 5

London and North Western Railway.

CARRIAGE DEPARTMENT.

Rates of Wages, Hours of Labour, and Conditions of Service

OF **OUT-DOOR GRADES** MENTIONED BELOW:—

Examiners and Repairers	Linen Attendants	Other Grades in Gas Works
Couplers	Cleaners	Stationary Enginemen
Lampmen	Electric-light Men	Boiler Attendants
Gas Fillers	Gasfitting Repairers	Footwarmer Attendants
Oilers	Gasmakers	Watchmen
	Assistant Gasmakers	

1. Rates of Wages.

The Rates of Wages are as shown on next page.

2. Piecework Rates for Carriage Cleaning.

OIL CLEANING (SCOURING):	Each.	ORDINARY INSIDE CLEANING :	Each.
4 and 6-wheeled Vehicles ...	1/9	Ordinary Carriages under 65 ft. in length	–/5
Vehicles 42 ft. and 45 ft. long ...	2/9	Saloons under 65 ft. in length ...	–/10
„ 47 ft. 6 in. 50 ft., 54 ft., 57 ft., 65 ft. 6 in., and upwards	3/–	65 ft. Saloons	1/4
		Post Offices under 65 ft. in length	1/–
LIGHT OIL CLEANING :		Break Vans	–/3
6-wheeled Vehicles. 42 ft., 45 ft., 47 ft. 6 in., and 50 ft. ...	1/–		
54 ft., 57 ft., 65 ft., and upwards	1/6	THOROUGH INSIDE CLEANING :	
		Ordinary Carriages under 65 ft. in length	2/–
DRY WIPING :		Saloons, 65 ft. and under ...	1/6
6-wheeled Vehicles, 42 ft., 45 ft., 47 ft. 6 in.. and 50 ft. ...	–/4	Break Vans	1/–
54 ft., 57 ft., 65 ft., and upwards	–/6	Post Offices	2/6

3. *Hours of Labour.

The hours of labour will be 67½ gross, 57 net, with meal times 10½ hours per week, oil gas making staff excepted.

No person will be called out for duty with less than an interval of 9 hours' rest after each completed turn of duty, except in cases of emergency.

4. Overtime.

All overtime made over the above hours will be paid for at rate and a quarter.

5. Sunday Duty.

Rate and a half will be paid for all time worked between midnight Saturday and midnight Sunday, except in cases of men finishing or commencing their week's work on Sunday.

*NOTE.—*These hours apply at Euston, Willesden, Broad Street, Carlisle, and Holyhead. At all other places they are 67½ gross, 58½ net, with meal times 9 hours per week. Oil Gas Making Staff work 48 hours per week, in six 8-hour Shifts, at all Gas Making Depôts.*

6. Difference of Pay (Temporary Duty).

Men working temporarily in higher grades will receive difference of pay to the minimum rate of the higher grade, or to the next higher scale of the higher grade, if the minimum does not give more than their present rate, when so employed for a period of one day.

7. Annual Holidays.

After one year's service, three days' holiday with pay ; after three years four days ; and after five years, six days will be allowed.

8. Christmas Day and Good Friday.

All permanently appointed staff will receive a day's pay at ordinary rate for Christmas Day and Good Friday, whether required to work or not, except when Christmas Day falls on Sunday.

9. Rates of Wages.

The scale of wages for Juniors will be :—

Years of age	14	15	16	17	18	19	20	
	8/-	9/-	11/-	13/-	15/-	17/-	19/-	per week.

The rates of wages for all other members of the staff will be :—

	Scale No. 1. LONDON.		Scale No. 2. LARGE TOWNS.		Scale No. 3. OTHER PLACES.	
	Minimum.	Maximum.	Minimum.	Maximum.	Minimum.	Maximum.
Examiner	26/-	32/-	26/-	30/-	26/-	29/-
Repairer						
Coupler	22/-	26/-	22/-	26/-	—	—
Lampman	22/-	26/-	22/-	24/-	21/-	23/-
Gas Filler						
Axlebox Oiler						
Linen Attendant						
Cleaner	21/-	24/	21/-	23/-	20/-	22/-
Electric Light Man	24/-	30/-	22/-	28/-	22/-	26/-
Gasfitting Repairer	24/-	30/-	24/-	28/-	22/-	26/-
Gas Maker	28/-	32/-	26/-	30/-	26/-	30/-
Assistant Gasmaker	24/-	26/	23/-	24/-	—	—
Other Grades in Gas Works	—	—	20/-	23/-	—	—
Stationary Engineman	28/-	30/-	—	—	—	—
Boiler Attendant	23/-	25/-	22/-	24/-	22/-	24/-
Watchman	24/-	30/-	23/-	28/-	—	—
Footwarmer Attendant	21/-	—	20/-	—	20/-	—

LARGE TOWNS (Scale No. 2).—Birmingham, Watford, Liverpool, Carlisle, Chester, Manchester, Leeds, Stockport, Crewe, Preston, Wolverhampton, Bolton, Patricroft, Warwick, Rugby, Hull, Leicester, Macclesfield, Tyldesley.

Annual advances to the maximum at the rate of 1/- per week.

NOTE.—In accordance with the agreement entered into between representatives of the Company and representatives of the Employees in the above grades, dated June 25th, 1912, these conditions of service will come into operation on July 5th, 1912, and continue in force until January 1st, 1915, and thereafter until they are varied, superseded, or nullified by agreement between the Company and the Employees, or by such machinery for the settlement of differences as may be hereafter established.

H. D. EARL,
Carriage Superintendent.

WOLVERTON.
July 1st, 1912.

B 3

London and North Western Railway.

CARRIAGE DEPARTMENT.

RATES OF WAGES, HOURS OF LABOUR, AND CONDITIONS OF SERVICE OF :—

SIGNALMEN AT WOLVERTON CARRIAGE WORKS.

	Rate per week of 54 hours.	
	Minimum.	Maximum.
Signalmen	19/–	22/–

---

1. HOURS OF LABOUR.

The standard week is 54 hours.

2. OVERTIME.

Will be paid at the rate of time and a quarter up to 10.0 p.m. and time and a half after 10.0 p.m.

3. SUNDAY DUTY.

Time and a half will be paid for all duty performed between midnight Saturday and midnight Sunday.

4. GOOD FRIDAY AND CHRISTMAS DAY.

Time and a half will be paid for all duty performed on Good Friday and Christmas Day.

H. D. EARL,
Carriage Superintendent.

WOLVERTON,
February, 1914.

A 8

London and North Western Railway.

LOCOMOTIVE DEPARTMENT.

RATES OF WAGES, HOURS OF LABOUR, AND CONDITIONS OF SERVICE OF
HYDRAULIC DEPARTMENT OUTDOOR STAFF AT GARSTON DOCKS.

1. RATES OF WAGES.

	Range of Rates of Pay per week.	
	Minimum Present.	Maximum Present.
Tippers	29/-	30/-
Hydraulic Cranemen (Adults)	21/-	27/-
Steam Cranemen	27/-	28/-
Hydraulic Enginemen	29/-	30/-
Hydraulic Firemen	26/-	26/-
Hydraulic Oilers	25/-	29/-

2. HOURS OF LABOUR.

The Tippers, Hydraulic Cranemen, Steam Cranemen, and Hydraulic Oilers have a standard week of 53½ hours, exclusive of meals.

Hydraulic Enginemen and Firemen have a standard week of 60 hours, including meals.

3. OVERTIME.

Tippers, Hydraulic and Steam Cranemen, and Oilers are paid time and quarter to 10.0 p.m. and time and half afterwards. When men of these grades are engaged unloading and loading vessels after 1.0 p.m. on Saturdays, they are paid at the rate of 1s. per hour, and these grades, if engaged on repairs to the Hydraulic Plant after 1.0 p.m. on Saturday, are paid at the rate of time and half, plus 1½d. per hour.

Hydraulic Enginemen and Firemen are paid bare time, except when engaged on repairs, when they are paid time and half.

4. SUNDAY DUTY.

In the case of Tippers, Hydraulic and Steam Cranemen, and Hydraulic Oilers, 1s. per hour if engaged unloading and loading vessels ; if engaged repairing plant, time and half, plus 1½d. per hour.

Hydraulic Enginemen and Firemen are paid time and half for all duties commencing and finishing on Sunday; also if the Saturday night turn of duty is extended beyond 6.0 a.m. on Sunday, they are paid time and half for any hours after 6.0 a.m.

5. CHRISTMAS DAY AND GOOD FRIDAY.

A day's pay is allowed for Good Friday, also for Christmas Day except when it falls on a Sunday. Any time worked on these days is paid for at the ordinary rates, in addition to the day's pay granted to the men.

CREWE,
January, 1914.

C. J. BOWEN COOKE,
Chief Mechanical Engineer.

16 Steam Shed

Morale at any steam shed was greatly influenced by the shed master. Too rigid an approach could produce a grudging compliance born out of fear; too indulgent an approach threatened slackness. In the closing years of the North Western, few sheds were better served than Rugby, where George W. Walton was in command. His charge included not only Rugby with over 160 engines and 570 men, but Peterborough, Stamford, Seaton, Market Harborough, Warwick and Coventry as well. 'GWW' espoused the old traditions, and right up to his retirement in the early 'twenties, arrived at the shed wearing a black silk top hat in winter and a straw boater in summer. George Walton undoubtedly brought style to the job, but it was not for his sartorial elegance alone that he was respected, but for a first-hand knowledge of running matters and a kindly and courteous manner. He had a knack of making even an unpleasant assignment acceptable, and when reproached for marking up one of his men for three consecutive Christmas turns, replied disarmingly: 'You're a good man I can rely on'. Although firm with his men, Walton stood ready to defend them from all comers, and would accept genuine error, though never slovenliness. Many men, who might have been dismissed by another chief, justified his faith in them.

Peterborough, Walton's most distant shed, was over 50 miles away, entailing plenty of travelling, for 'GWW' was a firm believer in the former LNWR General Manager George Findlay's old adage of being 'kept well posted in everything that is going on'. When the boss was away, it would fall to Jim Beck, his deputy, to keep things in order, but despite his many commitments, Walton made a point of seeing his chargehands, coalman and foreman before going out on the line, and attended to any defaulters in person.

Rugby shed was responsible for much of the express running on the Southern Division, and also for the Chester & Holyhead turns. The four 'Prince of Wales' 4-6-0s in the Holyhead link were seen as the plum jobs, for long after double manning had become widespread, they remained single manned. For many years, the link comprised Tom Hinks, Billy Ward, who had No 2275 *Edith Cavell*, Tom Russell and Jim Haggar. Leaving Rugby, the tender of the 'Irishman' would be stacked high with coal, nearly nine tons of it, to provide for the round trip, for coal was sometimes in short supply at Holyhead, and in any

George Walton's domain was the large steam shed on the up side of the line at the London end of the station. From L&B days, Rugby had been an important engine-changing venue, and as early as 1842 Whishaw wrote of 'a locomotive engine-house which will hold three engines and tenders'. By 1850, there was accommodation for 11 engines, but 22 were in steam daily. Within a few years there were separate Northern and Southern Division sheds, and by 1866, 100 engines were based at Rugby. Continued growth forced a move to the site depicted on the plan, with two 12-road sheds, the first dating from 1876 being erected to the standard 'Northlight' pattern. This survey depicts the depot in late LMS/early BR days, and as well as the steam shed it shows the LNWR erecting shop (see Chapter 18) and the track installed (open lines) for the Loco Testing Plant. The steam shed closed on 25 April 1965. The site lay bare for many years, but now houses a Grundig factory.

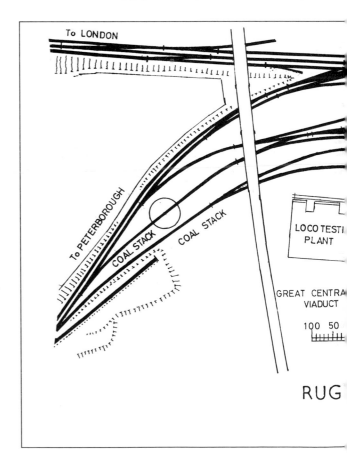

case, as Rugby men growled darkly. 'It was rum stuff that end'. Jim Haggar took over No 324, one of the 1921 Beardmore engines, and such was his belief in her that he would never willingly take a pilot. Partly it was pride, but much of his determination arose from horror at the thought of *his* 324 being drenched with water if the fireman of the pilot was slow with his scoop on the water troughs. Apart from the indignity to 324, it was always possible that the unwanted showerbath might wash out some of his bearings, with the ensuing 'hot box'. If need be, he was prepared to take 500 tons or more, well over the accepted figure for a 'Prince'. On one occasion when 324 had the down 'Irish Mail', it was not the engine but a diner which ran a hot box, and had to be put off at Wolverton. Although they picked up time to Crewe, adding a new diner resulted in an hour late departure, 28 minutes of which had been recovered by Holyhead!

It would have been a black mark against both Haggar and the shed if his engine had failed on the road, and desperate steps might be taken to get home. On one occasion as No 324 was pass-

ing Weedon, a few miles south of Rugby, her big end went, but Haggar was able to nurse her home. When they examined her, they found the 'bang top' missing from the big end. George Walton was at first inclined to blame Jim's fireman, Arthur Mason, for not screwing it down, but Jim and Arthur had worked together for quite a time, and Jim Haggar was not having anything said against his fireman.

One reason that the Holyhead run was so popular with the Rugby men was that it was over 150 miles, which counted for pay purposes as a full duty turn — originally of ten hours, later of eight. For the 'Irish Mail', the actual running time was from 10.12 am to 2.15 pm, or from booking on at 8.30 to booking off about 2.45 pm. It is a custom of all railways that one steam shed does not trust another, and the Rugby men were never happy leaving their beloved 'Princes' to the tender mercies of the Holyhead staff, but on one occasion, when Jim Haggar and Arthur Mason booked on again the following morning, Jim's worst fears had been fulfilled. Holyhead had stolen his beloved 324 to use on a mere local

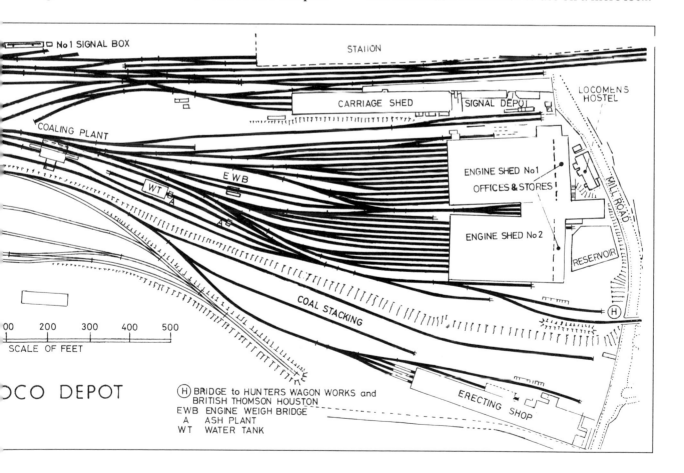

No 1803, built in 1897 as a class 'A' compound, and converted to a class 'C' simple in 1906, pauses on the shed approach roads, with the GCR London Extension as a backdrop, in about 1921. (Henry L. Salmon)

the previous afternoon, and, to add insult to injury, had replaced his personal coal with the rubbish they saw fit to call coal. Haggar's explosions, reinforced by George Walton's forceful comments to Crewe, resulted in a visit to Holyhead by a very exalted personage in the Locomotive Department to negotiate an armistice. Thereafter, no 324 was not tampered with! The four Holyhead 'Princes' worked the 'Irish Mail' for two weeks, then spent a week on the 5.15 pm Rugby to Euston, returning on the 9.20 pm, and a week on the early turn to Euston, returning on the down Midday. Annoying though it was to have to leave one's engine in the hands of philistines, the Rugby top link men rejoiced in one advantage, for it was into the Rugby erecting shop that No 324 went after her first 70,000 miles, and the shopmen knew that if there was anything wrong when she came out, Jim Haggar was ready to breathe fire, and was only a few yards down the line!

Apart from the four Holyhead 'Princes', there was a second less pampered set of six engines, double-manned for local work. Two were kept in steam for 24 hours, one on the up side and one on the down side for station pilot, relief and assistance work. In the early days they had been doubled-manned, but when the eight hour day came in at the end of the Great War, three crews were put on. The engines went on shed about 5.00 am, after the 'News' had gone, and came out again before 6.00 am.

The 'Claughton' link comprised six to eight engines of the class named after the Chairman, all double-manned with the crews alternating on turns weekly. They were usually to be found on the Euston and Crewe services. One of the 'Claughton' men, Bill Martin, was quite a character, with a lubrication system all his own. He regularly worked with 8.23 am Rugby–Euston, the 1.30 pm Euston to Crewe, and the following day took the 4.38 am Crewe–Euston and 9.30 am Euston–Rugby. He would go round the engine, look at all the trimmings, rub them down with sandpaper until he was entirely happy, then leave the engine to run the 300-mile-plus roster without deigning to look at them again (axleboxes, slide bars, horn cheeks etc, were fed with oil via wick-like 'trimmings' of worsted).

At a time when overheating was still a significant cause of failures, it was a striking demonstration of the value of careful preparation, and of confidence once that had been done.

The other six-coupled express engines, the Whale 'Experiments', were not so popular, and few Rugby men had a good word for them. Accordingly they tended to appear on locals or fast goods, unless a special or a failure cropped up. The sluggish performance of the non-superheated 'Experiments' has often been held up as their Achilles heel, but to the footplatemen it was not so such their performance as their coal consumption which, compared to the superheated Bowen Cooke engines, was high. On a railway as cost-conscious as the North Western, that did not make them popular, for a large chart hung in George Walton's office showing each driver's coal figures, and a bonus was paid to the most economical men. However skilful one's technique, a few days with an 'Experiment' could wreak havoc with the figures.

A good-natured battle went on between the coalmen and the enginemen over trying to 'win' the odd hundredweight of coal, and some drivers, if they espied a piece of coal lying in the yard, were not above sending their firemen to fetch it. Under such a system, a fireman who arrived on shed with a full grate and his safety valves lifting would earn a few caustic remarks. As running short of steam on the last few miles home was a still more heinous crime, firemen quickly learned to judge things to a nicety. As with everything to do with a steam locomotive, it was a partnership, and firemen also discovered the idiosyncrasies of individual drivers. One driver rarely well placed in the league was Jim Bassett, for he had come from the North Western shed at Colwick, in Nottingham, following a reorganization. Jim had spent years hammering the big eight-coupled 'D' goods locomotives over the GN & LNW Joint line through Melton Mowbray to Welham Junction with 40-wagon coals from the Notts coalfield. Brute power rather than finesse was called for, and his consumption figures remained high. On one occasion, when a former Rugby driver, Ike Ward, was riding as a footplate inspector, supervising some long-forgotten trial, he tried to instil a new attitude into Jim Bassett, getting him to 'think about them little black diamonds in that tender'. Ike's remark became a watchword at the shed, but made little

difference to Jim! After years on the Joint line, Jim Bassett believed engines were there to be thrashed, and was a staunch advocate of high pressure and superheating. On another occasion during the Great War, when Jim had the up 'Irish Mail', a Royal Flying Corps plane few alongside the train at Tring. Jim, no great admirer of flying machines, looked at it in disgust, and growled to his mate, 'If this one was pressured at 200 lbs, the man in that thing would never see us to London.' What is lost in the mists of time, if indeed it was ever known, was whether the RFC machine was an Avro 504, of which several thousands were built for training duties, or a front line Scout, which was much rarer in the skies over England. With the 82 mph flat-out of an Avro, considerably reduced in a head wind, Jim might well have won his race, but against the 120-plus of Camels and Bristols, it would have needed a performance eclipsing *Mallard*, then 20 years in the future.

There were usually about a dozen 'Precursor' and 'George the Fifth' 4-4-0s at Rugby, many on the 'Brum' turns. One of the 'Georges' was in its own special link, rivalling the 'Irish Mail' 'Princes' in prestige. Two drivers were in the link, one of them being George Leach, who was so diminutive in stature that he had a large wooden block to stand on to see through the front spectacle! On the day war broke out in 1914, George's regular fireman went off sick, and Arthur Mason, then more used to freight and local passenger turns, was roped in. George's remark, upon setting eyes on him, was acerbic: 'Where did they find HIM — the Co-op?' That evening, they went up to Euston on the 7.33 pm on a lodging turn, returning on Monday morning with the 10.00 am to Rugby, where George and Arthur came off the engine, and the second crew took her up to Crewe. As Arthur Mason was leaving the shed, he was told that George Walton wanted to see him. It was with considerable trepidation that he entered the office, for Walton relied heavily on his drivers' reports, and his first few minutes with George Leach had not been too happy. It was with relief that he realized that Walton was telling him that Leach, whose bark was worse than his bite, had asked for him until his regular man recovered. As the roster included the up 'Irish Mail', it was quite a feather in the cap of a junior fireman.

Apart from the 'Brummies' and George

Leach's engine, the remaining 4-4-0s worked semi-fasts on the main lines and some of the Stamford services. Several were entrusted to Extra Drivers, who took the excursion and assisting jobs at peak periods. One of the 'Precursor', No 1617 *Hydra*, was a complete enigma. No matter who drove or fired her, or what technique was used, *Hydra* had a mind of her own. Little and often — a thick fire — it did not matter, it was impossible to build up an adequate head of pressure. Crew after crew reporter her; the fitters tinkered and swore; George Walton looked at her, and still she would not build up pressure; but out on the road she performed as well with 30 lbs less on the gauge as the rest of the class with their regulation 175 psi! Another of the Rugby 4-4-0s earned her crew a welcome tip on account of her name. She was No 1631 *Racehorse*, one of the 'Georges', and after she had lived up to her name on a Birmingham–Euston express, a couple of 'toffs' came up to the driver and com-

plimented him on his steed. 'She can lick any racehorse' came the reply, whereupon one of the passengers revealed that they had two horses running, Furious in the Lincoln and Tritone in the National, and they hoped that *Racehorse* would be a lucky omen!

Just after the end of the Great War, another of the Rugby men, Hammond, had one of the 'Precursors' on a Euston semi-fast. At Bletchley, a well-dressed man swung up into the cab, flashed an imposing-looking document at them and settled himself into the fireman's seat. Their guest was none too communicative, but Hammond reasoned that quizzing one of the Crewe or Euston HQ people might not go down too well. As they got under way, both driver and fireman noticed that their 'official' seemed surprisingly excited and, as his suspicions mounted, Hammond hastily scribbled a note, wrapped it round a lump of coal and threw it on to the platform as they whipped through Watford. At

Euston, railway police were there to meet the train. It turned out that the supposed railway official had a £5 wager that he could bluff his way on to the footplate. He was later fined a tenner, but showed no ill will to the enginemen, giving them half a sovereign each!

In the days of the 'Railway Race to the North', Rugby men had made their mark with the diminutive Webb 'Precedent' 2-4-0s, and although their days as first link engines were long past, half a dozen were retained for piloting and working the Stamford and Peterborough trains. For many years, one of the Rugby men, Bill Read, had his own 'Jumbo' on the 8.30 am from Rugby and the 1.30 ex Peterborough. Bill and his venerable steed became an institution out in tranquil Leicestershire and Rutland. Another well-known Peterborough line driver was Alf Chadwick, whose antiquated 0-6-0 'DX' locomotive was just as familiar a sight on the local goods. Alf worked a lodging turn, sharing the link with a Peterborough man. It was a very leisurely turn, for as well as shunting at way stations, Alf was required to stop at the gatehouses *en route*, for the majority were never connected to the mains water supply, and depended on a couple of churns of water off the goods for their daily needs! To many drivers it would have been irksome, but not to Alf, who supplemented his 'six bob a day' wages by collecting eggs along the line at 6d a dozen, and selling them at the shed at 9d a dozen. Alf sometimes handled other produce, including chickens, with George Walton turning a diplomatic blind eye to one of his engines becoming a species of travelling shop! Somehow, the vision of the engine driver bartering for eggs is a picture one could associate with the Colonel Stephens lines or Will Hay more readily than the prestigious 'Premier Line', but away from officialdom, railwaymen are railwaymen the world over. On the same line, one of the authors once called at a wayside station in the 'sixties, where water was still delivered by churn, and enquired if it was possible to make any journeys with an LMS ticket? It was, but it was carefully explained to the author that although it was only Saturday midday, would he mind the ticket being dated for the following Monday, as no one ever brought a ticket on Saturday afternoons, and it saved having to rush things first thing on Monday morning if the dater was set in advance!

Individual mannerisms or stories could live on long after the person concerned had retired or died. George W. Walton believed that a good start in life was important for the youngsters who came to his shed. On his frequent inspections, the question was always the same: 'What are you doing, my son?' It became a catch-phrase at the shed, and was regaled to generations of men who joined the railway long after Walton's retirement; his mild rebuke, 'Now, we'll have none of that', when one of his lads used bad language, was another phrase which lived on.

A classic example of Walton's penchant for turning a blind eye, which is recalled to this day, concerned one of his drivers, the expressively nick-named 'Barrel' Griffiths. As with the engines he drove, 'Barrel' went best when adequately lubricated. His idea of adequate, 16 pints so legend has it, would have put most men under the table, but in his case he remained perfectly capable, and was as amiable as you could wish on the footplate. With inadequate lubrication, firemen recalled him being *as awkward as hell!* One of his regular turns was a lodging run to Longsight, where there was a strategically located pub just near the enginemen's barracks!

During the Great War, staff shortages were so acute at some sheds that firemen and cleaners had to be loaned from one depot to another; some of these loans went on for years after the end of hostilities. One young Rugby fireman was loaned to a Birmingham driver shunting at Spon Lane basin during or just after the war. The driver, an elderly man with a flowing beard, was oiling his steed one evening with the aid of an open-flame lamp when a gust of wind caught his beard and blew it into the flame. A good part of the beard was destroyed in the resulting conflagration, but as the driver was contemplating his loss, insult was added to injury by the antics of his young fireman, who was convulsed with laughter. Dignity had been outraged, and the driver took the heartless youth before the shed foreman the following morning. The foreman, contemplating the novel appearance of his driver, compounded the sin by bursting out laughing himself when told why the hapless fireman was before him!

A lodging house was provided at Rugby near the shed for visiting crews, and Rugby men, conscious of 'Barrel's' prowess, recalled the fate which befell two Edge Hill men with glee. The two men booked off duty and decided to sample

Above *Despite further upgrading to 'G', 'G1', 'G2' and 'G2a'. North Western men called them 'Ds'. Rugby fitters have dropped the buffer beam of this 'D' to attend to the left-hand cylinder, the inclination of which is apparent.*

Below *George Walton's district embraced six sub-sheds, including Coventry, depicted in 1911. Originally a two-road structure, it used to be said that when enlarged in 1897, flat lintels were used in both halves. This shows the opposite to be true — arched entrances were used, and the flat lintels were a later modification.*

the local Banks's bitter, which they did to such good effect that they filled not only the chamber pot but their boots as well before subsiding into insensibility. When it was time to return them to duty, they were still sleeping the beer off, and after repeated attempts to get them mobile they were lifted on to ordinary railway barrows, wheeled over to the station and loaded into the Liverpool train, the Rugby shed foreman again turning a blind eye to their misdeeds!

Some of the lodging houses frequented by Rugby men were primitive, to say the least. At Llandudno, the railway used a private lodging house, at which just one room was available. However, at peak weekends, with heavy excursion traffic, there might be a dozen crews turning up, and with the rest of the accommodation let out, there was slight overcrowding! Washing facilities consisted of a bucket of water in the back yard, and one crew gave up and went up the Great Orme to have a nap. Later on, an old sleeping car was provided. North Western crews working into Nottingham, via the LNW & GN Joint line, used a railway hostel in which a double bed was provided for the driver and fireman, and a single bed for the guard! Bletchley was not a shed at which Rugby men ordinarily lodged, not that they would have wanted to, as the lodge was the water tank house at the shed. It was cold and dank, and the normal method of warming beds was by use of a hot brick!

17 A CME's Lot

The story behind the evolution of any new class of locomotive, whether it is a North Western 'Precursor' or a Gresley 'A4', is always fascinating, and over the years many such accounts have appeared, recalling the cut and thrust between the Locomotive and Civil Engineers, the compromises which have to be made, and the stories of hopes fulfilled or shattered. We could be excused for believing that the 'Chief' spent his entire working life poring over the drawing-board, snatching just the odd moment away from his labours to ride forth do battle with the Civil Engineer. The reality was very different. Some Chief Mechanical Engineers may hever have designed an engine in their lives — Harry Wainwright of the SECR was, for example, a capable and good-natured leader and administrator, and possessed a brilliant touch in aesthetics, but it is debatable what his contribution to mechanical engineering was. Sir Henry Fowler was another chief whose forte was administration rather than design. Even those engineers with a massive contribution to steam locomotive design, men such as F.W. Webb, G.J. Churchward, C.J. Bowen Cooke or Nigel Gresley, relied heavily upon design teams they inherited or built up. Locomotive design *was* a matter of team work, and the running of the Locomotive Department even more so. Until the adoption of American ideas of separating locomotive design and maintenance from running, the Locomotive Department was responsible for designing, building, overhauling, servicing and running locomotives. The CME was responsible not just for design, but for everything which took place in his department. Naturally there was delegation, but with the wrong man in the wrong post, or carelessness or indifference, a Locomotive Department, no matter how fine its engines, would find itself in dire troubles all too soon.

This is the forgotten side of the CME's duties, but a vitally important one. Over the next few pages, we will look at extracts from the LNWR Conciliation Board minutes of 1915 to 1917, and see some of the problems which landed on Bowen Cooke's desk. At the best of times, running a Locomotive Department the size of the LNWR was no sinecure, but with the Great War raging, an already difficult job was made more so. With the Grand Fleet at its war bases of Scapa Flow, Invergordon and Rosyth, an endless stream of 'Jellicoe Specials' was required to feed its hungry furnaces. The demand on Bowen Cooke for motive power was intense, yet at the same time engines had to be handed over to the forces for use overseas. Crewe Works, with its massive industrial capacity, was soon at work producing cartridge cases, shell forgings, fuses, gun parts

No 1583 Henry Ward, *one of the first production 'George the Fifths' of November 1910, roars through Coventry the following summer at the head of a Birmingham–Euston 2-Hour Express.* (H.J. Stretton Ward)

MEMORANDUM OF MEETING

HELD IN MR. BOWEN COOKE'S OFFICE AT CREWE.

November 26th, 1915.

PRESENT

Company's Side.	*Employee's Side.*
Mr. C. J. BOWEN COOKE.	Mr. A. BELLAMY, J.P.
„ W. M. TURNBULL.	„ H. ELLISON.
„ D. E. TAPPLY.	
„ J. D. BROWN.	
„ W. H. B. JONES.	
„ W. F. BLACK.	
„ T. ARMSTRONG.	

56. Mr. Bellamy, representing the enginemen and firemen, explained that the enginemen were complaining that in many cases where they had been on duty for nearly 12 hours and asked for relief to be provided, the necessary steps were not being taken and relief was not obtained, although, if application had been made to the Locomotive Department, relief could have been supplied.

He further stated that where it was necessary on account of the War, or relief could not possibly be obtained, the whole of the men were willing to see the traffic through in the best interests of the Company and the Country.

After a discussion of details—

Mr. Bowen Cooke replied that he was afraid there had been some misunderstanding on the part of the Control Offices in their interpretation of the instructions on the subject, but stated that in all cases where enginemen applied for relief the Control Offices **must** pass the application forward to the Locomotive Department.

He was prepared, in conjunction with the Traffic Department, to issue an order instructing the Control Offices that before they work a man over 12 hours it must be ascertained from the Locomotive Department whether it is possible to provide relief, and if so, it must in all cases be supplied.

and even artificial limbs. Troop trains had to be run, munitions factories supplied, and always there were fresh demands on the Locomotive Department. If that were not enough, thousands of North Western men had enlisted, creating staff shortages and necessitating the use of unskilled labour. Bowen Cooke had indeed a multitude of problems on his mind — they ranged from how to supply sufficient engines to keep the trains moving and shell cases to keep the military happy, to such strange items as clogs and slops.

A

(f) Crewe.—Tank Filler A. Palin.

Palin is graded as " Tank Filler " and rated at 25s. per week for 54 hours. He asked to be paid at the rate of 6s. per day instead of 4s. 2d. for this work.

It was agreed that as Palin's reduction from engineman was due to failure of eyesight he should be paid at the rate of 6s. per day, and Mr. Cooke promised to go into the question generally to see whether a regulation could be adopted under which any extra driver or engineman put back through failure of eyesight, who might have to work in positions where they would be required to move engines in a locomotive shed or yard, would be paid at not less than 6s. per day.

It is agreed that this concession be granted in the case of enginemen put back through no fault of their own, and where they will be required to more engines in a locomotive shed or yard.

25

A

(j) Bushbury.—Drivers A. H. Moore and W. Brewer.

These men were reduced to local passenger working in January, 1916, owing to some of the London expresses being taken off. The concession granted in May last refers only to " 8s. men reduced owing to the reduction of mileage, through the temporary withdrawal of dining cars."

It is agreed as a concession that in future drivers rated at 8s. per day temporarily reduced to lower rated work, owing to war conditions, shall retain their 8s. rate.

This does not affect the agreement with reference to men reduced in grade owing to war conditions.

A

36

96. ### Application for guaranteed month to be made up.
Speke Junction.—Driver J. Tobin.

Tobin applies to be paid 18½ hours he was short of the 240 hours for the guaranteed period ending January 10th, 1917. Tobin is a driver in the No. 1 shunting link. All the shunting engines were discontinued from 6.0 p.m., December 23rd, to 12.0 night, December 26th, 1916. The engines required by the Traffic Department were ordered out specially, and the regular shunting drivers (who had been told to hold themselves in readiness during the time the regular work was discontinued) were sent for accordingly. Tobin booked on at 4.30 a.m. and off duty at 1.30 p.m. on Sunday, December 24th. An engine was ordered for 10.0 p.m. special shunting on the 24th. There were 10 shunting drivers at home when Tobin booked off, five of them had been found work, and the other five were not available when sent for. Tobin was then sent for, but did not come to work, stating he had only been off duty 8 hours. Consequently the job had to be put back until 1.10 p.m., Fireman H. J. Avery was then put on the work. Tobin was entered up as " not available," and was not required for work again until 4.30 a.m. on December 27th. He has been dealt with, so far as the guaranteed period is concerned, in accordance with the regulations; but Mr. Cooke agreed that his application should be granted, in view of the exceptional circumstances.

Right *Freight tonnage and engine mileage rose sharply in the mid-'nineties, taxing the Loco Department to the hilt, as this Coal Department letter explains!*

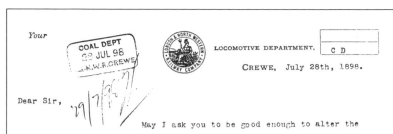

Your

COAL DEPT
28 JUL 98
L.N.W.R. CREWE

LONDON & NORTH WESTERN RAILWAY COMPANY

LOCOMOTIVE DEPARTMENT, | C D |

CREWE, July 28th, 1898.

Dear Sir,

        May I ask you to be good enough to alter the date of the enclosed, and make it available from the 12th to the 26th Aug.?

        I am sorry to trouble you but business is so pressing with us just now that I cannot possibly get away as I originally intended.

        Yours truly,

Enclo.

G. H. Wood, Esq.,

    Isle of Man Railway,

        Douglas.

Below *An NBL (Queens Park) Works ROD 2-8-0 (LNWR class 'MM') of 1919 at Crewe South in 1929. In the background is the 1920 mechanical coaling plant. Engine and coal plant were both reactions to the difficult aftermath of the First World War.*

A

117. **Application from the Camden Fuelmen employed on the Mechanical Coaling Plant for a ½d. per ton extra, which was taken off some time ago.**

 Camden—Fuelman T. Franklin and others.

 The tonnage of coal put on engines at the Elevator, Camden, has decreased through the discontinuance and deceleration of Passenger trains, commencing January 1st, 1917. The men applied on June 18th, 1917, for the piecework price to be advanced from 1¼d. to 1½d. per ton. This was not granted, but so that their earnings might be increased two alternative schemes were suggested, viz. :—

 (1) To take one man out of the gang and let the others work 12 hours instead of 8, or

 (2) To take one man off coaling on the 2.0 p.m. to 10.0 p.m. shift, and leave the other turns as before, but the men prefer to continue working as at present.

 They are now paid at the rate of 1¼d. per ton for coal put on engines at the Elevator, and 4½d. per ton for all coal put on shunting engines at the old coal stage.

 Owing to the January train alterations a large number of engines which were previously coaled at Camden are either discontinued or get their coal elsewhere, and in consequence the men have to work much longer hours to make their earnings what they were prior to the Elevator being put up.

 Mr. Cooke promised to have the matter looked into with a view to ensuring that the men are not in a worse position in respect of wages and hours of duty than when the old coal stage was in existence.

 It has been decided as a special case and without prejudice, to make up the wages of the Fuelmen at Camden during the period of the War to 36s., plus 15s. War Wage, for a week of 54 hours, providing they are available for duty the whole of the week, and deal with all engines requiring coal.

118. **Application for dating back of registration as Firemen.**

 Crewe.—Fireman C. W. Harrison and others.

 The petitioners appeal to be registered as firemen on or about December, 1911, instead of July, 1913. They are under the impression that they should have been promoted to firemen when they signed the Vacuum Brake Certificate. They have been told that the signing of the Vacuum Brake Certificate has nothing whatever to do with the question as to when a man should be passed as a fireman, except inasmuch as he cannot be made a fireman until he has passed the vacuum brake test.

 In consequence of a petition from cleaners to be made firemen in July, 1913, the whole question was fully inquired into, and the men who were entitled to be promoted (*i.e.*, those who were marked out on the working arrangement sheet for firing duty permanently so far as could be foreseen) were registered as firemen.

A

126. **Booking-off allowance.**

Rugby.—Extra Drivers Hinks and Stanton.

The above drivers forwarded the following resolution from the men at Rugby :—

"That this meeting protest against the small remuneration at present received by enginemen when booked off, and ask for the following increase:—1s. when booked off 15 hours, and 2s. 6d. when booked off 20 hours."

The allowances for booking off away from home are 1s. for first time of booking off, in addition to free lodging accommodation, and 3s. 6d. for the second time of booking. also for a period exceeding 20 hours. These allowances have been increased for the period of the War by 33⅓ per cent., the 1s. being advanced to 1s. 4d. and the 3s. 6d. to 4s. 8d.

The present application is for 1s. 4d. plus 1s.. equals 2s. 4d. for the booking off away from home 15 hours, and 4s. 8d. plus 2s. 6d., equals 7s. 2d. for booking off 20 hours.

It is stated that the traffic men are being treated better in this respect than those in the Locomotive Department.

Mr. Cooke promised to look into the question with a view to men booked off between 15 and 20 hours being dealt with on the same basis as men in the Traffic Department.

It is found that the Traffic Department pay the goods guards an allowance of 1s. extra (plus 33⅓ per cent. during the War) if booked off away from home exceeding 15 hours and under 20 hours. when working **unrostered** *trains only; and Mr. Cooke has therefore agreed to pay the drivers and firemen on the same basis.*

127. **Application for long booking-off allowance.**

Walsall.—Driver J. Fletcher and Fireman Dodson booked off away from home 19 hours and 25 minutes.

Mr. Cooke stated that any revised arrangements made in connection with the applications referred to in the previous minute would cover this case.

The men were working a **rostered** *train. and the application cannot, therefore. be granted.*

128. **Application for clogs and slops for boilerwashers.**

Rugby.—Boilerwasher J. J. Porter.

Mr. Cooke stated that he was prepared to recommend the supply of clogs and slops to boilerwashers, and undertook to look into the question with this end in view.

It has been decided to supply boilerwashers with one pair of clogs and two jean jackets annually.

18 Gee's Shops

Tens of thousands of words have been written about Crewe Works. Virtually from the day it opened, Crewe was a Mecca for engineers and later for lovers of railways. By comparison, little has appeared about another London & North Western Railway locomotive works, which played a vital role for decades in keeping the wheels rolling, and which survived for almost 70 years. Known to those who worked there as 'Gee's Shops' on account of its first, and long-serving manager, the Rugby erecting shop of the LNWR is virtually forgotten today.

At the start of F.W. Webb's long reign in 1871, the LNWR possessed some 1,800 engines, all of modest size. By the close of the Webb era, there were 3,100 locomotives, including a considerable number of large eight-coupled heavy freight engines, and the first mixed traffic 4-6-0s. Crewe had been a massive establishment under Ramsbottom, but under Webb production capacity was stepped up with improvement after improvement. It was vital, for with well over a 50 per cent increase in motive power, maintenance and building needs had soared. Despite these continual enlargements, Crewe was under intense pressure, with 15 or 16 per cent of motive power awaiting or under attention at Crewe in the early part of the Webb era. Engines which were out of traffic were not earning money; indeed, 'downtime', as we would now call it, was very expensive as additional motive power had to be built, or overtime paid to handle freight on Sundays, as it could not be moved during the week.

With land at a premium at Crewe, thoughts turned to cheaper sites, and at Rugby the North Western owned a substantial area of ground north of the running lines, and green fields adjoined the site. During 1892 a large new erecting shop took shape just north of the capacious steam sheds, and to provide further room, over and above the existing site, powers were secured under s19 of the LNWR (Additional Powers) Act 1892, for land between Brownsover Mill Road

on the north side of the line, and the LNWR Rugby & Stamford branch.

The new workshop opened on 31 December 1892, the local paper reporting that 'The extensive London & North Western repairing shops at Rugby have been opened during the past week, and already 30 men, including joiners, fitters and millwrights, have commenced work, but operations will not be in full swing for about a month, when no fewer than a hundred men will have

'Gee's shops' about 1959, with a pair of '2Ps', headed by No 40677, in the foreground. It is ironic that despite the Midlandization process, the North Western had the last laugh, with Midland-inspired engines carrying LNWR-inspired lining!

been drafted here, mainly from Crewe. In addition to the powerful gas engine and the two travelling cranes, there are in the workshops a dozen machines of various kinds.'

In the days before the Welfare State, company or staff benefit and pension schemes filled a vital role, and the North Western encouraged its men to form suitable societies. Often these were local affairs, and although a 'Locomotive Department Sick Benefit Society' already existed, a 'Rugby New Erecting Shop Sick Benefit Society' was formed on 2 January 1893. Other societies catering for North Western men in the town included the 'L&NWR Shed Club', the 'Rugby Loco.

United Football Club', the 'Rugby Steam Shed Brass Band', and the oldest of all, the 'Railway Institute', which opened its doors on 1 October 1887.

The erecting shops, in which 112 men were employed in 1908 under the Manager, Mr Gee, carried out a wide variety of repair work, although for many years between the wars, and in the latter days, it worked well below capacity. To the apprentices who trained there, one of the most vivid memories was the initiation ceremony! At Christmas, and again at Easter, the new boys had to swallow two treacle buns and down an entire bottle of lemonade in three minutes flat!

It sounds a daunting enough task, but to add to the fun the buns were suspended from a length of string, and were coated in thick black treacle, and the apprentice was *not* permitted to use his hands!

Lew Walton (who shared a surname with the steam shed foreman, although they were not related) was to work in the erecting shop for almost 20 years, and provided the authors with a vivid account of life in this forgotten North Western works. He started in January 1910, aged about 17. This was exceptionally late for an apprenticeship, but he had already spent two years at Crewe, where his father had been an LNWR water-pipe layer, and it was only through his father's transfer that he came to Rugby. Young Lew was offered a post in the steam shed or the erecting shop, and opted for the latter. He recalled Mr Gee as 'a real straight Jane — you had to do as you were told'. During his time at Crewe he had never touched an engine, working instead as a messenger much of the time. The erecting shop consisted of a long brick-built structure, with three tracks very closely spaced running for most of its length. So cramped was the building that men working at any of the machines along the walls had to stand aside whenever any parts were being barrowed to and from other engines!

Each road was under a chargehand, who had about 15 fitters and three or four apprentices under him. He was responsible for dividing his team amongst the engines on his track, as many as six at a time. Lew Walton was placed with chargehand Eaton, and a few days after he started his inexperience roused the manager's wrath. He recalled the incident vividly, 'When I first started as a lad, of course, I'd never used a file in my life before. Having to file left-handed on the hornplate was an awkward job, and you only had a wooden block to try to sit on. I started to file, but the file was going all ways. I wasn't aware that Mr Gee was standing behind me until he spoke. He was standing like this, with his hands behind his back, and he said, 'Damn it to Hell, man, file as if you mean to file, not see-saw'. With that, he went round to the fitter on the other side of the engine, and said, 'Go round and put the lad right; it'll be like an apple when he's finished there'.

Lew Walton described the arrival of an engine for shopping. 'A loco came in straight off the road. They used to bring it down to the outside of the shops, take the tender off, and the engine was stripped outside. All the motion, side rods, connecting rods and so on came off. If it rained, hailed or snowed, it still had to be done outside.' Removal of the side rods was a fraught business, for after the securing pins and collars had been removed, a bar was wedged between the rods and the wheel, and the rods edged sideways until they fell off. It paid to be nimble on one's feet!

Once the motion had been dropped, the engine was brought into the shops and made ready for lifting, using the two travelling cranes which could move the length of the shop. The engine was picked up, leaving the wheels on the rails, and positioned on heavy stands. The 'top work' now started, removing the cab roof and panels, lagging and other fittings, until the boiler could be lifted off. Space was often at a premium, so frequently the boiler was lifted, packing placed on the frames, and the boiler lowered back on to the packing. At other times, it was taken to the top of the shops, where a section was set aside for boiler work. Most of the stripping down was carried out by a fitter and an apprentice, assisted as necessary by men from the other engines on the row.

Although there were three gangs of fitters, part of the centre road was usually appropriated for wheels, which were turned down on a large lathe at the top end of the shops. All wheel turning was entrused to one skilled turner, the general fitters never handling this task. Another skilled hand looked after the motion work, connecting rods, coupling rods and so on.

Once the engine had been stripped down, re-assembly could begin, the fitter and apprentice being assisted far more frequently than during the stripping. Often there would be five or six men on the one engine. One of the most important jobs was re-wheeling the engine, for this entailed lifting the locomotive using both travelling cranes. Even for a small engine, such as a six-coupled goods, this required not just the crane-men and the chargehand, but at least six fitters and apprentices, to roll the wheels into place, and guide the loco down to see that the axleboxes entered the hornplates. Once this had been done, the keeps had to be fitted, and brake and other fittings connected, and the engine would require lifting again to turn the wheels into alignment to fit the side rods. Lew Walton recalled one

The erecting shop shortly before its closure in 1959. LMS and BR Standards have replaced LNWR power, but the belt drives to the works equipment survives! Note the clear walkway lines. (Leicester Mercury)

terrifying experience of cranework: 'One evening after tea, during the First World War I think, we had picked the engine up, and we'd all been underneath, and when we got the necessary work done, the crane picked it up again, and the chain broke and it came down. I think it was an eight-coupled coal engine. As luck had it, there was nobody underneath it. The loco had been generally overhauled, but it didn't hurt the loco at all, as it wasn't a great way off the floor. It had never happened before.'

Many jobs were unpleasant rather than hazardous. Although there was a separate gang under a chargehand who looked after tenders, the fitters had to look after side tanks or saddle tanks. Lew Walton reflected: 'We had to do the tanks on the tank engines; the lad had to crawl into the tanks and put the bolts in and the valves. That was a job I never did like. A murderous job on the coal tanks especially, as they were only so wide, and there were stays inside that you had to crawl under, and then over the splashers. You had to put the bolts in to hold them to the frames. You used to caulk them with string and red lead putty. When you had the bolt in, the other lad would be outside putting up the nut and tightening it up.' With the saddle tanks there were other problems on account of the awkward shape. Lew Walton recalled: 'They were shocking to

A 'piano-front G', LMS No 9090, receives attention at the outer end of the shops in about 1930. The removal of the covers shows the empty space left when these engines were converted to simples. At this time the travelling crane was still rope-driven from the gas engine. (H.J. Stretton Ward)

work in, but there were usually only the valves to see to; you used to grind them in with emery paper to bed them nicely to see they didn't leak, and then bed them in with red lead putty.'

Responsibility for boilers was split between the fitters and the boilermakers. One of the fitters' tasks was the removal of the roof-bars or stays between the inner and outer firebox wrappers. This commenced via the whistle stand, and the fitter had to push his arm through the opening and into the space between the wrappers to withdraw each stay. One day, one of the fitters, of portly build, had wriggled his arm in, but found it was trapped, and he could not get it out. Of course with the pressure it soon swelled up, and was even harder to move, and it was over three hours before he was freed, and his arm was a terrible sight.

Once some space had been made, two of the more slender apprentices would have to crawl into the boiler to remove the more distant stays. It was another foul job, as 'there was a days' work in getting them out, and you had to hold a big spanner up, whilst someone was bashing the hammer at you'. Rugby erecting shop could replace tubeplates, re-tube boilers and do minor patching work on fireboxes, but if a boiler was too far gone it was sent up to Crewe, which would send down a replacement. No float boilers were kept at the erecting shops. Most of the work had to be done by hand. The tubeplate holes sometimes became horizontally oval, and these had to be reamed out by hand, and liners or ferrules fitted to restore them to the proper diameter.

One job which was mechanized was cylinder boring. Once again, the work was entrusted to one hand, John Law, 'He had a proper boring machine for it. We unbolted the cylinder cover and took it off, and clamped the boring machine on to the head bolts, and then drove the machine off the works shafting.' One end of the boring tool was of course supported by a plate clamped to the cylinder, whilst a long rod, around which

'They used to leave the tender outside'. A Bowen Cooke tender of the 1916 pattern lies outside the fitting shop. Beyond, and secured to the wall, is the stores crane used to handle items such as buffers, wheel sets, etc. (H.J. Stretton Ward)

the cutter rotated, ran the length of the cylinder and protruded through the piston rod bearing at the far end. Rugby also re-cylindered engines when necessary, sending the scrap cylinders up to Crewe.

Albert Shirley was another skilled hand. He was the valve setter. As with the initial stripping, the work was chiefly done outside, with three or four fitters moving the engine back and forwards in the works yard. It was not a popular job!

Throughout Lew Walton's time, the workshop machinery was belt driven from a gas engine in the erecting shop itself. This also provided power for the travelling cranes and the shop lighting. Unfortunately the gas engine was not sufficiently powerful to meet the maximum level of demand. 'In the winter, you couldn't use the cranes in the morning before breakfast because it put the lights out. If it was dark, the crane was using too much gas.' In daylight, the cranes and the workshop

machinery could be worked, but although the lighting, which was ordinary jets and not incandescent mantles, was not exactly generous, it provided the straw which broke the camel's back. In the 1930s, after Lew Walton had left the erecting shop, the cranes were adapted for electric power, with motors on the travellers.

When an engine was ready for its trials, the steam shed sent over one of their hands to rebuild the brick arch in the firebox. A wooden former was put up inside the firebox and the bricks put up in the normal manner, then the arch removed when they had set. Steam was raised, and in due course the engine was ready for the trial trip. The fitter would go with the crew. 'Small engines, like a coal engine, or an 18-inch goods, we used to take to Welford; if it was a medium-sized passenger engine, like a 'Jumbo', we used to go to Market Harborough, and if it was a big engine, like a 'Precursor', we went to Northampton. Sometimes you used to take the lad with you, but you weren't allowed on the footplate until you were over 18.'

Lew Walton recalled working on a variety of engines from the small 17 and 18 inch goods or saddle tanks, through to the 'Claughtons', including No 1914 'Patriot', which was stabled at Rugby and came in on a couple of occasions for attention to a hot box. As a rule, they used to keep two pits at the outer end of the shop free so that they could cope with casualties. Although the steam shed had a drop pit which could cope with the smaller-wheeled engines, it was inadequate for the large diameter wheels of the express classes. They used to take the engine in one day, and have it ready the following morning. It was necessary to have the crane to lift the engine, and on one memorable occasion, as the engine was lifted clear, the driving wheels collapsed inwards due to a fractured axle.

As a subsidiary shop to Crewe, there were many jobs Rugby did not tackle. Driving wheels were turned but never re-tyred, being sent instead to Crewe. Safety valves were another item the works never touched. 'We never repaired safety valves at all; they always went to Crewe. We didn't keep a stock of safety valves, and we had to wait until they came to us.' Buffers were not normally kept in stock either, and if one was damaged, a replacement had to come down from Crewe. There was no separate paint shop, the two painters having to do their work, which consisted of patch painting or varnishing, in the erecting shop itself. Repair times varied, but six to eight weeks (for the largest engines) was not uncommon.

Lew Walton completed his time as an apprentice in June 1914, having served just 4½ years at Rugby instead of the usual seven because of his previous time at Crewe. In those days, it was common for most of the ex-apprentices to be discharged within a few weeks, and this was the rule throughout the railway workshops, but fate was to take a hand. 'The only thing that saved me was that I came out of my time in June, and the war broke out in August, otherwise I would have got the sack as they never kept many on.' Within a few weeks of war breaking out, over 66,000 railwaymen had joined the forces, of whom 10,725 were North Western staff, a vast number from Crewe alone. As early as September, the railways became seriously worried over the loss of skilled men, and after talks with the War Office, the latter issued an instruction to recruiting officers that railwaymen could only be accepted if they had written permission from their head of department that they could be spared. With this massive drain of experienced staff, the North Western abandoned any thought of dismissing its newly qualified junior fitters.

With a shortage of fitters on the steam shed, the erecting shop had to help out at weekends. 'During the war, the fitters had to go and take our turn at the steam shed, 6.00 am to 6.00 pm on Saturdays and Sundays, and if you had a big job — and it always was a big job that the steam shed foreman gave you — if you couldn't get it done by Sunday night, you had to go over from 6.00 pm until 10.00 pm, after you finished in the erecting shop on Monday, and each evening until you finished it.' Weekend shed duty came round every five weeks.

Ordinary hours in the fitting shop were from 6.00 am until 5.30 pm, with a break for breakfast from 8.15 until 9.00 am, and for dinner from 1.00 pm until 2.00 pm. When you reported for work, the time-keeper 'gave you a check; if you were more than a quarter of an hour late, you couldn't get a check, and you were kept out until after breakfast at 9.00 am.' At lunch you handed your check in, and collected it after lunch. On a Friday afternoon, after lunch, the men were given two checks, the second brass check being the pay check. Both were handed in upon leaving work, each man receiving his pay in a numbered metal tin, which he immediately emptied to see all was in order. He then handed in the pay tin and went on his way.

Apprentices worked their way up to 15 shillings (aged 20) in Lew Walton's younger days, and when they completed their time, at 21 years of age, jumped to 24 shillings (and usually dismissal!). The lucky few advanced a shilling a year until they were 25 years old, but then earning 28 shillings. The top rate was 30 shillings. Above the basic pay was the piecework system, which was applied over a whole gang and calculated on every five completed engines. 'You had to get five engines out complete before you got any piecework at all. We used to get our ordinary week's wages, and the piecework in what we called "the balance"; sometimes it was shillings, sometimes it was £5 or £6; in those days *that* was big money.' The piecework system could sometimes produce anomalies. 'We used to reckon that you got "time and a third" for piecework, but on one occasion the lad and I worked 500 hours, and our piecework came to five shillings.'

The rapid increase in prices during the war

led to a series of war bonus awards, as well as very unsettled conditions and, of course, a backlog of work, for whilst Rugby was not engaged in war production, Crewe was, and Rugby did not have a fraction of the capacity to make up for the loss of railway production at Crewe. Conditions remained difficult after the war, with the works busy catching up with years of neglect. Although Lew Walton worked on a very wide variety of North Western classes, he could never recall seeing one of the North Western steam railcars at the erecting shops, and assumed Crewe kept them separate on account of their many unusual design features. Crewe had no such sensitivities towards Rugby when the LNWR took over the 4ft gauge Wolverton & Stony Stratford tramway shortly before the Grouping. The tramway was widely used by the Wolverton carriage works employees, and it was for their sake that the North Western took the line over when it got into difficulties. One of the engines dated from 1900, the other was brand new, having been built in 1921, Lew Walton commented, 'We never had anything to do with the steam railcars, but there used to be some steam trams on the road. It would be about 1922-23. There were two of them I think, and we repaired the both of them. We dismantled them in the normal way.'

The top brass from Crewe sometimes used to come down, prior to which there would be a hurried clean-up and brush-up of the shops. 'Of course, in those days they didn't come down in an ordinary train, there was a special engine at Crewe with a coach attached. It used to come into the yard.' Lew Walton could remember visits by Bowen Cooke, and had heard of visits by A.R. Trevithick, though this would be during George Whale's time as CME. Trevithick, who detested Webb's three-cylinder compounds, was renowned for his whirlwind tours of Crewe yard, chalking ART — his initials — on locomotives to condemn them. If he pursued a similar course at Rugby it is likely that his visit would be vividly remembered by the fitters and talked of for years to come. J.O'B. Tandy was another of whom Lew Walton recalled fitters speaking, though without such intensity! Trevithick would probably have had plenty to inspect, for as Lew Walton commented, 'In those days, there was stacks and stacks of coal there for years, and there could be 20 engines waiting to come into the shops for repairs.' The stacks of coal persisted into LMS

days, as did the rows of engines. By that time, however, the engines were not all awaiting overhaul. With the eclipse of North Western motive power, often by Midland engines of equal or greater antiquity, many six-coupled tanks and tender engines and 'Jumbos' finished their lives with a period 'in store' amongst the coal stacks.

The Grouping brought new classes to Rugby to service, although this was a gradual process. Eventually the works were to tackle Stanier designs and, in the last days, even BR Standard 2-10-0s, but that was many years after Lew Walton had left. The 'Midlandization' process was not as deeply resented in Rugby as at Crewe, partly no doubt because Rugby had always been a subsidiary works, unlike Crewe, where the loss of autonomy would be felt keenly. One of the greatest worries was the LMS policy of closing down the smaller workshops inherited from the pre-Grouping companies. The rapid eclipse of formerly independent works, such as Stoke on the North Staffordshire Railway, or Inverness on the Highland, boded ill for Rugby, and with engine numbers falling due to ever more intensive use of motive power, the prospects for Rugby did not look particularly bright by the late 'twenties. Lew Walton, foreseeing problems, looked for alternative work, and with two major electrical engineering firms in the town, English Electric and the British Thomson Houston Co, was able to go into turbine fitting in 1929. Both concerns had been attracted to Rugby around the turn of the century for the same reasons as the LNWR just a few years earlier, low-cost green-field sites right alongside the line, good rail communications and proximity to the Warwickshire and Leicestershire coalfields. With the depression sweeping away jobs, this foresight paid off, for over the next few years apprentices were discharged as a matter of course on finishing their time, and even qualified men were reduced in numbers.

Surprisingly, in view of LMS general policy of closing smaller works, the erecting shop *did* survive, and was once again invaluable during the Second World War. Well into the 'fifties, the works was completing two 'intermediate' shoppings a week, but with the eclipse of steam its days were numbered, and the last locomotive left the shops on 4 July 1959. The building was partially demolished, but the lower part of the walls provided the basis of a new District Electric

Depot in the early days of West Coast electrification, although its role was confined to inspection and minor servicing.

The erecting shop had been very cramped with its three roads, and opportunity was taken during the rebuild to reduce the depot to two tracks, each about 300 feet in length. Office accommodation had always been limited, and a new block paralleled the fitting shop. This contained offices for the District Engineer, conference and classroom facilities, mess rooms, a large workshop and the electric control room to monitor the 25Kv overhead wiring from Weedon to Rugeley and throughout the Birmingham area. The new depot, about twice the size of its predecessor, appeared to have a bright future, but it was soon realized that maintenance facilities for 25Kv loco-

motives and multiple units were not necessary in Rugby. Multiple unit refurbishing provided a stopgap, but longer term stability came when maintenance of 'on line' track machines was switched to Rugby. Rugby became headquarters to one of British Rail's 'Area Mechanical & Electrical Engineers'. However, a re-organization saw the end of the AM&EE structure, with Mr F.R. Walker, the last AM&EE, retiring in April 1989, ending more than a century of association between Rugby and the Locomotive Department. Previous North Western officers stationed at Rugby included A.L. Mumford and C.J. Bowen Cooke, and it was appropriate that Ray Walker came from a North Western family, and had indeed trained at Crewe.

When Rugby steam shed closed in 1965, the Loco Department War Memorial was transferred to the Diesel & Electric Depot, which used the shell of the erecting shop. The photograph and inscription at the top are a memorial to Bowen Cooke.

The Roll of Honour for the First and Second World Wars. When No 45500 Patriot, *the LMS replacement for the LNWR War Memorial engine, was withdrawn, its nameplate was added to the memorial, which was refurbished by the AM&EE, Ray Walker, prior to an Open Day in 1986.*

19 Finale

We opened this book with the words of Sir Richard Moon, the longest-serving and best-known of North Western Chairmen. Under the Railways Act 1921, the LNWR was merged with the Midland, Caledonian, Furness, Glasgow & South Western, Highland and various other companies to form the London, Midland & Scottish Railway Company. From 1 January 1923, the LNWR was no more, but certain formalities had to be observed, including a final meeting of the Court of Proprietors, still bearing that dignified name. It met on 23 February 1923, and there could be no better way of closing this book than by allowing the last Chairman of the LNWR to take the stage, The Hon Charles Napier Lawrence.

'Our next business is to read the minutes of the proceedings of the Special General Meetings of the 28th February 1922 and 4th November 1922, which I presume you will agree to take as read.

'Since we met 12 months ago, the Company has suffered a very grievous loss by the death, in March last, of Lord Manton, who, although he was only on our Board for a comparatively short time, having been a member of the board of the Lancashire & Yorkshire company, had already impressed us with his sterling business qualities. Another matter of interest in connection with the Directors is that in the honours which were recently announced, we were delighted to see that a well merited baronetcy had been conferred upon our esteemed colleague Mr J.H. Kaye.

'You have all been supplied with a copy of the Statement of Accounts, and I do not think that any useful purpose would be served by going through the figures in detail, for as I informed you 12 months ago, the North Western Company ceased to exist on the 31st December 1921, being succeeded by the new company of the same name, but you will see that the accounts for 1922 are the result of the working, not only of the old North Western, but also of the Lancashire & Yorkshire, North London and Dearne Valley Railway companies, so that they are of no use for comparative purposes. Having regard, however, to the fact that we are able to recommend an increase of one per cent in our dividend notwithstanding the very serious depression in the trade of the country, you will gather that we are quite satisfied with the results. The gross receipts for the past 12 months were £45,496,005, and the net receipts £8,978,717, and after paying all prior charges the amount available for the ordinary stock dividend is £5,034,450, out of which we recommend you to pay a dividend on the Consolidated Stock at the rate of 5½ per cent, making with the interim dividend of 3 per cent, paid in August last, 8½ per cent per annum, and leaving a balance to carry forward of £170,021. The old London & North Western Company in 1913 paid 7 per cent, and in the eight succeeding years an average of 6.7 per cent. Whilst I do not think it necessary to go into details of the Accounts in view of the changed circumstances, it will, I feel sure, be of interest to the shareholders to know that since 1846 when the Company's capital was £17,878,090, this figure has been increased to £191,494,391 at 31st December last, and the gross receipts have grown from £2,072,965 to £45,496,005.

'The past year or two have been very trying to the management, but notwithstanding the adverse conditions which have obtained throughout the country, we have by dint of careful and wise economy reduced our expenses so that our net receipts are more than they were in the previous year, when, of course for almost eight months we had the Government behind us. I am happy to say that there are many signs of a better state of affairs in the trade of the country, and I can assure you that when the full revival of trade does take place we are in a position to deal adequately with all the traffic that we can secure. In reducing expenses we have, of course, been materially assisted by the fall in the rates of wages, and by the reduced cost of coal and other materials, although I may say in regard to coal the price is still much too high, being 85 per cent above 1913, but in addition your Board and the officials have used every means within their power to reduce the expenses, and their efforts have met with considerable success. A further factor has been the reduction in ''Rates and Taxes''. When we met in February last, I informed you that an

London and North Western Railway. (No 630.)

No. 39555

SECRETARY'S OFFICE, EUSTON STATION,
LONDON, N.W. 1, 1st *March*, 1923.

Referring to the Resolution passed at the Annual Meeting of the Proprietors held on the 23rd ultimo declaring Dividends on the several Stocks mentioned below for the Half-year ending 31st December last, I have in accordance with your instructions paid to the Bank named the amount due to you for Dividend, as per Statement at foot.

I hereby certify that the amount of Income Tax deducted will be paid by the Company to the proper Officer for the Receipt of Taxes.

Proprietors requiring exemption from Income Tax are informed that the Inland Revenue will receive this Statement as a Voucher in claiming the same.

R. C. IRWIN, *Secretary.*

Name JAMES C. STITT &
MARY A. STITT
PER BANK OF LIVERPOOL LTD.
WATER STREET, LIVERPOOL.
A/C SANDERS.

CHANGE OF POSTAL ADDRESS.
Proprietors should keep the Company informed of the above to prevent loss of Dividend Warrants, &c. Forms for giving orders to the Company to pay Dividends direct to Bankers can be obtained on application to the Secretary, Euston Station, N.W.1.

DIVIDEND STATEMENT—HALF-YEAR ENDING 31st DECEMBER, 1922.

	Per cent.	Amount of Stock. £	Amount of Dividend. £	s.	d.
CONSOLIDATED (ORDINARY) STOCK	*£5 :10 : 0				
* making with the Interim Dividend already paid a total Dividend for the year of 8½ per cent					
CONSOLIDATED 4% GUARANTEED STOCK	£2 : 0 : 0				
CONSOLIDATED 4% PREFERENCE STOCK	£2 : 0 : 0	200	4	.	.
4% PREFERENCE STOCK (1902)	£2 : 0 : 0				
5% REDEEMABLE PREFERENCE STOCK	£2 :10 : 0				
(To be redeemed on the 30th June, 1926)					
Less Income Tax:—	s. d.	£ s. d.			
Consolidated (Ordinary) Stock at 5/3 in the £...					
(*Being the average rate for the year 1922, viz.:—3 months at 6/- and 9 months at 5/-*).					
Guaranteed & Preference Stocks at 5/- in the £			1	.	.
		£	3	.	.

This Statement to be forwarded to the Proprietor by the Banker.

Ex d. /

On 1 March 1923, Richard Irwin sent out the last ever dividend statements of the LNWR, and on that day the Company passed from everyday life to history.

arrangement had been arrived at with the National Conference of Assessment Committees.

'As you are all aware, this is the last meeting at which the name of the London & North Western Railway Company will appear, as henceforth it will be merged into the much larger Corporation to be known as the London, Midland and Scottish Railway Company, and whilst it is, of course, a matter of regret that the old name, which has been in existence since 1846, when it was formed by an amalgamation of the Grand Junction, the London & Birmingham, and the Manchester & Birmingham Railways, disappears, the change has been rendered necessary consequently upon the larger territory to be operated. We have, over a long period of years, consistently tried to preserve the great traditions which our company inherited from such men as George Stephenson, Sir George Findlay and Sir Richard Moon, and we look forward with hope to the future as the result of blending together

the best traditions of all the Companies forming the new undertaking.

'With regard to the future, there never has been, during the whole history of [railways], a time when greater wisdom and care was necessary than the present. The task of welding 35 railway companies — eight of them being constituent companies — into one new undertaking is stupendous and complex, and will call for the loyalty and co-operation of the staff and all concerned, but I am sanguine enough to believe that in the course of a very short time the new undertaking will be working with the smoothness and ease which has characterized the management of the several railway companies forming the new Company. So far, terms on the basis approximately of the 1919 figures have been agreed between all the constituent companies except one, and we have received the approval of the Tribunal set up under the Railways Act to the amalgamation and absorption of the following companies; the L&NWR (including the LYR), the MR, the FR, G&SWR, HR, Dearne Valley Railway, Shropshire Union Railways & Canal Co, and the Yorkshire Dales Railway.

Terms have also tentatively been agreed with the following companies:- the NSR, Cleator & Workington Junction; Cockermouth, Keswick & Penrith; Maryport & Carlisle; Mold & Denbigh Junction; North & South Western Junction; Stratford-upon-Avon & Midland Junction; Tottenham & Forest Gate; Arbroath & Forfar; Callander & Oban; Cathcart District; Dornoch Light; Lanarkshire & Ayrshire; Portpatrick & Wigtownshire; Solway Junction and the Wick & Lybster Light Railway. These will be dealt with very shortly before the Railways Amalgamation Tribunal... you will recognize that we have had a period of extremely strenuous work and have accomplished a very great deal in preparing and agreeing schemes for submission to the Amalgamation Tribunal. I may say, personally, that we have got very much further than I anticipated 12 months ago.

'In getting up our organization special steps have been taken to provide means whereby the public can be supplied with information regarding our facilities. We have formed a Commercial Department, both for goods and passenger traffic, and the officers in charge of these departments will lay themselves out to deal promptly with any enquiries they may receive and make every possible arrangement for the speedy transit of all descriptions of traffic, and we are satisfied that this action will have the effect of bringing the public and ourselves into much closer contact.

'Having regard to the size of the new undertaking it was thought desirable to delegate the management of the section north of the Tweed, where different conditions of law and trade are met with, to a body of gentlemen intimately associated with those special conditions, and the work of the Scottish portion of the undertaking, therefore, will be carried on by a Scottish Local Committee representative of the principal Scotch Companies in our group, on which four members of the Central Board will sit. We are passing over to the new Company a line as well equipped as any in the country. Our financial position is also stronger than it ever has been in the history of the Company, ample provision having been made for contingencies. I may say that practically the whole of the money we have received from the Government payable under the Railways Act 1921 [re Government use of the railway in wartime, etc] has been preserved intact, and is now safely invested in Government securi-

ties, where it will remain as a reserve for carrying out deferred maintenance works which are overdue, and the provision of increased facilities for traders and the public generally.

'As you are aware the companies forming the North Western and Midland Group approved an application to Parliament for powers to conduct road motor transport, and so far as this company was concerned this action was endorsed by a Special General Meeting, held on the 28th February 1922. After a long debate in the House of Commons, the Bill received its second reading and was committed to a Select Committee of the House, which took evidence at length from all parties interested, including the Ministry of Transport, whose representative at a very late date suggested certain amendments in regard to charges which, if adopted, would have rendered the Bill valueless to the promoters. The Bill was, therefore, withdrawn. The Select Committee, in a special report to the House of Commons, drew attention to the unnecessary expense caused to the parties owing to the delay on the part of the Ministry of Transport on notifying their objection to the principle of charging suggested in the Bill and intimated that, subject to the possibility of eliminating unfair competition, they were unanimously of the opinion that it would be in the public interest to allow the railway companies of the Group, and all competitors, to participate in road transport. As is well known, railway companies are amongst the largest... payers of rates to Local Authorities, and it is not too much to expect that they should be allowed to use the roads to which they contribute such large sums to maintain.

'In conjunction with other railway Chairmen and General Managers, I attended a conference in November last with the Prime Minister and other members of the Government, with the object of seeing whether the Railway Companies, as large employers of labour, could provide some remunerative work for the benefit of the unemployed, who as such are drawing very heavy sums for their maintenance, such sums being doles. During the war, railway construction was of necessity largely restricted. Most railway Boards had many schemes under contemplation which would add to the amenities of railway travel and transit. We, of course, sympathize with the men out of work, particularly those who fought in the war, and fully appreciating the anxiety of the

*The LNWR Chairman spoke of 'blending together the best tra-
ditions of all the companies'. A more hawkish attitude prevailed
at Derby; 'The Midland Railway Company is dead; long live
the Midland Railway Company'. Midland officers aimed to make
sure it happened. Midland livery was adopted so rapidly that
a few engines were repainted before the LMS 'crest' was available, so a small 'LMS' had to be painted on the cabside. 'Prince
of Wales' No 1290* Lucknow *is so garbed as LMS No 5729
at Crewe in 1924. It was a fine livery, but the tactless way
in which proud traditions were trampled underfoot was to bedevil
the LMS for decades.*

Prime Minister we decided to put such necessary works in hand at once. I may say that in
every case we were quite satisfied that the expenditure which would be entailed was thoroughly
justified. In addition to meeting the wishes of the
Government and providing work for the unemployed, the best interests of the undertaking are
being safeguarded.

'Dealing with the future; 12 members of your
Board will join the Board of the new company
which as at present constituted will consist of 26
members. The inevitable consequence of a merg-
ing of this character is that certain of our colleagues on the Board, whose faces have long been
familiar to you, must retire. They have rendered
yeoman service to the Company in the past, and
I feel sure it will be your pleasure, as well as your
duty, that in addition to voting them a certain
sum, and on this point a resolution will be moved

in due course, that you should also pass them
a very cordial vote of thanks for the very valuable services they have rendered to you, in many
cases, over a long period of years.

'So far as the officers are concerned, most of
them become officers of the new company, and
whilst on this topic it affords me much pleasure
to express our very deep indebtedness for the
effective work they have performed during the
past 12 months. The General Manager, Officers
and Staff have worked loyally and hard, and but
for this fact the results we present to you today
would have been far different. You will be doing
less than your duty if you do not authorize me
to express to them, on your behalf, your very
heartiest thanks.

'Whilst on this phase of our work, I would also
like to express my very hearty appreciation of the
relations which exist between ourselves, as a
Board, and our employees. For a short time after
the termination of hostilities our men were not
working well, but in the last year or two the relations have improved very considerably.

'Each holder of stock of this Company, as well
as any other company that has been absorbed
or amalgamated will, no doubt, be anticipating
that new certificates will be issued in exchange
for the certificates that are now held, and I am
therefore taking this opportunity of calling attention to the fact that under the Amalgamation

Scheme approving the formation of the London, Midland and Scottish Railway Company, the certificates of stock in the several railway companies that are now held are deemed to be certificates of the stocks of the new company for the proportional amount allocated. This provision was made in the scheme because there are some hundreds of thousands of certificates held by proprietors, and, although they must be exchanged ultimately, the work will have to be spread over a considerable period. Shareholders will, however, be communicated with as and when it becomes necessary for them to forward their certificates for the purpose. Perhaps proprietors will note this, as it will save them making enquiries as to the exchange of certificates.

'Under the provisions of the Railways Act with which I dealt very fully in my remarks a year ago, we are commencing a new era in railway work. The changed conditions are not of our seeking, but have been imposed upon us by the Government of the country. We have loyally accepted their verdict, and shall do our best to make the new conditions successful. It is too early yet to make any forecast as to whether the amal-

gamations will result in the economies prophesied in Parliament; one thing certainly you can rely on — the Directors will leave nothing undone to administer the new undertaking in the most economical way consistent with proper maintenance and efficiency and with the utmost endeavour to stimulate the trade of the country. . . Public efficiency and financial stability will always be the goal held in view by the London, Midland & Scottish Board of Directors.'

It was thus that the London & North Western Railway Company, the 'Premier Line', the 'largest joint stock corporation in the world', passed from the everyday world of business into the pages of history.

It is high summer, and Rockingham station, on the Stamford line, slumbers between trains. It is 1966, and although more than four decades have elapsed since the LNWR passed into history, there is little to show that the company is not still in business. From Euston to Carlisle, and Cambridge to the Welsh coast, this was the 'hardware' that North Western men used. How they used it, and what they thought of it all, is what we have sought to discover. We hope you gained as much enjoyment watching the story unfold as we did.

Index